WILLIAM SHAKESPEARE

POET, DRAMATIST, AND MAN

BY

HAMILTON WRIGHT MABIE

AUTHOR OF "MY STUDY FIRE," "UNDER THE TREES AND
ELSEWHERE," "THE LIFE OF THE SPIRIT," ETC.

NEW EDITION

WITH A NEW PREFACE

New York

THE MACMILLAN COMPANY

LONDON: MACMILLAN & CO., LTD.

1904

Norwood Press
J. S. Cushing & Co. — Berwick & Smith
Norwood Mass. U.S.A.

To
My Mother
and
To the Memory of
My Father

PREFACE

THIS account of Shakespeare, planned nearly four years ago, has been prepared with the hope that it may bring the greatest of English poets more distinctly before the minds of some of his readers, and widen the interest in a body of poetry rich beyond most literature in the qualities which not only give deep and fresh interest to life, but which make for the liberation and enrichment of the human spirit. As the Spokesman of a race to which has fallen a large share of the government of the modern world, and as the chief exponent in literature of the fundamental conception of life held by the Western world at a time when the thought of the East and the West are being brought into searching comparison, Shakespeare must be studied in the near future with a deeper recognition of the significance of his work and its value as a source of spiritual culture. In these chapters the endeavour has been made to present the man as he is disclosed by the results of the long and loving study of a group of scholars, chiefly English, German, and American, who have searched the whole field of contemporary literature, records, and history with infinite patience and with keen intelligence, by the history of his time, and by a study of his work. The plays have been presented in those aspects which throw light on the dramatist's life, thought, and art; the many and interesting questions which have been discussed with great ingenuity and at great length by Shakespearean scholars have been touched upon only as they directly affect the history, thought, or art of the poet. The writer is under obligations to the entire body of Shakespearean scholars, who have brought together a fund of knowledge open to the world, but collected at great cost of time and thought. He desires to acknowledge his special indebtedness to Mr. Halliwell-Phillipps, Mr. F. J. Furnivall, Dr. Horace Howard Furness, Mr. Sidney Lee, Mr. George Wyndham, Mr. Israel Gollancz, Professor C. H. Herford, and Mr. A. W. Ward.

As the result of independent study of the plays the writer found himself reaching conclusions with regard to the significance of the order in which they were written which follow, in certain respects, the lines marked out years ago by Dr. Edward Dowden, a critic who has rendered very important service to Shakespearean scholarship. The word

Preface

Romance as happily descriptive of the later plays has been taken from Dr. Dowden, from whom the writer has received for years past, in this as in other fields, both suggestion and stimulus. To Dr. William J. Rolfe he is indebted for many kindnesses of a personal nature.

Mr. William Winter has made Shakespeare's country familiar to a host of readers in America and England, and has reproduced the atmosphere in which the poet lived as boy and youth with such sympathetic charm and fidelity that he has laid all lovers of Shakespeare under obligations which it is a pleasure to recognize.

ON SHAKESPEARE

What needs my Shakespeare for his honoured bones
The labour of an age in pilèd stones?
Or that his hallowed reliques should be hid
 Under a star-ypointing pyramid?
Dear son of memory, great heir of fame,
What need'st thou such weak witness of thy name?
Thou in our wonder and astonishment
Hast built thyself a livelong monument.
For whilst, to the shame of slow endeavouring art,
Thy easy numbers flow, and that each heart
Hath from the leaves of thy unvalued book
Those Delphic lines with deep impression took,
Then thou, our fancy of itself bereaving,
Dost make *us* marble with too much conceiving,
And so sepúlchered, in such pomp dost lie
That kings for such a tomb would wish to die.

JOHN MILTON. 1630.

CONTENTS

xi

Contents

INTRODUCTION TO FOURTH EDITION

THE appearance of this biography of Shakespeare in a fourth edition within two years of the date of its publication may be interpreted, without assumption on the part of the author, as one of the many evidences of the growth of interest in the work of the foremost poet who has used our language. As the peoples who speak that language are driven more and more by their world-wide activities and responsibilities to study their own motives and the sources of their power they will turn with deepening concern to the man who, more profoundly than any other who has given expression to their spirit and genius, has comprehended their view of life, of character, and of history, and interpreted it in dramatic form.

Consciously or unconsciously Shakespeare has formulated that underlying conception of the interdependence of thought and action, of the fundamental significance of character in relation to truth,

Introduction

which is the key to the spirit and achievement of the English-speaking peoples. The more impressively this conception is disclosed in action and institution the deeper will be the craving for clear comprehension of its nature and significance; and in the search for this deeper understanding of themselves the peoples of English blood will turn more and more eagerly to the greatest text-book of their race.

In this study of Shakespeare it has been the endeavour of the writer to present the poet as a man, not as a series of problems associated with a name; to reveal the dramatist in the growth of his spirit, his thought, and his art by filling in the background of landscape, educational opportunity, social condition, and race activity, which, in connection with his work, give his face distinctness of outline and feature. It is hardly necessary to remind students that the uncertainties and doubts with regard to Shakespeare which have been widely discussed, and to which an importance has sometimes been attached out of all proportion to their reality and weight, found their opportunity at a time when Shakespearean scholarship was far less rich and thorough than it has become of late years, and have their root very largely in lack of familiarity

Introduction

with the conditions under which the dramatist did his work, or in lack of literary insight and feeling.

The kindly reception which this study has received at the hands not only of students of Shakespeare, but of scholars of standing here and abroad, has confirmed the writer in his conviction that there was room for a biography which, in an unassuming spirit, should put aside the numberless technical questions and approach the author of "Hamlet" as one approaches the author of "In Memoriam" or of "Pippa Passes."

The edition of the plays and poems in connection with which this biography now appears possesses the highest authority both as regards text and critical apparatus. The text is based on the work of the editors of the Cambridge and Globe Shakespeares, and it is hardly necessary to say that no better textual work has been done in the field of Shakespearean scholarship. It involved an exhaustive collocation of the four Folios and of all the Quarto editions, and of all the later editions and commentaries. Professor Herford's Introductions present, in a very interesting form, the historical and literary data relating to the sources of the plays and poems, and an interpretation of their place and meaning in Shakespeare's work as a whole; while the notes indicate the radical departures from the old texts, suggest the most probable readings in those passages in which the old texts are " incorrigib¹y corrupt," and supply such other information with regard to allusions, references, and other matters as are essential to a good understanding of the text.

WILLIAM SHAKESPEARE

POET, DRAMATIST, AND MAN

WILLIAM SHAKESPEARE:

POET, DRAMATIST, AND MAN

CHAPTER I

THE FORERUNNERS OF SHAKESPEARE

THE history of the growth of the drama is one of the most fascinating chapters in the record of the spiritual life of the race. So closely is it bound up with that life that the unfolding of this art appears, wherever one looks deeply into it, as a vital rather than a purely artistic process. That art has ever been conceived as the product of anything less rich and deep than an unfolding of life shows how far we have been separated by historic conditions from any first-hand contact with it, any deep-going and adequate conception of what it is, and what it means in the life of the race. It requires a great effort of the imagination to put ourselves into the attitude of those early men who had the passions and were doing the work of men, but who had the fresh and responsive imagination of childhood; who were so closely in touch with nature that the whole world was alive to them in every sight and sound. Personification was not only natural but inevi-

table to a race whose imagination was far in advance
of its knowledge. Such a race would first create and
then devoutly believe the story of Dionysus : the wandering god, master of all the resources of vitality ;
buoyant, enthralling, mysterious, intoxicating ; in whom
the rising passion, the deep instinct for freedom, which
the spring let loose in every imagination, found visible
embodiment ; the personification of the ebbing and
rising tide of life in Nature, and, therefore, the symbol of the spontaneous and inspirational element in
life ; the personification of the mysterious force of
reproduction, and therefore the symbol of passion and
license.

The god was entirely real ; everybody knew that a
group of Tyrrhenian sailors had seized him as he sat
on a rock on the seashore, bound him with withes,
and carried him to the deck of their tiny piratical
craft ; and everybody knew also that the withes had
fallen from him, that streams of wine ran over the
ship, vines climbed the mast and hung from the yards,
garlands were twined about the oars, and a fragrance
as of vineyards was breathed over the sea. Then suddenly a lion stood among the sailors, who sprang over-
board and were changed into dolphins ; while the god,
taking on his natural form, ran the ship into port. Such
a being, appealing alike to the imagination and the
passions, personifying the most beautiful mysteries and
giving form to the wildest longings of the body and the
mind, could not be worshipped save by rites and ceremonies which were essentially dramatic.

The seed-time and harvest festivals furnished natural

occasions for such a worship; the worshippers often wore goatskins to counterfeit the Satyrs, and so gave tragedy its name. Grouped about rude altars, in a rude chorus, they told the story of the god's wanderings and adventures, not with words only, but with gesture, dance, and music. The expression of thought and feeling was free from self-consciousness, and was like a mirror of the emotions of the worshipper. This ballad-dance, which Mr. Moulton describes as a kind of literary protoplasm because several literary forms were implicit in it and were later developed out of it, was a free, spontaneous, natural act of worship; it was also a genuine drama, which unfolded by easy gradations into a noble literary form. The frequent repetition of the story threw its dramatic element into more striking relief: the narrative gradually detached itself from the choral parts and fell to individual singers; these singers separated themselves from the chorus and gave their parts increasing dramatic quality and distinctness; until, by a process of rude and almost unconscious evolution, the story was acted instead of narrated, and the dramatic poet, when he arrived, found all the materials for a complete drama ready to his hand. It is sober history, therefore, and not figurative speech, that the drama was born at the foot of the altar.

And more than eighteen hundred years later the drama was born again at the foot of the altar. Whatever invisible streams of tradition may have flowed from the days of a declining theatre at Rome through the confused and largely recordless life of the early Middle Ages, it may safely be assumed that the modern drama began, as the ancient drama had begun, in the development of worship along dramatic lines. In the history of fairy tales and folk-lore, the explanation of striking similarities between the old and the new is to be sought, probably, in the laws of the mind rather than in the direct transmission of forms or materials. When spiritual and intellectual conditions are repeated, the action or expression of the mind affected by them is likely to be repeated. In every age men of a certain temperament dramatize their own experience whenever they essay to describe it, and dramatize whatever material comes to their hand for the purpose of entertaining others. The instinct which prompts men of this temper to make a story of every happening by selecting the most striking incidents, rearranging them, and heightening the effect by skilful grouping, has made some kind of drama inevitable in every age. When the influence of Menander, modified and adapted to Roman taste by Terence, Plautus, and their successors, was exhausted, farces, with music, pantomime, and humorous dialogue, largely improvised, met the general need with the coarse fun which suited a time of declining taste and decaying culture. The indecency and vulgarity of these purely popular shows became more pronounced as the Roman populace sank in intelligence and virtue ; the vigour which redeemed in part their early license gave place to the grossest personalities and the cheapest tricks and feats of skill.

The mimes, or players, carried this degenerate

drama into the provinces, where taste was even less exacting than in Rome, and the half-heathen world was entertained by cheap imitations of the worst amusements of the Capital. At a still later date, in market-places, on village greens, in castle yards, and even at Courts, strolling players recited, postured, sang, danced, played musical instruments, and broke up the monotony of life at a time when means of communication were few, slow, and expensive. It is difficult for modern men to realize in imagination the isolation of small communities and of great castles in the Middle Ages. The strolling player was welcome, not only because he was entertaining, but because he brought the air of the remote world with him.

The vulgarity and indecency of shows of such an origin, everywhere adapting themselves to popular taste at a time when popular taste was coarse to the last degree, were inevitable. Then, as now, society had the kind of entertainment for which it asked; then, as now, the players were bent on pleasing the people. The Church, having other ends in view, tried to purify the general taste by purifying the amusements of the people, and in the fifth century the players of various kinds — mimes, histriones, joculatores — were put under formal ecclesiastical condemnation. The Church not only condemned the players; she excluded them from her sacraments.

The players continued to perform in the face of ecclesiastical disapproval, and they found audiences; for the dramatic instinct lies deep in men, and the only way to shut out vulgar and indecent plays is to replace them by plays of a better quality. The play persists, and cannot be successfully banned. This degenerate practice of a once noble art came into England after the Norman Conquest, and the players became, not only the entertainers of the people, but the story-tellers and reporters of the period. They made the monotony of life more bearable.

How much indirect influence this humble and turbid stream of dramatic activity may have had on the development of the English drama cannot be determined; the chief influence in the making of that drama came from the Church. The Church condemned the manifestation of the dramatic instinct, but it did not fall into the later error of condemning the instinct itself; on the contrary, it was quick to recognize and utilize that instinct. It had long appealed to the dramatic instinct in its worshippers; for the Mass is a dramatization of certain fundamental ideas generally held throughout Christendom for many centuries. From the sixth century the Mass was the supreme act of worship throughout western Europe. "In the wide dimensions which in course of time the Mass assumed," says Hagenbach, "there lies a grand, we are almost inclined to say an artistic, idea. A dramatic progression is perceptible in all the symbolic processes, from the appearance of the celebrant priest at the altar and the confession of sins, to the *Kyrie Eleison*, and from this to the grand doxology, after which the priest turns with the Dominus vobiscum to the congregation, calling upon it to pray. Next, we listen to the reading of the Epistle and the Gospel.

The Forerunners of Shakespeare

Between the two actions or acts intervenes the *Graduale* (a chant), during which the deacon ascends the lectorium. With the *Halleluia* concludes the first act; and then ensues the Mass in a more special sense, which begins with the recitation of the Creed. Then again a Dominus vobiscum and a prayer, followed by the offertory and, accompanied by the further ceremonies, the Consecration. The change of substance — the mystery of mysteries — takes place amid the adoration of the congregation and the prayer for the quick and the dead; then, after the touching chant of the Agnus Dei, ensues the Communion itself, which is succeeded by prayer and thanksgiving, the salutation of peace, and the benediction."

In the impressive and beautiful liturgy of the Mass the dramatization of the central mystery of the Christian faith was effected by action, by pantomime, and by music. There was no purpose to be dramatic; there was a natural evolution of the instinct to set forth a truth too great and mysterious to be contained in words by symbols, which are not only more inclusive than words but which satisfy the imagination, and by action.

The Church did not stop with a dramatic presentation of the sublimest of dramatic episodes, the vicarious death of Christ; it went further and set forth the fact and the truth of certain striking and significant scenes in the New Testament. As early as the fifth century these scenes were reproduced in the churches in living pictures, with music. In this manner the people not only heard the story of the Adoration of the Magi and of the Marriage of Cana, but saw the story in tableaux. In course of time the persons in these tableaux spoke and moved, and then it was but a logical step to the representation dramatically, by the priests before the altar, of the striking or significant events in the life of Christ.

Worshippers were approached through every avenue of expression : the churches in which they sat were nobly symbolical in structure ; the windows were ablaze with Scriptural story; altar-pieces, statues, carvings, and pictures continually spoke to them in a language of searching beauty. In some churches the priests read from rolls upon which, as they were unfolded toward the congregation, picture after picture came to view. Christmas, Good Friday, and Easter services inevitably took on dramatic forms, and became beautiful in their reproduction of the touching and tender scenes in the life of Christ, and grewsome in their literal picturing of his sufferings and death. The dramatic instinct had been long at work in the development of worship ; a play on the Passion, ascribed to Gregory of Nazianzen, dated back to the fourth century. This early drama was a succession of monologues, but it plainly predicted the mystery drama of the twelfth and thirteenth centuries.

There was nothing forced or artificial in the growth of this later and more complete drama ; a description of a Durham Good Friday service makes us see the easy progression toward well-defined drama : " Within the church of Durham, upon Good Friday, there was a marvellous solemn service, in which service time, after the Passion was sung, two of the eldest monks took a goodly large crucifix all of gold, of the semblance of our Saviour Christ, nailed upon the Cross. . . . The service being ended, the said two monks carried the Cross to the Sepulchre with great reverence (which Sepulchre was set up that morning on the north side of the choir, nigh unto the High Altar, before the service time), and then did lay it within the said Sepulchre with great devotion."

It is easy to follow the dramatic development of such a theme, and to understand how beautiful and impressive worship became when the divine tragedy was not only sung and described, but acted before the high altar by gorgeously robed priests. Thus the drama was born a second time at the foot of the altar.

But the time came when the drama parted company with the liturgy, and, as in its development in Greece, took on a life of its own. The vernacular was substituted for Latin; laymen took parts of increasing importance; the place of representation was changed from the church to the space outside the church; the liturgical yielded to the dramatic; humour, and even broad farce, were introduced; the several streams of dramatic tradition which had come down from an earlier time were merged in the fully developed Mystery or Miracle play.

The trade guilds had become centres of organized enterprise in the towns, and the presentation of plays, in which popular religious and social interest was now concentrated, fell into their hands. Cities like York, Chester, and Coventry fostered the growing art with enthusiasm and generosity. By the beginning of the fifteenth century the presentation of the dramas was thoroughly systematized. In some places the Mayor, by proclamation, announced the dates of presentation ; in other places special messengers or heralds made the round of the city and gave public notice. The different guilds undertook the presentation of different acts or scenes. Two-story wagons took the place of the stage in front of the church or in the square ; on these wagons, or pageants, as they were called, the rude dressing-rooms were on the lower and the stage on the upper story. These movable theatres, starting from the church, passed through all the principal streets, and, at important points, the actors went through their parts in the presence of throngs of eager spectators in the windows, galleries, doorways, squares, and upon temporary scaffolds. The plays were in series and required several days for presentation, and the town made the occasion one of general and hilarious holiday.

On the pageants, handsomely decorated, the spectators saw scenes acted, with which they had been made familiar by every kind of teaching. The drama in the Garden of Eden was presented with uncompromising realism, Adam and Eve appearing in appropriate attire ; the devil played a great and effective part, furnishing endless amusement by his buffoonery, but always going in the end to his own place. Pilate and Herod divided popular attention by their semi-humorous or melodramatic rôles, and Noah's wife afforded an opportunity for the play of monotonous and very obvious masculine wit on the faults and frailty of woman. The construction of these semi-sacred dramas, dealing with high or picturesque events and incidents in Biblical story, was rude ; the mixture of the sacred and the comic so complete that the two are constantly merged ; the frankness of speech and the grossness almost incredible to modern taste. It would be a great mistake, however, to interpret either the intermingling of the tragic and the comic or the gross-ness of speech as indicating general corruption ; they indicate an undeveloped rather than a corrupt society. The English people were morally sound, but they were coarse in habit and speech, after the manner of the time. There was as much honest and sober living as to-day ; the grossness was not a matter of character, but of expression. Men and women saw, without any consciousness of irreverence or incongruity, the figure of Deity enthroned on a movable stage, with Cherubim gathered about Him, creating the world with the aid of images of birds and beasts, with branches plucked from trees, and with lanterns such as were carried about the streets at night.

Religion was not a department or partial expression of life ; it was inclusive of the whole range of feeling and action. It embraced humour as readily as it embraced the most serious conviction and the most elevated emotion. It was, therefore, entirely congru-ous with the deepest piety of the time that grotesque figures, monstrous gargoyles, broadly humorous carv-ings on miserere stalls, should be part of the structure of those vast cathedrals which are the most sublime

William Shakespeare

expressions in art of the religious life of the race. To read into the grossness and indecency of expression in the fifteenth century the moral significance which such an expression would have in the nineteenth century is not only to do a grave injustice to many generations, but to betray the lack of a sound historic sense. The great dramatists who followed these early unknown playwrights understood that the humorous cannot be separated from the tragic without violating the facts of life ; and religion, in its later expressions, would have been saved from many absurdities and much destructive narrowness if the men who spoke for it had not so strangely misunderstood and rejected one of the greatest qualities of the human spirit — that quality of humour which, above all others, keeps human nature sane and sound.

To the Mysteries and Miracle plays succeeded the Moralities. Whether these later and less dramatic plays were developed out of the earlier dramatic forms is uncertain ; that they were largely modelled along lines already well defined is apparently well established. No line of sharp division as regards time, theme, or manner can be drawn between the two ; although certain broad differences are evident at a glance. The mediæval mind dealt largely with types, and only secondarily with individuals ; and the break in the slow and unconscious progression from the type to the sharply defined person, which registers the unfolding not only of the modern mind but of modern art, is not inexplicable. The characters in the Mysteries and Miracle plays were received directly or indirectly from Biblical sources; in the Moralities there was, apparently, an attempt to create new figures. These figures were more abstract and far less human than their immediate predecessors in the pageants, but they may have had the value of a halting and uncertain attempt to create instead of reproduce. The first result was, apparently, a retrogression from the dramatic idea: the earlier plays had shown some skill in the development of character; in the Moralities the stage was surrendered to the personifications of abstract virtues. In place of a very real Devil, revelling in grotesque humour, and an equally real Herod, who gave free play to the melodramatic element so dear to the uncultivated in every age, appeared those very tenuous and shadowy abstractions, the World, the Flesh, the Devil, not as actors in the world's tragedy, but as personifications of the principle of evil; with Genus Humanum, Pleasure, Slander, Perseverance, and the Seven Deadly Sins. These prolix and monotonous plays cover a wide range of subjects, from the popular " Everyman," which deals, not without dignity, with the supreme experience of death, to "Wyt and Science," which doubtless, on many a school stage, set forth the charms of knowledge, and presented one of the earliest pleas for athletics.

The Moralities beguiled the darkest period in the literary history of England; the tide of the first dramatic energy had gone out, the tide of the second and greater dramatic movement had not set in. There were freedom, spontaneity, fresh feeling, poetic

imagery, in the ballads; but the Moralities were mechanical, rigid, laboured, and uninspired.

The Moralities marked, however, one important
step in the development of the English drama: they
created opportunities for professional actors, and made
acting as a profession possible. The earlier plays
had been in the hands of amateurs; men who had, in
many cases, considerable skill in acting, but who were
members of guilds, with other and different occupations. Side by side with the Mystery and Miracle
plays there had percolated through the long period
when the English drama was in the making many
kinds of shows, more or less coarse and full of buffoonery, in the hands of roving pantomimists, singers,
comedians — a class without habitation, standing, or
character. These wandering performers, many of
them doubtless men of genuine gifts cast upon an un-
propitious time, found place at this period in companies supported by noblemen and attached to great
houses, or in companies which presented plays in
various parts of the country in the courts of inns and,
on great occasions, in large towns and cities. For all
classes dearly loved the bravery, excitement, and di-
version of the pageant, the masque, and the play of
every kind. The parts were entirely in the hands
of men; no women appeared on the stage until after
the time of Shakespeare; the female characters were
taken by boys.

The transition from the Moralities to the fully developed play was gradual, and was not marked by
logical gradations. The tendency to allegory gave

place slowly to the tendency to character-drawing, to the unfolding of a story, and to the humour and liveliness of the comedy. One of the earliest forms which comedy took was the Interlude — a transitional dramatic form with which the name of John Heywood is identified. A London boy, believed to have sung for a time in the choir of the Chapel Royal, Heywood studied at Oxford, was befriended by that great Englishman, Sir Thomas More, and early became attached to the Court of Henry the Eighth as a player. Players were still under social and religious interdict, but Heywood's sincerity as a Catholic withstood the test of the withdrawal of the royal favour at a time when a king's smile was fortune in a most tangible form. There was a manly integrity in the nature of John Heywood, as in that of many of his fellow-actors. The Interlude in his hands was less ambitious in construction than a play; shorter, more vivacious, and much closer to the life of the time. It was often rude, but it was oftener racy, direct, and effective in expression ; using the familiar colloquial speech of the day with great effectiveness. The interest turned on a humorous situation, and the dialogue was enlivened by the play of shrewd native wit. In the " Four P's " the characters were so well known that the audience hardly needed the stimulus of wit to awaken its interest. The Palmer, the Poticary, the Pedlar, and the Pardoner brought the playwright and his auditors into easy and immediate contact, and furnished ample opportunity to satirize or ridicule the vices, hypocrisies, and follies of the time. The structure of the Interlude was simple, and its wit not too fine for the coarse taste of the time; but it was a true growth of the English soil, free from foreign influence; the virility, the gayety, and the license of the early English spirit were in it.

"Ralph Roister Doister," the earliest comedy, was produced not later than 1550 — perhaps twenty years after the production of the "Four P's." Heywood had shown how to set character in distinct outlines on the stage; Nicholas Udall, an Oxford student, a scholar, holding the head-mastership first of Eton College and later of Westminster School, brought the comedy to completeness by adding to the interest of characters essentially humorous the more absorbing interest of a well-defined plot. Udall was a school-master, but there was no pedantry in him; he felt the deep classical influence which had swept Europe like a tide, but he took his materials from the life about him, and he used good native speech. He had learned from the Latin comedy how to construct both a plot and a play, and his training gave him easy mastery of sound expression; but he composed his comedies in terms of English life. "Roister Doister" was a type of man instantly recognized by an English audience of every social grade; a coward who was also a boaster, whose wooing, like that of Falstaff, affords ample opportunity for the same rollicking fun. The significance of the piece lay in its freshness, its freedom, and its ease — qualities which were prophetic of the birth of a true drama.

"Gammer Gurton's Needle," a broad, coarse, but

effective picture of rustic manners, generally believed to have been written by John Still, a Lincolnshire man by birth, a Cambridge man by education, and a Bishop by vocation, marks the first appearance of the fully developed farce in English, and is notable for vigorous characterization in a mass of vulgar buffoonery. That such a piece should come from the hand of the stern divine, with Puritan aspect, who lies at rest in Wells Cathedral, and that it was performed before a college audience in Cambridge, shows that the social and intellectual conditions which permitted so close a juxtaposition of the sacred and the vulgar in the Mystery and Miracle plays still prevailed. The saving grace of this early dramatic writing was its vitality; in this, and in its native flavour and its resistance to foreign influence, lay its promise.

The earlier development of comedy as compared with tragedy is not difficult to account for. Tragedy exacts something from an audience; a certain degree of seriousness or of culture must be possessed by those who are to enjoy or profit by it. Comedy, on the other hand, appeals to the untrained no less than the trained man; it collects its audience at the village blacksmith's or the country shop as readily as in the most amply appointed theatre. Moreover, it kept close to popular life and taste at a time when the influence of the classical literatures was putting its impress on men of taste and culture. Italy, by virtue of its immense service in the recovery of classical thought and art, and in the production of great works of its own in literature, painting, sculpture, and archi-

tecture, was the teacher of western Europe ; and such
was the splendour of her achievements that what ought
to have been a liberating and inspiring influence became a danger to native originality and development.
Italian literature came into England like a flood, and,
through a host of translations, some of which were of
masterly quality, the intellectual inequality of a difference of more than two centuries in culture was equal-
ized with astonishing rapidity. In that age of keen
appetite for knowledge, the art and scholarship of a
more mature people were assimilated with almost
magical ease. The traditions of the classical stage for
a time threatened the integrity of English art, but in
the end the vigour of the English mind asserted itself;
if the classical influence had won the day, Ben Jonson
would have secured a higher place, but Shakespeare
might have been fatally handicapped.

"Ferrex and Porrex," or, as the play is more generally known, "Gorbordoc," was the earliest English
tragedy, and is chiefly interesting as showing how
the influence of Seneca and the sturdy vigour of the
English genius worked together in a kind of rude
harmony. The manner shows the Latin influence,
but the story and the spirit in which it is treated are
genuinely English. Sir Philip Sidney, whose culture
was of the best in point of quality, found "Gorbordoc"
full of "stately speeches and well-sounding phrases,
climbing to the height of Seneca his style," but notes
the failure to comply with the traditional unity of time.
Sackville, one of the authors of this vigorous play,
stood in relations of intimacy with the Court of Eliza-

beth, became Chancellor of the University of Oxford, and Lord High Treasurer of England. His work in "The Mirrour of Magistrates" brings out still more clearly the deep seriousness of his spirit. Norton, who collaborated with him in the writing of "Gorbordoc," was a man of severe temper, a translator of Calvin's Institutes, and a born reformer. Such men might be affected by the classical influence ; they could hardly be subdued by it. In the excess of action, the rush of incident, the swift accumulation of horrors, which characterize this sanguinary play, Seneca would have found few suggestions of his own methods and temper. The blank verse in which it is written, however, came ultimately from Italy through the skilful adaptation of Surrey.

The integrity of the English drama was assured when the playwrights, now rapidly increasing in numbers, turned to English history and produced the long series of Chronicle plays, to which Shakespeare owed so much, and which furnished an inaccurate but liberalizing education for the whole body of the English people. In these plays, probably covering the entire field of English history, the doings and the experiences of the English race were set forth in the most vital fashion ; English history dramatically presented became a connected and living story. They developed the race consciousness, deepened the race feeling, made love of country the passion which found splendid expression in "Henry V.," and prepared the way for the popular appreciation of the noblest dramatic works. This dramatic use of national history made the drama the natural and inevitable expression of the English spirit in Elizabeth's time, and insured an art which was not only intensely English but intensely alive. The imagination trained by the Chronicle plays was ready to understand "Hamlet" and "Lear."

Bale's "King Johan," "The True Tragedy of Richard III.," "The Famous Victories of Henry V.," "The Contention of the Two Famous Houses of York and Lancaster," "Edward III.," and kindred plays, not only furnished material for Shakespeare's hand, but prepared Shakespeare's audiences to understand his work. These plays practically cover a period of four centuries, and bring the story of English history down to the Armada.

In close historical connection with the Chronicle plays must be placed the long list of plays which, like "Cardinal Wolsey," "Duchess of Norfolk," "Duke Humphrey," and "Hotspur," drew upon the treasury of English biography and dramatized individual vicissitude and fate ; and the plays which, like the "Downfall of Robert Earl of Huntington," developed the dramatic uses of legendary history. It would not be easy to devise a more stimulating method of educating the imagination and preparing the way for a period of free and buoyant creativeness than this visualization of history on the rude but intensely vitalized stage of the sixteenth century.

One more step in this vital expression of the English spirit was taken by Shakespeare's immediate predecessors and by some of his older contemporaries.

The Forerunners of Shakespeare

Such a play as "Arden of Feversham," which has been credited to Shakespeare by a number of critics, brought the dramatic form to a stage where it needed but the hand of a poet of genius to perfect it. There was still a long distance between the plays of this period, however, and the balance, harmony, and restraint of Shakespeare. "Arden of Feversham," and a host of dramas of the same period, are charged with power; but he who reads them is fed with horrors. Lyly's comedies were acted, with one or two exceptions, before Queen Elizabeth, and were mainly, as Mr. Symonds suggests, elaborately decorated censers in which incense was lavishly burned to a Queen incredibly avid of adulation and flattery. As a writer of comedies for the Court, the author of "Euphues" influenced the language of the later dramatists far more deeply than he influenced the drama itself. He made an art of witty dialogue, and repartee became in his hands a brilliant fence of words; it remained for Shakespeare to carry both to perfection in "Much Ado About Nothing."

When Shakespeare reached London about 1586, he found the art of play-writing in the hands of a group of men of immense force of imagination and of singularly varied gifts of expression. During the decade in which he was serving his apprenticeship to his art England lost Peele, Kyd, Greene, and Marlowe; Lodge, having become a physician, died in 1625. Every member of this group, with the exception of Marlowe, was born to good conditions; they were gentlemen in position, and scholars by virtue of university training. They were careless and, in some cases, violent and criminal livers ; men born out of due time, so far as adjustment between genius and sound conditions was concerned ; or committed by temperament to unbalanced, disorderly, and tragical careers. Greene, after a life of dissipation, died in extreme misery of mind and body ; Peele involved himself in many kinds of misfortune, and became the victim of his vices ; Nash lived long enough to lament the waste and confusion of his career ; and the splendid genius of Marlowe was quenched before he had reached his thirtieth year. He who would pass a sweeping and unqualified condemnation on this fatally endowed group of ardent young writers would do well to study the times in which they lived, the attitude of society towards the playwright, the absence of normal conditions for the expression of genius such as they possessed, and the perilous combination of temperament and imagination which seems to have been made in each. It is futile and immoral to conceal or minimize the faults and vices of men of genius ; but it is equally futile and immoral to attempt to determine in any individual career the degree of moral responsibility.

Greene was a born story-teller, without having any marked gift for the construction of strong and well-elaborated plots ; his study of character was neither vigorous nor convincing. Nash was, on the other hand, a born satirist, with a coarse but very effective method and a humour often grotesque but always virile. Peele was preëminently a poet of taste, with a gift for graceful and even elegant expression, a touch of tenderness, and a sensitiveness of imagination which showed itself in his use of the imagery of mythology. Lodge wrote dull plays and lightened them by the introduction of charming songs.

Marlowe was the creative spirit of this group of accomplished playwrights. The son of a Canterbury shoemaker, he took his Bachelor's degree at Cambridge, and arrived in London, "a boy in years, a man in genius, a god in ambition." His ardent nature, impatient of all restraint and full of Titanic impulses, found congenial society on the stage and congenial work in play-writing. His life was as passionate and lawless as his art; his plays were written in six turbulent years, and his career was one of brief but concentrated energy. The two parts of "Tamburlaine," "The Massacre at Paris," "The Jew of Malta," "Edward II.," and "Dr. Faustus," the glowing fragment of "Hero and Leander," and a few short compositions, among them the exquisite "Come live with me and be my love," evidence the depth and splendour of Marlowe's genius and the lack of balance and restraint in his art. He gave English tragedy sublimity, intensity, breadth, and order; he freed blank verse from rigidity and mechanical correctness, and gave it the freedom, harmony, variety of cadence, and compelling music which imposed it upon all later English tragedy. Neither in his life nor in his art did Marlowe accept the inevitable limitations of human power in action and in creation; he flung himself passionately against the immovable barriers, and grasped at the impossible.

William Shakespeare

But his failures were redeemed by superb successes. He breathed the breath of almost superhuman life into the English drama both as regards its content and its form; for he was even greater as a poet than as a dramatist :

> . . . his raptures were
> All air and fire . . . ;
> For that fine madness still he did retain
> Which rightly should possess a poet's brain.

He left but a single step to be taken in the full unfolding of the drama, and that step Shakespeare took : the step from the Titan to the Olympian.

CHAPTER II

THE charm of Stratford-on-Avon is twofold; it is enfolded by some of the loveliest and most character-istic English scenery, and it is the home of the greatest English literary tradition. Lying in the very heart of the country, it seems to be guarded as a place sacred to the memory of the foremost man of expression who has yet appeared among the English-speaking peoples. It has become a town of some magnitude, with a pros-perous trade in malt and corn; but its importance is due wholly to the fact that it is the custodian of Shakespeare's birthplace, of the school in which he was trained, of the house in which he courted Anne Hathaway, of the ground on which he built his own home, and of the church in which he lies buried. The place is full of Shakespearean associations; of localities which he knew in the years of his dawning intelligence, and in those later years when he returned to take his place as a householder and citizen; the old churches with which as a child he was familiar are still standing, substantially as they stood at the end of the sixteenth century; the grammar school still teaches the boys of to-day within the walls that listened to the same reci-tations three hundred years ago; the houses of his

25

children and friends are, in several instances, still secure from the destructive hand of time; there are still wide stretches of sloping hillside shaded by the ancient Forest of Arden; there are quaint half-timbered fronts upon which he must have looked; the "bank where the wild thyme blows" is still to be found by those who know the foot-path to Shottery and the road over the hill; the Warwickshire landscape has the same ripe and tender beauty which Shakespeare knew; and the Avon flows as in the days when he heard the nightingales singing in the level meadows across the river from the church, or slipped silently in his punt through the mist which softly veils it on summer nights.

When Shakespeare was born, on April twenty-second or twenty-third, in the year fifteen hundred and sixty-four, Stratford was an insignificant hamlet, off the main highways of travel, although within reach of important towns like Coventry, and of stately old English homes like Warwick and Kenilworth castles. The streets were narrow, irregular, and, like most streets in most towns in that unsanitary age, badly kept and of an evil odour; the houses were set among gardens or in the open, with picturesque indifference to modern ideas of community orderliness; the black-oak structure showing curious designs of triangles and squares through the plaster. Thatched roofs, projecting gables, rough walls, unpaved lanes, foot-paths through the fields, the long front of the Guild Hall with the Grammar School, the Guild Chapel, the Church of the Holy Trinity, the bridge across the

Birth and Breeding

Avon built by Sir Hugh Clopton in the time of Henry VII., made up the picture which Shakespeare saw when he looked upon the place of his birth. On High Street, when he came back from London to live in Stratford, he found, not far from his house in New Place, the carved half-timbered front of the house in which tradition says the mother of John Harvard was born.

The population of Stratford is now about nine thousand; in 1564 it was probably less than fifteen hundred. It was surrounded by fields which were sometimes white with grain, and were always, in the season, touched with the splendour of the scarlet poppy. The villagers were sturdy English folk with more vigour than intelligence, and with more capacity than education. Many of them were unable to sign their own names, and among these John Shakespeare, the father of the poet, has sometimes been included : documents exist, however, which bear what is believed to be his signature. There was nothing unusual in this lack of literary training ; comparatively few Englishmen of the station of John Shakespeare had mastered, in that period, the art of writing. Men who could not sign their own names were often men of mark, substance, and ability.

The family name was not uncommon in Warwickshire, and was borne by a good yeoman stock. When John Shakespeare applied, in 1596, for the right to use a coat of arms, he declared that Henry VII. had made a grant of lands to his grandfather in return for services of importance. The college of heraldry has been so prolific of fictitious genealogies that this claim is open to suspicion; what is certain is the substantial character of the poet's ancestors, their long residence in Warwickshire, and the fact that some of them were farmers, land-renters, and land-owners. The grandfather of the poet was probably Richard Shakespeare, a farmer who lived within easy walking distance of Stratford. John Shakespeare removed to Stratford about the middle of the sixteenth century, and became a trader in all manner of farm produce. Then, as now, malt and corn were staple articles of commerce in Stratford; John Shakespeare dealt in these and in wool, skins, meat, and leather. He has been called a glover and a butcher; he was both, and had several other vocations besides.

Henley Street was then one of the thoroughfares of Stratford, and got its name from the fact that it led to Henley-on-Avon, a market town of local importance. That John Shakespeare was an active man of affairs, with a keen instinct for business, if not with a sound judgment, is clear, not only from the variety and number of his business interests, but from the frequency of the suits for the recovery of small debts in which he appeared. His early ventures were successful, and he soon became a man of substance and influence. His prosperity was increased by his marriage, in 1557, to Mary Arden, the youngest daughter of a well-to-do farmer of Wilmcote, not far from Stratford. She brought her husband a house and fifty acres of land, some money, and other forms of property. During the year before his marriage John Shakespeare had purchased the house, with a garden, in Henley Street, which is now accepted as the birthplace of the poet. In the following year his growing influence was evidenced by his election as a tester of the quality of bread and of malt liquors. Various public duties were devolved upon him. He was elected a burgess or member of the town council; he became a chamberlain of the borough; and later was advanced to the highest position in the gift of the municipality, that of Bailiff. There were two daughters who died in infancy; then came the first son, William, who was christened, the parish register tells us, on the 26th day of April, 1564. The custom of the time with regard to the interval between birth and baptism was so well settled that there seems no reason to doubt that the poet was born on the 22d or 23d of the month. There were then two detached houses standing in Henley Street where the present house now stands; tradition assigns the house to the west as the place of the poet's birth. This house finally came into the possession, by the bequest of the poet's granddaughter, of the family of his sister Joan Hart, and until 1806 was occupied by them; the adjoining house to the east was let as an inn. In 1846 both houses were secured for preservation, restored as far as possible to the condition in which they were in the poet's time, joined in a single structure, and made one of the most interesting museums in the world. In this structure there is every reason to believe that Shakespeare was born. The continued possession of the part which was once the western house by the poet's kinsfolk was probably the basis for a tradition which runs back for an indefinite period.

The Birthplace, as it is called, is a cottage of plaster and timber, two stories in height, with dormer windows, and a pleasant garden in the rear — all that remains of a considerable piece of land. It stands upon the street, and the visitor passes at once, through a little porch, into a low room, ceiled with black oak, paved with flags, and with a fireplace so wide that one sees at a glance what the chimney-corner once meant of comfort and cheer. On those seats, looking into the glowing fire, the imagination of a boy could hardly fail to kindle. A dark and narrow stair leads to the little bare room on the floor above in which Shakespeare was probably born. The place seems fitted, by its very simplicity, to serve as the starting-point for so great a career. There is a small fireplace; the low ceiling is within reach of the hand; on the narrow panes of glass which fill the casement names and initials are traced in irregular profusion. This room has been a place eagerly sought by literary pilgrims since the beginning of the century. The low ceiling and the walls were covered, in the early part of the century, with innumerable autographs. In 1820 the occupant, a woman who attached great importance to the privilege of showing the house to visitors, was compelled to give up that privilege, and, by way of revenge, removed the furniture and whitewashed the walls of the house. A part of the wall of the upper room escaped the sacrilegious hand of the jealous custodian, and names running back to the third decade of the

Birth and Breeding

last century are still to be found there. Other and perhaps more famous names have taken the places of those which were erased, and the walls are now a mass of hieroglyphs. Scott, Byron, Rogers, Tennyson, Thackeray, Dickens, have left this record of their interest in the room. No new names are now written on these blackened walls; the names of visitors are kept in a record-book on the lower floor.

In a small room behind the birth-room what is known as the Stratford portrait of the poet is shown. On the first floor, opening from the room into which the visitor enters, is a larger room in which are collected a number of very interesting articles connected with the poet. There are to be seen the deed which conveyed the property to his father; the letter in which Richard Quiney, whose son Thomas married the poet's youngest daughter, Judith, in 1616, asked him for a loan of money; the seal ring on which the letters W. S. are engraved; the desk which stood in the Grammar School three hundred years ago; and many other curiosities, memorials, documents, and books which find proper place in such a museum. In the garden, sweet with the fragrant breath of summer, there are pansies and violets, columbines and rosemary, daisies and rue — flowers which seem to belong to Shakespeare, since they bloom in the plays as if they first struck root in the rich soil of his imagination. This property, which remained continuously in the possession of Shakespeare's kin until the beginning of the present century, is now set apart forever, with the home of Anne Hathaway, the ground which the poet purchased in 1597, and where he built his own home, and the adjoining house, as memorials of the poet's life in Stratford.

John Shakespeare prospered in private fortune and in public advancement for nearly a decade after the birth of the poet. His means were very considerable for the time and place, and as Bailiff and chief Alderman he was the civic head of the community. An ingenious attempt has been made to prove that he was a man of Puritan temper and associations ; but the fact that he applied for a grant of arms, and that as Bailiff he welcomed the actors of the Earl of Worcester's Company and the Queen's Company to Stratford in 1568, would seem to indicate that, whatever his religious convictions and ecclesiastical tendencies may have been, he did not share the fanatical temper of some of his contemporaries.

The child William, then four years old, may have seen these companies, bravely dressed, with banners flying, drums beating, and trumpeters sounding their ringing tones, riding over Clopton bridge and halting in the market-place where High and Bridge Streets intersect, and where the market, with its belfry and clock, now stands. The players of the day led a wandering life, full of vicissitude, but, in fair weather and a hospitable community, they brought with them a visible if sometimes shabby suggestion of the great London world, which made their occasional coming into a quiet town like Stratford an unforgettable occurrence. The horses they rode were gayly caparisoned, the banners they carried were splendidly emblazoned with the arms of their patrons, their costumes were rich and varied, and they were accompanied by grooms and servants of all sorts. A goodly company they must have seemed to a child's imagination, with an air of easy opulence worn as a part of their vocation, but as purely imitative as the parts they played to crowds of open-mouthed rustics. Their magnificence, however shabby, and their brave air, however swaggering, made rural England feel as if it had touched the great new world of adventure and fame and wealth, of which stories were told in every chimney corner.

To these companies of players Stratford appears to have given exceptional hospitality; the people of the place were lovers of the drama. In the course of two decades the town enjoyed no less than twenty-four visits from strolling companies; a fact of very obvious bearing on the education of Shakespeare's imagination and the bent of his mind toward a vocation. In such a community there must have been constant talk about plays and players, and easy familiarity with the resources and art of the actor. It follows, too, that the presence of so many players in the little village brought boys of an inquiring turn of mind into personal contact with the comedians and tragedians of the day. As a boy, Shakespeare came to know the old English plays which were the stock in trade of the travelling companies; he learned the stage business, and he was undoubtedly on terms of familiarity with men of gift and art. For the purposes of his future work this education was far more stimulating and formative than any which he could have secured at Eton or Winchester during the same impressionable years. Scott's specific training for the writing of the Waverley novels and the narrative poems which bear his name was gained in his ardent reading and hearing of old Scotch ballads, romances, stories, and history, rather than in the lecture-rooms of the University of Edinburgh. Shakespeare has sometimes been represented as a boy of obscure parentage and vulgar surroundings; he was, as a matter of fact, the son of a man of energy and substance, the foremost citizen of Stratford. He has often been represented as wholly lacking educational opportunities; he was, as a matter of fact, especially fortunate in educational opportunities of the most fertilizing and stimulating kind. The singular misconception which has identified education exclusively with formal academic training has made it possible to hold men of the genius of Shakespeare, Burns, and Lincoln before the world as exceptions to the law that no art can be mastered save through a thorough educational process. If Burns and Lincoln were not so near us, the authorship of "Tam o' Shanter" and the Gettysburg address would have been challenged on the ground of inadequate preparation for such masterpieces of expression.

These three masters of speech were exceptionally well educated for their art, for no man becomes an artist except by the way of apprenticeship; but their education was individual rather than formal, and liberating rather than disciplinary. The two poets were saturated in the most sensitive period in the unfolding of the imagination with the very genius of the people among whom they were to work and whose deepest instincts they were to interpret. Their supreme good fortune lay in the fact that they were educated through the imagination rather than through the memory and the rationalizing faculties. Homer, Æschylus, and Sophocles were educated by the same method; so also was Dante. A man sometimes gets this kind of education in the schools, but he oftener misses it. He is always supremely fortunate if he gets it at all. Shakespeare received it from several sources; one of them being the love of the drama in the town in which he was born, access to its records of every sort, and acquaintanceship with the custodians of its traditions and the practitioners of its art.

But he was by no means lacking in educational opportunities of a formal kind. The Grammar School on Church Street, adjoining the Guild Chapel and across Chapel Lane from the site of the poet's later home, one of the oldest and most picturesque buildings now standing in Stratford, was founded at the close of the fifteenth century. It was part of an older religious foundation, of which the Chapel still remains, and which once included a hospital. After passing through many vicissitudes, the school was reconstituted in the time of Edward VI. The Chapel was used in connection with it, and, if tradition is to be accepted, was occasionally employed for school purposes. It was built about the middle of the thirteenth century, and is a characteristic bit of the England which Shakespeare saw. The low, square tower must have been one of the most familiar landmarks of Stratford in his eyes. He saw it when he came, a schoolboy, from his father's house in Henley Street, and turned into High Street ; and from his own home at New Place he must have looked at it from all his southern windows. The interior of the Chapel has suffered many things at the hands of iconoclasts and restorers, but remains substantially as Shakespeare knew it. The low ceilings and old furnishings of the Grammar School, blackened with time, make one aware, like the much initialed and defaced forms in the older rooms at Eton, that education in England has a long history.

In Shakespeare's time the Renaissance influence was at its height, and the schools were bearing the fruits of the new learning. Education was essentially literary, and dealt almost exclusively with the humanities. Greek was probably within reach of boys of exceptional promise as students ; but Latin was every boy's daily food. With Plautus and Terence, the masters of Latin comedy, with Ovid, Virgil, and Horace, the masters of Latin poetry, with Cicero the orator and Seneca the moralist, Shakespeare made early acquaintance. When Sir Hugh Evans, in the "Merry Wives of Windsor," listens to the recitation, so familiar to all boys of English blood, of *Hic*, *Hæc*, *Hoc*, we are doubtless sharing a reminiscence of the poet's school days. The study of grammar and the practice of conversation prepared the way for the reading of the classic writers, and furnished an education which was not only disciplinary but invigorating. Without being in any sense a scholar, there is abundant evidence that Shakespeare knew other languages and literatures than his own. His knowledge was of the kind which a man of his quality of mind and educational opportunities might be expected to possess. It was entirely subordinate to the end of furnishing the material he wished to use; it was vital rather than exact; it was used freely, without any pretension to thoroughness; it served immediate ends with the highest intelligence, and is inaccurate with the indifference of a poet who was more concerned with the sort of life led in Bohemia than with its boundary lines. The great artists have been noted for their insight rather than their accuracy; not because they have been untrained, but because they have used facts simply to get at truth. Shakespeare could be as accurate as a scientist when exactness served his purpose, as the description of the Dover Cliff in " King Lear" shows.

In the plays there are recurring evidences that the poet knew Virgil and Ovid, and had not forgotten Lily's grammar and the "Sententiæ Pueriles," which the schoolboys of his time committed to memory as a matter of course. In a number of instances he used the substance of French and Italian books of which English translations had not been made in his time. The command of French and Italian for reading purposes, to a boy of Shakespeare's quickness of mind and power of rapid assimilation, with his knowledge of Latin and the widespread interest among men of his class in the literature of both countries, was easily acquired. It must be remembered that for thirty years Shakespeare was on intimate terms with men of scholarly tastes and acquirements. The most splendid tribute among the many which he received from his contemporaries came from the most thoroughly trained of his fellow-dramatists; one who stood preëminently for the classical tradition in the English drama. Shakespeare was neither by instinct nor opportunity a scholar in the sense in which Ben Jonson was a scholar; but he had considerable familiarity with four languages; he had access to many books; he had read some of them with the most vital insight; and he was exceptionally well informed in many directions.

He knew something of law, medicine, theology, history, trade; and this knowledge, easily acquired, was readily used for purposes of illustration; sometimes used inaccurately as regards details, as men of imagination have used knowledge in all times and are using it to-day; but used always with divination of its spiritual or artistic significance. A careful study of Shakespeare's opportunities and a little common sense in reckoning with his genius will dissipate the confusion of mind which has made it possible to regard him as uneducated and therefore incapable of writing his own works. Aubrey's statement that " he understood Latin pretty well " is abundantly verified by the plays; they also furnish evidence that he understood Italian and French.

That he studied the Bible, either in the Genevan version or in the revision of 1568, is equally apparent. His references to incidents in Biblical history and his

Birth and Breeding

use of Biblical phrases suggest a familiarity acquired in boyhood rather than a habit of reading in maturity. The direct suggestions of the influence of the Bible are numerous; but there is also the impression of a rich and frequent use of Biblical wisdom and imagery. Mr. Locke Richardson has suggested that when Falstaff " babbled of green fields " his memory was going back to the days when, as a schoolboy, the Twenty-third Psalm was often in his ears or on his lips; and there are many places in the plays where Shakespeare seems to be remembering something which he learned from the Bible in youth. No collection of books could have brought him richer material for his view of life and for his art, not only as regards its content but its form.

The Grammar School, in which Cicero and Virgil have been taught in unbroken succession since Shakespeare's time, was a free school, taking boys of the neighbourhood from seven years upwards, and keeping them on the benches with generous disregard of hours. There were holidays, however, and there was time for punting on the river, for rambles across country, and for those noisy games, prolonged far into the evening by the long English twilight, which make the meadows across the Avon as vocal as the old graveyard about the church is reposeful and silent.

Boys in Shakespeare's station in life rarely went to school after their fourteenth year, and the growing financial embarrassments of John Shakespeare probably took his son out of the Grammar School a year earlier. The tide of prosperity had begun to recede from the active trader some time earlier; whether his declining fortunes were due to lack of judgment or to the accidents of a business career it is impossible to determine. It is clear that he was a man of energy and versatility; that he was successful at an unusually early age and in an unusual degree; and that later, for a time at least, he was overtaken by adversity. In 1578, when the poet was fourteen years old, John Shakespeare mortgaged his wife's property at Wilmcote for the sum of forty pounds, or about two hundred dollars — the equivalent of more than a thousand dollars in present values. In the following year another piece of property at Snitterfield was disposed of for the same amount. Unsatisfied or dissatisfied creditors began to bring suits; taxes went unpaid; other properties were sold without arresting the downward movement; in 1586, when the poet went up to London to seek his fortune, John Shakespeare had ceased to attend the meetings at Guild Hall, and lost his right to wear the Alderman's gown in consequence; later his goods were seized by legal process and warrants for his arrest as an insolvent debtor were issued. There is a story of a considerable loss through the generous act of standing as surety for a brother; and it is known that there was, during these years, great distress in several branches of trade in Warwickshire.

If it cost nothing to send a boy to the Grammar School, it cost something to keep him there; and by the withdrawal of his son when losses began to press heavily upon him John Shakespeare may not only have cut off one source of his expense, but gained some small addition to his income from the industry of another wage-earner in the family. After leaving school the son may have assisted his father, as Aubrey reports, or he may have entered the office of a lawyer, as a contemporary allusion seems to affirm ; nothing definite is known about his occupations between his fourteenth and eighteenth years. There is no reason why anything should have been remembered or recorded ; he was an obscure boy living in an inland village, before the age of newspapers, and out of relation with people of fashion or culture. During this period as little is known of him as is known of Cromwell during the same period ; as little, but no less. This fact gives no occasion either for surprise or scepticism as to his marvellous genius ; it was an entirely normal fact concerning boys growing up in unliterary times and rural communities. That these boys subsequently became famous does not change the conditions under which they grew up.

CHAPTER III

THE England of Shakespeare's boyhood and youth was not only dramatic in feeling but spectacular in form ; the Queen delighted in those gorgeous pageants which symbolized by their splendour the greatness of her place and the dignity of her person. Her vigorous Tudor temper was thrown into bold relief by her intensely feminine craving for personal loyalty and admiration. One of the keenest and most adroit politicians of her time, her instincts as a woman were sometimes postponed to the exigencies of the State, but they were as imperious as her temper. Denied as Queen the personal devotion which as a woman she craved, she fed her unsatisfied imagination on flattery and imposing ceremonies. In the summer of 1575, when Shakespeare was in his twelfth year, the Queen made that memorable visit to Kenilworth Castle which has found its record in Scott's brilliant novel. Four years earlier, the royal presence at Charlecote (Sir Thomas Lucy, the future Justice Shallow, playing the part of host) had brought the Court into the immediate neighbourhood of Stratford. Kenilworth is fifteen miles distant, but the magnificent pageants and stately ceremonies with which Leicester welcomed the Queen were matters of general talk throughout Warwickshire long before the arrival of Elizabeth.

The Queen's visit was made in July, when nature supplemented with lavish beauty all the various art and immense wealth which Leicester freely drew upon for the entertainment of his capricious and exacting mistress. Pageants and diversions of every kind succeeded one another in bewildering variety for ten days. The Queen was addressed by sibyls, by giants of Arthur's age, by the Lady of the Lake, by Pomona, Ceres, and Bacchus. There was a rustic marriage for her entertainment, and a mock fight representing the defeat of the Danes. Returning from the chase, Triton rose out of the lake and, in Neptune's name, prayed for her help to deliver an enchanted lady pursued by a cruel knight; and straightway the lady herself appeared, with an escort of nymphs; Proteus, riding a dolphin, following close behind. Then, suddenly, from the heart of the dolphin, a chorus of ocean deities sang the praises of the great and beautiful Queen. The tension of these splendid mythological and allegorical pageants was relieved by the tricks of necromancers, the feats of acrobats, and by fights between dogs and bears. The prodigality, semi-barbaric taste, and magnificence of the age were illustrated for a royal spectator with more than royal lavishness.

On a summer day the way from Stratford to the Castle lies through a landscape touched with the ripest beauty of England; a beauty not only of line and structure, but of depth and richness of foliage,

of ancient places slowly transformed by the tender
and patient and pious care of centuries of growth
into masses of greenness so affluent and of such depth
that it seems as if fountains of life had overflowed into
great masses of foliage.

The summer days were doubtless long and weari-
some to the boys in the Grammar School in the quiet
village. The nightingale had ceased to sing along the
Avon ; the fragrance was gone from the hedges with
their blossoms ; midsummer was at its height ; there
was the smell of the new-cut grass in the meadows,
touched here and there with the glory of the scarlet
poppy. Whether the coming of the Queen was made
the occasion of granting a holiday it is much too late
to assert or deny,; that the more adventurous took
one is more than probable. In those days even the
splendour of the wandering players paled before that
of the Queen. She had been seventeen years on the
throne. She had all the qualities of her family : the
Tudor imperiousness of temper, and the Tudor instinct for understanding her people and winning them.
The Armada was thirteen years in the future, and the
full splendour of a great reign was still to come ; but
there was something in the young Queen which had
already touched the imagination of England ; something in her spirit and bearing which saved the poets
of the time from being mere flatterers. Elizabeth was
neither beautiful nor gracious ; the romantic charm
which captivated all who came into the presence of
her unhappy contemporary Mary Stuart was not in
her. But what she lacked as woman she easily pos-

sessed as queen; she had the rare gift of personifying her rank and place. The sense of sovereignty went with her. In a time of passionate energy and lust of life she was not only the centre of organized society, but the symbol of unlimited opportunity, fortune, and greatness.

Where the Queen was, there was England; she was not only its ruler, but the personification of its vitality and force. When she came into Warwickshire, the whole country was stirred with the sense of the presence of something splendid and significant. Stories of the preparations at the Castle had been carried by word of mouth across the countryside. There were no newspapers; no means of rapid communication with the outer world; there were, for the vast majority of people, no books; most men never went out of their native shires; travellers from a distance were few. Tales of Leicester's honours and emoluments were told and listened to like modern fairy stories; his rapid advancement lent a kind of magic to the splendour of his state; and the Queen was the magician whose touch made and marred all fortunes. In the time of Elizabeth as in that of Victoria, the Queen personified the English State and the majesty of the English race. Through this kind of symbolism a deep and formative educational influence has been silently put forth and unconsciously received. The Queen was in many ways the incarnation of the spirit of Shakespeare's time, and her coming into Warwickshire was like the advent of the world-element into a life which had felt only local influences.

William Shakespeare

Chief among those influences was that of the lovely scenery by which the poet's young imagination was enfolded. Whether he was one of the throng which waited for the Queen on some old-time highway, or stood with the eager crowd who gathered about the Castle gates on the great day of the royal visit, is of no consequence : it can hardly be doubted that the imaginative boy of eleven did not lose that splendid spectacle ; what is certain is his familiarity with the Warwickshire landscape — that fortunate landscape beautiful in itself and appealing to every imagination because it was Shakespeare's country.

There are more striking outlooks than those which are found between Kenilworth and Stratford ; there are more fertile and garden-like stretches of country ; but there is nowhere in England happier harmony of the typical qualities of the English country : gentle undulation of wold and wood, groups of ancient trees, long lines of hedges, slow rivers winding under over-hanging branches and loitering in places of immemorial shade ; stately homes rich in association with men and women of force or craft, or possessed of the noble art of gentleness in ungentle times ; a low, soft sky from which clouds are rarely absent, and an atmosphere which softens all outlines, subdues all sounds, and works magical effects of light and distance. These qualities of ripeness and repose are seen in their per-fection from the ruined Mervyn's Tower, in which Amy Robsart was imprisoned. As far as the eye can reach, the landscape is full of a tender and gracious beauty. Nothing arrests and holds the at-

tention, for the loveliness is diffused rather than concentrated; it lies like a magical veil over the whole
landscape, concealing nothing and yet touching everything with a modulating softness which seems almost
like a gift from the imagination. In midsummer, when
the grain stands almost as high as a man's head, the
foot-path which runs through it can be followed for a
long distance by the eye, so sharply cut through the
waving fields is it. Those winding foot-paths, which
take one away from the highroads into the heart of
the country, are nowhere more alluring to the eye and
the imagination than in Warwickshire. They make
chances for intimacy with the landscape which the
highways cannot offer. The long-travelled roads are
old and ripe with that quiet richness of setting which
comes with age; they rise and fall with the gentle
movement of the country; they are often arched with
venerable trees; they wind up hill and down in leisurely,
picturesque curves and lines; they cross slow-moving
streams; they often loiter in recesses of shade which
centuries have conspired to deepen and widen.

But it is along the quiet by-paths that one comes
upon all that is essential and characteristic in Warwickshire. These immemorial ways put any man who
chooses to follow them in possession of the landscape;
they cross the most carefully tended fields, they
penetrate the most jealously guarded estates, they
offer access to ancient places of silence and seclusion.
The narrow path between the hedges is one of those
rights of the English people which evidence their
sovereignty over possessions, the titles to which have

been lodged for centuries in private hands. They silently affirm that, though the acres may be private property, the landscape is the inalienable possession of the English people. In May, when the hawthorn is in bloom and the nightingale is in full song, a Warwickshire foot-path leads one into a world as ideal as the island in "The Tempest" or the fairy-haunted country of the "Midsummer Night's Dream." That Shakespeare knew these pathways into the realm of the imagination there is ample evidence; that he was familiar with these byways about Stratford is beyond a doubt. Does not one of them still lead to Shottery?

Kenilworth, which was a noble and impressive stronghold in Shakespeare's boyhood, ample enough to entertain a court with long-continued and magnificent pageants, is not less imposing in its vast ruins than in the day when knights rode at one another, spears at rest, in the tilting-yard and the Queen was received at the great gate by Leicester. In the loveliness of its surroundings, the beauty of its outlook, the romantic interest of its ivy-covered ruins, and the splendour and tragedy of its historic fortunes, it symbolizes the harmony of natural and human association which invests all Warwickshire with perennial charm. Much of this charm has come since Shakespeare's time, but it was there in quality and characteristic when he roamed afield on summer afternoons, or, on holidays, made his way to Kenilworth, Warwick, or Coventry. It was in key with his own poised and harmonious spirit; its quality is diffused through his work. For nature in the plays is always subordinate to the unfolding of character through action, but is so clearly limned, so constantly in view, so much and so significantly a part of the complete impression which conveys not only a drama but its setting and atmosphere, that it must have had large space in the poet's spiritual life.

There are touches of Warwickshire in all Shakespeare's work : in " The Winter's Tale " the flowers of Warwickshire are woven together in one of the most exquisite calendars of season and blossom in the whole range of poetry ; in " As You Like It " the depths and hollows and long stretches of shade of the old Forest of Arden rise before the imagination ; in " A Midsummer Night's Dream " there are bits of landscape which are now in fairyland, but were once good solid Warwickshire soil. The valley of the Tweed and the mountains about the Scotch lakes form a natural background for Scott's poetry ; the Ayrshire landscape rises into view again and again in the verse of Burns ; the lake district of Cumberland, with its mists and multitudinous voices of hidden streams, lies behind Wordsworth's verse. In like manner, Warwickshire lies always in the background of Shakespeare's mind, and gives form, quality, and colour to the landscape of his poetry. Unless dramatic necessity imposes catastrophic effects upon him, as in " Lear " and " Macbeth," Shakespeare's landscape is reposeful, touched with ripe and tender beauty, happily balanced between extremes in temperature, happily poised between austerity and prodigality in beauty. Its loveliness has more solidity and substance than that which the New England poets loved so well, and the fragrance of which, as delicate as that of the arbutus, they have caught and preserved; while, on the other hand, it has not the voluptuous note, the beguiling and passionate sensuousness, of the Italian landscape. The beauty of the country in which Rosalind wanders and Jacques meditates is more harmonious with man's spiritual fortunes and less sympathetic with his passion than that in which Romeo and Juliet live out the brief and ardent drama of that young love which sees nothing in the world save the reflection of itself. The landscape of the Forest of Arden knows all the changes of the season, and bends the most obsequious courtier to its conditions; it has a quiet and pervasive charm for the senses, but its deepest appeal is to the imagination; there is in it a noble reticence and restraint which exact much before it surrenders its ultimate loveliness, and in its surrender it reinvigorates instead of relaxing and debilitating. Its beauty is as much a matter of structure as of form; as much a matter of atmosphere as of colour. And this is the charm of Warwickshire.

It does not know the roll and thunder of the sea, which Tennyson thought were more tumultuous and resonant on the coast of Lincolnshire than anywhere else in England; it is not overlaid with the bloom which makes Kent a garden when the hop-vines are in flower; it lacks that something, half legendary and half real, which draws to Cornwall so many lovers of the idylls of Arthur; the noble largeness of the Somerset landscapes is not to be found within its boundaries; but its harmonious, balanced, and ripe loveliness is its own and is not to be found elsewhere.

There are many points at which one feels this characteristic charm. From Kenilworth to Stratford, if one goes by the way of Warwick and Charlecote, it is continuous. There are sweet and homely places along the road where the houses seem to belong to the landscape and the roses climb as if they longed for human intercourse; there are stretches of sward so green and deep that one is sure Shakespeare's feet might have pressed them; there are trees of such girth and circumference of shade that Queen Elizabeth might have waited under them; there are vines and mosses and roses everywhere; and everywhere also there are bits of history clinging like old growths to fallen walls, and densely shaded hill, and stately mansion set far back in noble expanse of park. Through the trees the low square tower guides one to an ancient church set among ancient graves, with a sweet solemnity enfolding it in silence and peace. The fields are richly strewn with wild flowers, and every cliff, stone, and bit of ruined wall is hung deep with vine and moss, as if nature could not care enough for beauty in a country in which men care so much for nature.

Warwick is a busy town on court and market days, but the old-world charm is still in its streets. Its ancient and massive gates prepare one for its quaint and narrow streets, on which half-timbered houses still stand; the venerable and picturesque Leicester hospital, founded by Lord Dudley in 1571, rising above the narrow entrance to the town, as one approaches it from Stratford, like a custodian of the old-time ways and men. The stream of sightseers which pours through the Castle cannot lessen its impressiveness, nor dull the splendour of the ancient baronial life which invests it with perennial interest. The view from the plant house, with the lovely stretch of sward to the Avon, the old-fashioned garden on the left, the Castle rising in massive lines, the terraces bright with flowers, the cedars of Lebanon dark in the foreground, is one of the loveliest in England for its setting of opulent and dignified English life.

But the view which Shakespeare must have loved is that from the Avon below the ruined bridge, whose piers, crowned with foliage, rise out of the quiet water in monumental massiveness. It was a fortunate hour which relieved them from the everyday work of a highway for traffic and made them tributary to its romantic interest and beauty. The dark tower rising from the river's brink, the long, massive front set with a multitude of shining windows, the gardener's cottage blossoming with roses to the very apex of the roof, the quiet river in which, on soft afternoons, all this beauty and grandeur seem to sink into the heart of nature — this is Warwickshire; where nature, legend, and history commingle in full and immemorial stream to nourish and enrich an ancient and beautiful landscape.

Warwick Castle is a type of the great baronial home; Charlecote belongs to another and more gracious order of architecture. It is a stately house, with the characteristic environment of a great English estate —

the long reaches of park-like country, the fine approaches, the herd of mottled deer feeding at a distance with that intent alertness which shows that these shy creatures are at home only in the deep woods. No lover of Shakespeare can look at Charlecote or think of it without a vision of these wild creatures grazing at high noon under the shade of wide-spreading oaks, or stealing like phantoms through the soft moonlight. Such a one has no curiosity about the present ownership or occupancy of the house; there lived, nearly three centuries ago, and there will always live, the immortal Justice Shallow. The great gates open upon one of the loveliest roads; opposite is the tumbledown stile, a curiosity in itself, but concerning whose Shakespearean associations one must not inquire too closely. The house dates back to the year 1558, and the noble oaks, chestnuts, limes, and elms which stand in great groups or in isolated beauty in the park must have a still older date. In its long, rambling structure the architecture of Elizabeth's time is preserved in spite of later changes. It must be seen from the Avon if its spacious structure and rich setting are to be discerned; from the highway it is stately and dignified, but it is not beautiful. As one approaches it on the quiet river it discloses itself as part of the landscape. Octagonal towers, turrets, oriel window and belfry; the mellow red of long-standing walls relieved by great masses of green; the walled terrace with great urns which in the blossoming season are overflowing fountains of colour; the quiet loveliness of the terraced ground from the river to the house; the broad steps

which make the Avon companionable and approach-
able ; the dignity, seclusion, and stately beauty of the
landscape of which the house seems the focal point —
all these separable features sink into the mind and
leave a single rich, harmonious impression of noble
and characteristic English life. A herd of deer feeding under the trees looks up startled and seems to
melt into the deeper wood : the river has the placidity
of a stream which has never been awakened by the
clamour of trade, although it turns a wheel here and
there in its winding course ; the note of a hidden
waterfall penetrates the silence and deepens it.

The Avon knows no gentler landscape than that
through which it passes as it glides out of the shadow
of Hampton Lucy bridge, an old mill close at hand
and a waterfall not far distant. On a summer day,
when the grain is ripening in the fields, it would not
be easy to find a more charming epitome of rural
England : the gray church tower rising above a noble
group of elms ; the little village gathered about it as
if for safety and companionship ; the murmur of the
river as it drops into a lower channel ; the wide sun-
lighted fields, with glimpses of scarlet through the
green and gold, and the larks rising out of their hidden
nests, mounting swiftly until they become mere points
against the soft blue of the low sky or the white
masses of drifting cloud, hanging poised in mid-air
and pouring out a flood of sweet, clear, haunting notes,
full of the sound of running water, of deep woods
where the sun sets them aflame, and of the great open
spaces of the meadows. No other bird has a note so

jubilant with the unspent freshness of nature ; a sound in which there is no pathos of human need or sorrow, but the overflowing joyousness of that world in which the deep springs are fed and the roots of flowers nourished.

> Hark ! hark ! the lark at heaven's gate sings,
>   And Phœbus 'gins arise,
> His steeds to water at those springs
>   On chaliced flowers that lies;
> And winking Mary-buds begin
>   To ope their golden eyes.

The lark's note of unforced joyousness is often heard in Shakespeare's plays ; its buoyant music, rising as if from inexhaustible springs, was akin to his own fresh and effortless melody.

Between Hampton Lucy and Stratford the distance is not great, but the river moves with a leisurely indifference to time which is amply justified by the beauty of its course. When that course lies enfolded in green and shaded loveliness, it is doubtful whether any point has a more compelling charm than the quiet graveyard where Holy Trinity keeps watch and ward over its ancient dead. On a moonlit night there is enchantment in the place ; the moment one leaves the street and enters the arching avenue of limes, the England of to-day becomes the England of long ago. The spire of the church, rising above the trees, seeming to bring into more striking relief the long, narrow, dark nave ; the graves, grass-grown and so much a part of the place that they suggest the common mortality of the race rather than solitary death or individual loss; the level common across the river, which nightingales love when the bloom of May is on the hedges; the deep shadows in which the river loses itself as one looks toward the mill, and the dark outlines and twinkling lights as one turns toward the village : all these aspects of the place, under the spell of one great memory, touch the imagination and make it aware of a brooding presence which, although withdrawn from sight, still loves and haunts this place of quiet meditation and of a beauty in which joy and pathos are deeply harmonized. Apart from the sentiment which the place of Shakespeare's burial must inevitably evoke, there is that in the scene itself which interprets Shakespeare's spirit and makes his genius more near and companionable.

On such a night one turns instinctively toward Shottery with the feeling that the poet must have taken the same course on many another night as silent and fragrant. The old foot-path is readily found, and the meadows on either side are sleeping as gently in the soft, diffused light of the mid-summer night as when the poet saw them in his youth. The little hamlet, a mile to the eastward, is soon reached, and the cottage in which Anne Hathaway spent her girlhood is so well impressed on the memory of the English-reading world that it is recognizable at a glance. The elms rise over it as if to protect it from the harsh approaches of wind and storm; it is so embosomed in vines that it seems to be part of the old-time garden whose flowers bloom to the very

stepping-stones of entrance. Its thatched roof, tim-
bered walls, and projecting eaves have preserved its
ancient aspect; and the story of its age is told still
more distinctly in its low and blackened ceilings, its
stone floors, its broad hearth and capacious chimney-
seats.

To the west and north of Stratford the Forest of
Arden once covered a great stretch of territory, and
traces of its noble beauty are still to be discerned in
the trees which spread a deep shade over hollow and
hillside as one rambles across the Welcombe hills.
In the distance the clustered chimneys of Charlecote
are seen, and the ridge where the battle of Edge Hill
was fought. The Forest of Arden has been a place of
refuge for the imagination ever since the time when,
by the alembic of Shakespeare's genius, it was trans-
ferred from Warwickshire to that world in which time
does not run nor age wither; enough remains of ancient tree and shadowy silence to make its noble
beauty credible. The foot-path brings one past the
gates of Clopton — a spacious and dignified house,
with a charming outlook, fine old gardens, some very
interesting pictures, a rich heritage of ghost stories,
and a generous host. The stone effigies of the Clop-
tons now fill the ancient pew in Holy Trinity, but
they were long the foremost family at Stratford, men
of force and benefactors of the town. Sir Hugh
Clopton, who built the bridge over the Avon, and
rebuilt the Guild Chapel, became Lord Mayor of London; and others who bore the name honoured it. In
the tower of the Guild Chapel there is a quaint recital

of the virtues and generosity of Sir Hugh: "This monumental table was erected A.D. 1708, at the request of the Corporation (by Sir John Clopton, of Clopton, Knt., their Recorder), in memory of Sir Hugh Clopton, Knt. (a younger branch of yt ancient family), whose pious works were so many and great, they ought to be had in everlasting remembrance, especially by this town and parish, to which he was a particular benefactor, where he gave £100 to poor housekeepers and 100 marks to twenty poor maidens of good name and fame, to be paid at their marriages. He built ye stone bridge over Avon, with ye causey at ye west end; farther manifesting his piety to God, and love to this place of his nativity, as ye centurion in ye Gospel did to ye Jewish Nation and Religion, by building them a Synagogue; for at his sole charge, this beautiful Chappel of ye Holy Trinity was rebuilt, temp H. VII, and ye Cross Ile of ye parish Church. He gave £50 to ye repairing bridges and highways within 10 miles of this town." Then follows a recital of a number of benefactions to London and other parts of the country, closing with the words: "This charatable Gent died a Bachelr 15 Sept. 1496, and was buried in Saint Margaret's Church, Lothbury, London."

In this country Shakespeare's young imagination was unfolded; against this background of tender and pervasive beauty he came to consciousness, not, perhaps, of the quality and range of his genius, but of the nobility of form and loveliness of colour against which the comedy and tragedy of human life are set as upon a divinely ordered stage.

CHAPTER IV

MARRIAGE AND LONDON

THERE are traditions but no records of the period between 1577, when Shakespeare's school life ended, and the year 1586, when he left Stratford. In this age, when all events, significant and insignificant, are reported; when biography has assumed proportions which are often out of all relation to the importance or interest of those whose careers are described with microscopic detail; when men of letters, especially, are urged to produce and publish with the greatest rapidity, are photographed, studied, described, and characterized with journalistic energy and industry, and often with journalistic indifference to perspective; and when every paragraph from the pen of a successful writer is guarded from the purloiner and protected from plagiarist by laws and penalties, it seems incredible that so little, relatively, should be known about the daily life, the working relations, the intimate associations, the habits and artistic training, of the greatest of English poets.

And this absence of biographic material on a scale which would seem adequate from the modern point of view has furnished, not the ground — for the word ground implies a certain solidity or basis of fact—

but the occasion, of many curious speculations and of some radical scepticism. Absence of the historical sense has often led the rash and uncritical to read into past times the spirit and thought of the present, and to interpret the conditions of an earlier age in the light of existing conditions. Taking into account the habits of Shakespeare's time; the condition of life into which he was born; the fact that he was not a writer of dramas to be read, but of plays to be acted, and that, in his own thought and in the thought of his contemporaries, he was a playwright who lived by writing for the stage and not a poet who appealed to a reading public and was eager for literary reputation; recalling the inferior position which actors occupied in society, and the bohemian atmosphere in which all men who were connected with the stage lived, it is surprising, not that we know so little, but that we know so much, about Shakespeare.

Mr. Halliwell-Phillipps has covered this ground with admirable clearness and precision: "In this aspect the great dramatist participates in the fate of most of his literary contemporaries, for if a collection of the known facts relating to all of them were tabularly arranged, it would be found that the number of the ascertained particulars of his life reached at least the average. At the present day, with biography carried to a wasteful and ridiculous excess, and Shakespeare the idol not merely of a nation but of the educated world, it is difficult to realize a period when no interest was taken in the events in the lives of authors, and when the great poet himself, notwithstanding the immense popularity of some of his works, was held in no general reverence. It must be borne in mind that actors then occupied an inferior position in society, and that in many quarters even the vocation of a dramatic writer was considered scarcely respectable. The intelligent appreciation of genius by individuals was not sufficient to neutralize in these matters the effect of public opinion and the animosity of the religious world, — all circumstances thus uniting to banish general interest in the history of persons connected in any way with the stage. This biographical indifference continued for many years, and long before the season arrived for a real curiosity to be taken in the subject, the records from which alone a satisfactory memoir could have been constructed had disappeared. At the time of Shakespeare's decease, non-political correspondence was rarely preserved, elaborate diaries were not the fashion, and no one, excepting in semi-apocryphal collections of jests, thought it worth while to record many of the sayings and doings, or to delineate at any length the characters, of actors and dramatists, so that it is generally by the merest accident that particulars of interest respecting them have been recovered."

History, tradition, contemporary judgments scattered through a wide range of books and succeeded by a "Centurie of Prayse," the fruits of the critical scholarship of the last half-century, the Record in the Stationers' Register taken in connection with the dates of the first representations of the different plays; and, finally, the study of Shakespeare's work as a whole, have, however, gone a long way toward making good the absence of voluminous biographic material. Enough remains to make the story of the poet's career connected and intelligible, the record of his growth as an artist clear and deeply significant, and the history of his spiritual development legible and of absorbing interest.

The kind of occupation which fell to Shakespeare's hands during the five years of his adolescence between 1577 and 1582 is a matter of minor interest ; the education of sense and imagination which he received during that impressionable period is a matter of supreme interest. That he early formed the habit of exact observation his work shows in places innumerable. No detail of natural life escaped him; the plays are not only saturated with the spirit of nature, but they are accurate calendars of natural events and phenomena ; they abound in the most exact descriptions of those details of landscape, flora, and animal life which a writer must learn at first hand and which he can learn only when the eye is in the highest degree sensitive and the imagination in the highest degree responsive. A boy of Shakespeare's genius and situation would have mastered almost unconsciously the large and thorough knowledge of trees, flowers, birds, dogs, and horses which his work shows. Such a boy sees, feels, and remembers everything which in any way relates itself to his growing mind. The Warwickshire landscape became, by the unconscious process of living in its heart, a part of his memory, the background of his conscious life. He knew it passively in numberless walks, loiterings, solitary rambles; and he knew it actively, for there is every reason to believe that he participated in the sports of his time, and saw fields and woods and remote bits of landscape as one sees them in hunting, coursing, and fishing. He was in a farming country, and his kin on both sides were landowners or farmers; he had opportunities to become acquainted not only with the country, but with the habits of the birds and animals that lived in it.

He loved action as well as meditation, and his life was marvellously well poised when one recalls what perilous stuff of thought, passion, and imagination were in him. It was perhaps through physical activity that he worked off the ferment of adolescence, and went through the storm-and-stress period without serious excess or mistake of direction. Sport would have furnished a natural outlet for such a nature as his at a time when self-expression in some form was inevitable; and the spirit of sport, once aroused in a youth of ardent temperament, was not careful of the arbitrary lines which property draws across the landscape. To the sportsman the countryside is one unbroken field.

There may have been, therefore, some basis of fact for the tradition which has long affirmed that an unsuccessful poaching adventure in Charlecote Park led to the poet's departure from Stratford. This story was told succinctly by Rowe nearly a century after Shakespeare's death. "He had, by a misfortune common enough to young fellows, fallen into ill company, and, among them, some, that made a frequent practice of deer-stealing, engaged him with them more than once in robbing a park that belonged to Sir Thomas Lucy of Charlecote, near Stratford. For this he was prosecuted by that gentleman, as he thought, somewhat too severely ; and, in order to revenge that ill-usage, he made a ballad upon him, and though this, probably the first essay of his poetry, be lost, yet it is said to have been so very bitter that it redoubled the prosecution against him to that degree that he was obliged to leave his business and family in Warwickshire and shelter himself in London.''

Facts have come to light in late years which seem to show that the deer-park at Charlecote was not in existence until a much later date, and it has been assumed by some, who are perhaps overanxious for Shakespeare's reputation, that the poaching story is entirely legendary. It rests entirely on tradition ; but the tradition was persistent during many decades, and finds some support in the fact that Justice Shallow is beyond doubt a humorous study of the Sir Thomas Lucy of prosecuting temper. No trace of the ballad mentioned by Rowe remains. Poaching of this kind, although punishable by imprisonment, was not regarded at that time as a very serious offence against good morals, although not without grave provocation to landowners. Young men at the universities were not unfrequently detected in the same forbidden but fascinating sport. It is perhaps significant that Sir Peter Lucy, about this time, publicly advocated the passage of more stringent game laws.

The evidence is neither direct nor conclusive, but,

taken as a whole, it seems to confirm the poaching tradition. It was, in any event, a much more serious matter for the owner of Charlecote than for the Stratford youth who fell into his hands; for Justice Shallow has been accepted by later generations as a portrait rather than a caricature; and what Shakespeare left undone in the way of satirizing the landowner against whom he had offended, another poet of Warwickshire birth, Walter Savage Landor, completed in his brilliant "Citation and Examination of William Shakespeare." It ought not to be forgotten, however, that the victim of the satirical genius of Shakespeare and Landor wrote these touching words for the tomb of his wife in Charlecote church:

"All the time of her Lyfe a true and faithfull servant of her good God; never detected of any crime or vice; in religion most sound; in love to her husband most faithfull and true. In friendship most constant. To what in trust was committed to her most secret; in wisdom excelling; in governing her House and bringing up of Youth in the feare of God that did converse with her most rare and singular; a great maintainer of hospitality; greatly esteemed of her betters; misliked of none unless the envious. When all is spoken that can be said, a Woman so furnished and garnished with Virtue as not to be bettered, and hardly to be equalled of any; as she lived most virtuously, so she dyed most godly. Set down by him that best did know what hath been written to be true. Thomas Lucy."

Sir Thomas may have had the qualities which Shakespeare imputed to him, but the likeness of the author of this touching inscription can have been caught only by the license of caricature in Justice Shallow.

The poaching episode, if it has any historical basis, probably took place in 1585, when Shakespeare had been three years married, and, although barely twenty-one years old, was the father of three children. Richard Hathaway, described as a "husbandman," was the owner of a small property at Shottery, a mile distant from Stratford, and reached not only by the highway but by a delightful footpath through the fields. The thatched cottage, so carefully preserved by the trustees of the Shakespeare properties, has doubtless suffered many changes since 1582, but remains a picturesque example of a farmhouse of Shakespeare's time. It did not pass out of the hands of the Hathaway family until about the middle of the present century, and Mrs. Baker, the custodian, who died in 1899, was a Hathaway by descent. Although Shottery is in the parish of Stratford, no record of Shakespeare's marriage to Anne, the daughter of Richard Hathaway, has been found in the parish register. In the Edgar Tower at Worcester, however, a bit of parchment in the form of a marriage bond furnishes conclusive contemporary evidence. By the terms of this bond, signed by Fulk Sandells and John Richardson, husbandmen of Shottery, it is affirmed that no impediment existed to the marriage of William Shakespeare and Anne Hathaway. The document is dated November 28, 1582, and the bondsmen make themselves responsible in the sum of forty pounds in case any impediment should be disclosed subsequently. The bond stipulates that the friends of the bride shall consent to her marriage, and, in that event, the customary reading of banns in church may be dispensed with and the marriage tâke place at once.

Three parishes within the diocese in which the contracting parties lived are, in accordance with the law and custom of the time, named in the bond, in any one of which the marriage might have taken place. The registers of two of the parishes have been searched without result; the register of the third parish disappeared at the time of the fire which destroyed the church at Luddington in which it was kept. Marriage bonds were not uncommon in Shakespeare's time, but they were not often entered into by persons in Shakespeare's position; the process was more expensive and complicated than the "asking of the banns," but it offered one advantage : it shortened the time within which the ceremony might take place. The bridegroom in this case was a minor by three years, and the formal assent of his parents ought to have been secured ; the bond, however, stipulates only that the friends of the bride shall give their consent.

In such bonds the name of the groom or of his father usually appears ; in this case no member of Shakespeare's family is named ; the two bondsmen were not only residents of Shottery, but one of them is described in the will of the bride's father as "my trustie friende and neighbour." The circumstances seem to suggest that the marriage was secured, or at least hastened, by the family of the bride; and this surmise finds its possible confirmation in the fact that the marriage took place about the time of the execution of the bond on November 28, 1582, while the poet's first child, his daughter Susannah, was christened in Holy Trinity, at Stratford, on the 26th day of May, 1583. It has been suggested on high authority that a formal betrothal, of the kind which had the moral weight of marriage, had taken place. The absence of any reference to the groom's family in the marriage bond makes this doubtful. These are the facts so far as they have been discovered; it ought to be remembered, as part of the history of this episode in Shakespeare's life, that he was a boy of eighteen at the time of his marriage, and that Anne Hathaway was eight years his senior.

That he was an ardent and eloquent lover it is impossible to doubt; the tradition that he was an unhappy husband is based entirely on the assumption that, while his family remained in Stratford, for twelve years he was almost continuously absent in London, and that he seems to speak with deep feeling about the disastrous effects of too great intimacy before marriage, and of the importance of a woman's marrying a man older than herself:

> . . . let still the woman take
> An elder than herself; so wears she to him,
> So sways she level in her husband's heart.

This is, however, pure inference, and it is perilous to draw inferences of this kind from phrases which a dramatist puts into the mouths of men and women who are interpreting, not their author's convictions and feelings, but a phase of character, a profound human experience, or the play of that irony which every playwright from Æschylus to Ibsen has felt deeply. The dramatist reveals his personality as distinctly as does the lyric poet, but not in the same way. Shakespeare's view of life, his conception of human destiny, his attitude toward society, his ideals of character, are to be found, not in detached passages framed and coloured by dramatic necessities, but in the large and consistent conception of life which underlies the entire body of his work; in the justice and sanity with which the external deed is bound to the inward impulse and the visible penalty developed out of the invisible sin; in the breadth of outlook upon human experience, the sanity and balance of judgment, the clarity and sweetness of temper which kept an imagination always brooding over the tragic possibilities of experience, and haunted by all manner of awful shapes of sin, misery, and madness, poised in health, vigour, and radiant serenity.

It is perilous to draw any inference as to the happiness or unhappiness which came into Shakespeare's life with his rash marriage. It is true that he spent many years in London; but when he had been there only eleven years, and was still a young man, he secured a home for himself in Stratford. He became a resident of his native place when he was still in middle life; there is evidence that his interest in Stratford and his communication with it were never interrupted;

that his care not only for his family but for his father was watchful and efficient; there is no reason to doubt that, taking into account the difficulties and expense of travel, his visits to his home were frequent; there is no evidence that his family was not with him at times in London. In this aspect of his life, as in many others, absence of detailed and trustworthy information furnishes no ground for inferences unfavourable to his happiness or his integrity.

The immediate occasion of Shakespeare's leaving Stratford is a matter of minor importance; the poaching episode may have hastened it, but could hardly have determined a career so full of the power of self-direction. Sooner or later he must have gone to London, for London was the one place in England which could afford him the opportunity which his genius demanded. It cannot be doubted that through all the ferment and spiritual unrest through which such a spirit as his must have gone — that searching and illuminating experience which is appointed to every great creative nature — his mind had moved uncertainly but inevitably toward the theatre as the sphere for the expression of the rich and passionate life steadily deepening and rising within him. The atmosphere and temper of his time, the growing spirit of nationality, the stories upon which his imagination had been fed from earliest childhood, the men whom he knew, the instinct and impulse of his own nature — these things determined his career, and, far more insistently than any outward circumstance or happening, drew him to London.

Marriage and London

His daughter Susannah was born in May, 1583 ; in February, 1585, his twin children, Hamnet and Judith, were baptized. He had assumed the gravest responsibilities, and there is no reason to doubt that he felt their full weight. Stratford offered him nothing which would have been anything more than drudgery to such a nature as his. To London, therefore, in 1586 he made his way in search of work and opportunity.

There were two well-established routes to London in that day of few, bad, and dangerous roads ; one ran through Banbury and Aylesbury, and the other, which lay a little farther to the west and was a little longer, ran through Oxford and High Wycombe. The journey was made in the saddle or on foot ; there were no other methods of travel. Goods of all kinds were carried by packhorses ; wagons were very rude and very rare ; it was fifty years later before vehicles began to run regularly as public conveyances. If Shakespeare, after the custom of the time, bought a horse for the occasion, he probably sold it, as Mr. Halliwell-Phillipps suggests, on reaching Smithfield, to James Burbage, who was a livery-man in that neighbourhood — the father of the famous actor Richard Burbage, with whom the poet was afterwards thrown in intimate relations. It was the custom among men of small means to buy horses for a journey, and sell them when the journey was accomplished. Tradition has long affirmed that Shakespeare habitually used the route which ran through Oxford and High Wycombe. The Crown Inn, which stood near Carfax, in Oxford, was the centre of many associations, real or imaginary,

William Shakespeare

with Shakespeare's journeys from the Capital to his home in New Place. The beautiful university city was even then venerable with years and thronged with students. Shakespeare's infinite wit and marvellous charm, to which there are many contemporary testimonies, made him later a welcome companion in one of the most brilliant groups of men in the history of literature. The spell of Oxford must have been upon him, and volumes of biography might well be exchanged for a brief account of one evening in the commons room of some college when the greatest and most companionable of English men of genius was the guest of scholars who shared with him the liberating power of the new age; for Shakespeare was loved by men of gentle breeding and of ripest culture.

Dickens once said that if he sat in a room five minutes, without consciously taking note of his surroundings, he found himself able, by the instinctive action of his mind, to describe the furnishing of the room to the smallest detail. This faculty of what may be called instinctive observation Shakespeare possessed in rare degree; he saw everything when he seemed to be seeing nothing. It is not impossible that, as Aubrey declares, " he happened to take the humour of the constable in ' Midsummer Night's Dream' in a little town near Oxford." There is no constable in Shakespeare's single fairy-play, and Aubrey was probably thinking of Dogberry or Verges. Shakespeare was constantly " taking the humour" of men and women wherever he found himself, and although Oxford is connected with his life only by a faint tradition, it may have furnished him with more than one sketch which he later developed into a figure full of reality and substance. It would have been quite in keeping with the breadth and freedom of his genius to find a clown in Oxford more interesting than some of the scholars he met; for clowns occasionally have some touch of individuality, some glimmer of humour, while scholars are sometimes found without flavour, pungency, or originality. Shakespeare's principle of selection in dealing with men was always vital; he put his hand unerringly on significant persons.

In 1586 he reached London, without means, in search of a vocation and a place in which to exercise it. The time was fortunate, and coöperated with him in ways which he did not, then or later, understand; for, however clearly a man may comprehend his gift and master his tools, he is too much a part of his age to discern his spiritual relations to it as these are later disclosed in the subtle channels through which it inspires and vitalizes him, and he in turn expresses, interprets, and affects it.

To the youth from the little village on the Avon, London was a great and splendid city; but the vast metropolis of to-day, with a population of more than five million people, was then a town of about one hundred and fifty thousand inhabitants. The great fire which was to change it from a mediæval to a modern city was almost a century distant; and the spire of old St. Paul's was seen, as one approached, rising over masses of red-roofed, many-gabled houses, crowded into the smallest space, and protected by walls and trenches. The most conspicuous objects in the city were the Tower, which rose beside the Thames as a symbol of the personal authority of the monarch; the Cathedral, which served as a common centre of community life, where the news of the day was passed from group to group, where gossip was freely interchanged, and servants were hired, and debtors found immunity from arrest; and old London Bridge, a town in itself, lined with buildings, crowded with people, with high gate-towers at either end, often ghastly with the heads that had recently fallen from the block at the touch of the executioner's axe.

The streets were narrow, irregular, overhung with projecting signs which creaked on rusty hinges and, in high winds, often came down on the heads of unfortunate pedestrians. These highways were still foul with refuse and evil odours; within the memory of men then living they had been entirely unpaved. Their condition had become so noisome and dangerous fifty years earlier that Henry VIII. began the work of paving the principal thoroughfares. Round stones were used for this purpose, and were put in position as they came to hand, without reference to form, size, or regularity of surface. Walking and riding were, in consequence, equally disagreeable. The thoroughfares were beaten into dust in summer and hollowed out into pools in winter; a ditch, picturesquely called "the kennel," ran through the road and served as a gutter. Into these running streams, fed with the refuse which now goes through

Marriage and London

the sewers, horses splashed and pedestrians often slipped. The narrow passage for foot-passengers was overcrowded, and every one sought the space farthest away from the hurrying pedestrians and litter-carriers and reckless riders. Two centuries later Dr. Johnson divided the inhabitants of London into two classes — the peaceable and the quarrelsome, or those who "gave the wall" and those who took it. To add to the discomfort, great water-spouts gathered the showers as they fell on the roofs of houses and shops, and discharged them in concentrated form on the heads of passers-by.

The London of that day was the relatively small and densely populated area in the heart of the modern metropolis which is known as the City. Its centre was St. Paul's Cathedral; and Eastcheap, which Falstaff loved so well, was a typical thoroughfare. A labyrinth of foul alleys and dingy, noisome courts covered the space now penetrated by the most crowded streets. Outside the limits of the town stretched lonely, neglected fields, dangerous at night by reason of footpads and all manner of lawless persons, in an age when streets were unlighted and police unknown. St. Pancras, surrounded by its quiet fields, was a lonely place with extensive rural views in all directions. Westminster was separated from the city by a long stretch of country known later as the Downs; cows grazed in Gray's Inn Fields.

The Thames was the principal thoroughfare between London and Westminster, and was gay with barges and boats of every kind, and noisy with the cries and oaths of hundreds of watermen. The vocabulary of profanity and vituperation was nowhere richer; every boat's load on its way up or down the stream abused every other boat's load in passing; the shouts "Eastward Ho!" or "Westward Ho!" were deafening.

In 1586 London was responding to the impetus which rapidly increasing trade had given the whole country, and was fast outgrowing its ancient limits. Neither the Tudor nor the Stuart sovereigns looked with favour on the growth of the power of a community which was never lacking in the independence which comes from civic courage and civic wealth. James I. said, with characteristic pedantry, that "the growth of the capital resembleth that of the head of a rickety child, in which an excessive influx of humours draweth and impoverisheth the extremities, and at the same time generateth distemper in the overloaded parts." The instinct which warned the father of Charles I. against the growth of London was sound, as the instincts of James often were; but there was no power within reach of the sovereign which could check the growth of the great city of the future. That growth was part of the expansion of England; one evidence of that rising tide of racial vitality which was to carry the English spirit, genius, and activity to the ends of the earth.

CHAPTER V

A YOUTH of Shakespeare's genius and charm of nature needed only a bit of earth on which to put his foot in the arena of struggle which London was in that day, and still is, in order to make his way to a secure position. That bit of ground from which he could push his fortunes forward was probably afforded by his friendship with Richard Field, a Stratford boy who had bound himself, after the custom of the time, to Thomas Vautrollier, a printer and publisher in Blackfriars, not far from the two theatres then in existence, The Theatre and The Curtain. Richard was the son of " Henry ffelde of Stratford uppon Aven in the countye of Warwick, tanner," a friend of John Shakespeare. Young Field, who had recently ended his apprenticeship, came into the possession of the business by marriage about this time, and his name will always be kept in memory because his imprint appears on the earliest of Shakespeare's publications, the "Venus and Adonis," which was first issued in 1593 and reissued in 1594 and 1596; and on the title-page of "The Rape of Lucrece" in 1594. The relation of this printer and his predecessor to the poet was intimate in the true sense of the word:

William Shakespeare

Field not only gave to the world Shakespeare's earliest poems, but brought out several books which deeply influenced the young poet; in 1589 he printed Puttenham's "Arte of English Poesie" and fifteen books of Ovid's "Metamorphoses"; and he brought out at least five editions of North's translation of Plutarch's "Lives," that "pasturage of noble minds," upon which Shakespeare must have fastened with avidity, so completely did his imagination penetrate and possess Plutarch's great stories.

The theory that Shakespeare worked for a time in the printing establishment is pure surmise; there is not even tradition to support it. Friendship with James Burbage, one of the leading actors of the day, with whom Shakespeare became intimately associated, has been taken for granted on the assumption that Burbage was a man of Stratford birth; and on the same ground it has been assumed that he knew John Heminge, who became at a later time his associate and friend; it is improbable, however, that either of these successful actors was a native of Warwickshire. Nor is there good ground for the surmise that the poet began his career as a lawyer's clerk; his knowledge of legal terms, considerable as it was, is more reasonably accounted for on other grounds.

Tradition is doubtless to be trusted when it connects Shakespeare from the beginning of his career with the profession which he was later not only to follow with notable practical success, but to practise with the insight and skill of the artist. His mastery of the mechanism of the play as well as of its poetic resources was so complete that his apprenticeship must have begun at once. Assuming that he connected himself with the theatre at the very start, that period of preparation was amazingly brief. It is highly probable that the stories which associate him with the theatre in the humblest way are true in substance if not in detail. The best known of these is that which declares that he began by holding, during the performances, the horses of those who rode to the theatres. It was the custom of men of fashion to ride; Shakespeare lived in the near neighbourhood of both theatres; and James Burbage, the father of Shakespeare's friend the actor, was not only the owner of The Theatre, but of a livery stable close at hand, and may have given him employment. This story first appeared in print in 1753, and it was then an old tradition. The poet was not long in finding his way from the outside to the inside of the theatre.

If he did not attain eminence as an actor, he knew the stage business and the management of a theatre from first-hand knowledge, and down to the minutest detail. No man has ever kept the theory and the practice of an art more thoroughly in hand or in harmony. The plays hold the first place in poetry to-day because their literary quality and value are supreme; they were successful in the poet's time largely because they showed such mastery of the business of the playwright. Shakespeare the craftsman and Shakespeare the artist were ideal collaborators. Rowe's statement that " he was received into the company then in being at first in a very mean rank " has behind it two credible and probable traditions : the story that he entered the theatre as a mere attendant or servitor, and the story that his first service in his profession was rendered in the humble capacity of a call-boy. The nature of the work he had to do at the start was of no consequence ; what is of importance is the fact that it gave him a foothold ; henceforth he had only to climb ; and climbing, to a man of his gifts and temper, was not toil but play.

Shakespeare began as an actor, and did not cease to act until toward the close of his life. His success as a playwright soon overshadowed his reputation as an actor, but, either as actor or shareholder, he kept in closest touch with the practical and business side of the theatre. He was for many years a man of great prominence and influence in what would to-day be known as theatrical circles ; and while his success on the stage was only respectable, his success as share- holder and manager was of the most substantial kind. It is clear that he inherited his father's instinct for business activity, and much more than his father's share of sound judgment and wise management. His good sense stands out at every stage in his mature life in striking juxtaposition with his immense capacity for emotion and excess both of passion and of brooding meditation. His poise and serenity of spirit were shown in his dealing with practical affairs ; and his success as a man of affairs is not only a rare fact in the history of men of genius, but stood in close relation to his marvellous sanity of nature. He steadied his spirit by resolute and wholesome grasp of realities.

The London Stage

It was a rough school in which Shakespeare found himself in the years of his apprenticeship; the profession he chose, although associated in our minds, when we recall his time, with some of the gentlest as well as the most ardent and gifted spirits, was not yet reputable; the society into which he was thrown by it was bohemian, if not worse; and the atmosphere in which he worked, but which he seemed not to breathe, was full of passion, intrigue, and license. No occupation is so open to moral peril as that which constantly stimulates the great passions and evokes the great emotions; and in Shakespeare's time the stage hardly felt the steadying force of public opinion. Lying under a social ban, it paid small attention to the standards and tastes of serious-minded men and women. The theatre of Shakespeare's time owed its immense productiveness to the closeness of its relations with English life and the English people, but that very closeness of touch charged it with perilous forces; the stage was the scene of tumultuous passions, of fierce emotions whose tidal volume and intensity swept everything before them; of violence, cruelty, and bloodshedding. The intense vitality which gave the age its creative energy in statesmanship, in adventure, in organization, and in literature, showed itself in perilous excesses of thought and conduct; the people, although morally sound, were coarse in speech; the vices of the Italian Renaissance did not seriously taint the English people, but they were familiar on the English stage; the actor was not received as a member of society; he was still a social outcast. Under such conditions the tragic fate of Shakespeare's immediate predecessors seems almost inevitable ; and it is a matter of surprise that Shakespeare's friends in his profession were men, on the whole, of orderly life.

There was ground, in the atmosphere which surrounded the stage in Shakespeare's youth, for the growing opposition of the Puritan element in London to the theatre ; but fortunately for the free expression of English genius, Elizabeth was of another mind. She, rather than her Puritan subjects, represented the temper and spirit of the people. She loved the play and was the enthusiastic patron of the player. In 1574, twelve years before Shakespeare came to London, the Queen had given a Royal Patent, or license, empowering Lord Leicester's servants to "use, exercise, and occupy the art and faculty of playing Comedies, Tragedies, Interludes, Stage-plays . . . as well for the recreation of our loving subjects, as for our solace and pleasure, when we shall think good to see them." Lord Leicester's company had appeared at Court on many occasions ; henceforth they called themselves "The Queen's Majesty's Poor Players." They were given the privilege of playing, not only in London, but throughout England ; but the plays they presented were in all cases to pass under the eye of the Master of the Revels, and no performance was to be given "in the time of Common Prayer, or in the time of great and common Plague in our said City of London." Such a license was rendered necessary by an Act of Parliament adopted three years earlier ; without it the players might have been apprehended as vagabonds.

The London Stage

The Earl of Leicester's company of players bore his name and secured their privileges through his influence, but were not subsidized by him. Two years after receiving the royal license, they occupied in Shoreditch the first public theatre erected in London; so widespread was the popular interest, and so ripe the moment for the development of the drama, that at the death of Elizabeth London had no less than fifteen or eighteen playhouses. When Shakespeare arrived on the scene, two theatres had been built and several companies of actors regularly organized. Choir-boys frequently gave performances, and the choirs of St. Paul's, the Chapel Royal, and the school at Westminster were organized into companies, furnished players for women's parts, and practically served as training-schools for the stage. Of these companies, that which bore the name of Lord Leicester soon secured a foremost place; became, in the time of Elizabeth's successor, the King's Players; included among its members Richard Burbage, the greatest tragedian of his time, John Heminge and Henry Condell, who laid posterity for all time under lasting obligations by editing the first folio edition of Shakespeare's plays in 1623, and Augustus Phillips — all Shakespeare's intimate and lifelong friends. With probably not more than two exceptions, his plays were first brought out by this company. With this company Shakespeare cast in his fortunes soon after his arrival in London, when it was performing in The Theatre, with the Curtain as its only rival; and he kept up his connection with it until his final retirement to Stratford.

William Shakespeare

The first theatres were rude in structure and bore evidence of the earlier conditions under which plays had been presented. The courtyard of the old English inn, with its open space surrounded on three sides by galleries, reappeared with modifications in the earliest London theatres. These structures were built of wood, and the majority of the audience sat in the open space which is now known as the orchestra but was then called the "yard" and later the pit, under the open sky. The Globe, which was the most famous theatre of Shakespeare's time, and with which his own fortunes were closely identified, was shaped like a hexagon; the stage was covered, but the private boxes, which encircled the central space or yard, were not roofed. The Fortune, which stood in Cripplegate and was one of the results of the great success of the Globe, was a square of eighty feet on each side. The stage was nearly forty-five feet in depth; three tiers of boxes encircled the yard. The stage stood upon pillars and was protected by a roof. The greater part of the audience sat in the "yard" and were called "groundlings"; those who were able to pay a larger fee found places in the boxes or galleries; the men of fashion, with the patrons of the drama, sat on the stage itself.

The audience in the yard was made up of citizens of London, apprentices, grooms, boys, and a more dissolute and boisterous element who paid two or three pennies for admission. If it rained, they were wet; if the sun shone, they were warm; they criticised the actors and ridiculed the dandies on the stage; they ate and drank and occasionally fought one another, after the fashion of the time. They were sometimes riotous. When the air of the yard became disagreeable, juniper was burned to purify it. The nobles and men of fashion paid sixpence or a shilling for a three-legged stool on the stage. These gentlemen, who were dressed, as a rule, in the extreme of the prevailing mode, were scornful of the people in the yard, and often made themselves obnoxious to the actors, with whose exits and entrances they sometimes interfered, and upon whose performances they made audible and often insulting comments. There were no women on the stage, and few, and those usually not of the best, in the boxes.

The performances were given at three o'clock in the afternoon, and were announced by the hoisting of flags and the blowing of trumpets — a custom which has been revived in our time at Bayreuth. Playbills of a rude kind were distributed; if a tragedy was to be presented, these bills were printed in red letters. In place of the modern ushers were boys who sold tobacco, nuts, and various edibles, without much attention to the performance or the performers. The stage was strewn with rushes, and partially concealed by a curtain. When the trumpets had been blown for the third time, this curtain was drawn aside and an actor, clad in a mantle of black velvet and wearing a crown of bays over a capacious wig, came forward to recite the Prologue. This speech was often interrupted and sometimes ended by the violence of the "groundlings" or the late arrival of some rakish gentleman upon the stage. The people in the yard were, as a rule, more respectful to the plays and players than those on the stage.

The costumes were often rich, and the stage was not devoid of gorgeous properties; but the scenery was of the simplest and rudest description, and the stage devices were elementary and transparent. The stage was narrow, projected into the audience, was partly filled by spectators, and was open to view on all sides save at the back. There were crude representations of rocks, trees, animals, cities. A placard on the walls of one of these wholly undeceptive cities announced that it was Verona or Athens or Rome; the audience needed nothing more; a hint to the imagination was enough.

"You shall have Asia of the one side, and Africka of the other," writes Sir Philip Sidney, "and so many other under-kingdoms, that the Plaier when he comes in, must ever begin with telling where hee is, or else the tale will not be conceived. Now shall you have three Ladies walke to gather flowers, and then wee must beleeve the stage to be a garden. By and by we heare newes of shipwracke in the same place, then wee are to blame if we accept it not for a rocke; . . . in the meane time two armies flie in, represented with foure swordes and bucklers, and then what hard heart will not receive it for a pitched field?"

Against a background so meagre, heroes rode in on hobby-horses, and young women, whose chins were not always as closely shaven as they might have been, were frightened by pasteboard dragons of the simplest devices; and yet no one was made ridiculous, and the disparity between the stage and the action was not perceived ! The imagination is more subtle than the most skilful stage carpenter, and more vividly creative than the greatest stage artist. " The recitation begins," wrote Emerson ; " one golden word leaps out immortal from all this painted pedantry and sweetly torments us with invitations to its own inaccessible homes."

This absence of visible scenery imposed on the dramatist the task not only of creating the plot and action, but the background of his play ; and much of the most exquisite poetry in our language was written to set before the imagination that which the theatre could not set before the eye. The narrow stage with its poor devices was but the vantage-ground from which the poet took possession of the vast stage, invisible but accessible, of the imagination of his auditors; on that stage alone, in spite of modern invention and skill, the plays of Shakespeare are adequately set.

The theatre was the channel through which the rising life of the people found expression, and accurately reflected the popular taste, feeling, and culture ; it was the contemporary library, lecture-room, and newspaper, and gave expression to what was uppermost in the life of the time. The drama was saturated with the spirit of the age ; it was passionate, reckless, audacious, adventurous ; indifferent to tradition but throbbing with vitality ; full of sublimity when a great poet was behind it, and of rant and bluster when it came from a lesser hand ; it was insolent, bloody, vituperative, coarse, and indecent ; it was noble, pathetic, sweet with all tenderness and beautiful with all purity ; there was no depth of crime and

foulness into which it did not descend; there was no
height of character, achievement, sacrifice, and service to which it did not climb with easy and victori-
ous step. At its best and its worst it was intensely
alive; and because it was so intensely alive it became
not only the greatest expression of English genius, but
the mirror of English spiritual and social life.

"Rude as the theatre might be, all the world was
there," writes Green. "The stage was crowded
with nobles and courtiers. Apprentices and citizens
thronged the benches in the yard below. The rough
mob of the pit inspired, as it felt, the vigorous life,
the rapid transitions, the passionate energy, the reality, the lifelike medley and confusion, the racy dialogue, the chat, the wit, the pathos, the sublimity, the
rant and buffoonery, the coarse horrors and vulgar
bloodshedding, the immense range over all classes of
society, the intimacy with the foulest as well as the
fairest developments of human temper, which characterized the English stage. The new drama represented 'the very age and body of the time, his form
and pressure.' The people itself brought its nobleness and its vileness to the boards. No stage was
ever so human, no poetic life so intense. Wild, reckless, defiant of all past traditions, of all conventional
laws, the English dramatists owned no teacher, no
source of poetic inspiration, but the people itself."

This vital relationship between the English people
and the English drama explains the growing interest
in the stage during Shakespeare's career as actor and
dramatist, and the prosperity which attended many

theatrical ventures and notably his own venture. When he joined Lord Leicester's company at The Theatre, which stood in Shoreditch, in the purlieus of the City, the Curtain, which was a near neighbour, was the only rival for popular patronage. But these houses were not long in possession of the field. The Rose was built on Bankside, Southwark, not far from the tavern from which Chaucer's pilgrims set out on their immortal pilgrimage. To this theatre Shakespeare's company ultimately removed, and it is probable that on its narrow stage he began to emerge from obscurity both as an actor and a playwright. He had gone a long way on the road to fame and fortune when Richard Burbage built the Globe Theatre in the neighbourhood of the Rose. Here his fortunes of every kind touched their zenith, and, by reason of his intimate association with its early history, the Globe has become and is likely to remain the most famous theatre in the annals of the English drama. In the management of the Globe Shakespeare came to hold a first place, with a large interest in its profits. It soon secured, and held until it was destroyed by fire in 1613, the first place in the hearts of the London public. Edward Alleyn was the greatest actor of his time outside the company with whom Shakespeare associated himself; for a time the company known as the Admiral's Men, with whom he acted, combined with Shakespeare's company and gave what must have been the most striking representations which English audiences had ever seen. The two companies soon separated, however, and the Fortune was built to fur-

nish suitable accommodation for the Admiral's Men,
of whom Alleyn was the star; Shakespeare's company, now generally known as the Lord Chamberlain's
Men, being its chief competitor, with Richard Burbage
as its leading actor, supported by Heminge, Condell,
Phillips, and Shakespeare. The Blackfriars Theatre,
built by the elder Burbage on the site now occupied
by the offices of the London *Times* in Victoria Street,
was probably not occupied by the Lord Chamberlain's
Men until the close of Shakespeare's life in London.

Shakespeare's name appears on many lists of principal actors in his own plays, and in at least two of
Ben Jonson's plays; according to Rowe, his most
notable rôle was that of the Ghost in " Hamlet "; one
of his brothers, in old age, remembered the dramatist's
rendering of the part of Adam in " As You Like It ";
he is reported to have " played some kingly parts in
sport." The stage tradition, as expressed by an actor
at a later period, declared that he " did act exceeding well." That he was not a great actor is evident;
it was fortunate for him and for the world that his
aptitude for dealing with the theatre was sufficient to
give him ease and competence, but not enough to
divert him from the drama. His experience as actor
and manager put him in a position to do his work as
poet and dramatist. He learned stage-craft, which
many dramatists never understand; his dramatic instinct was reënforced by his experience as an actor.
He must have been an intelligent and careful actor,
studious of the subtleties and resources of his art,
keenly sensitive to artistic quality in voice, intonation,

gesture, and reading. His address to the players in "Hamlet" is a classic of dramatic criticism.

That Shakespeare kept in intimate relation with the theatre as actor and manager until 1610 or 1611 there is no question; his interest as shareholder was probably kept up until his death. In 1596, when he had gained some reputation, he was living in Southwark, not far from the theatres. The theatre of the day was crude and elementary in arrangement, scenery, and the sense of order and taste; but there was a vital impulse behind it; popular interest was deepening in the face of a rising opposition; and it offered opportunities of moderate fortune. The companies into which actors organized themselves were small, often numbering only eight persons, and rarely exceeding twelve. The men who took the inferior and subordinate parts were called hirelings, and were paid small fixed sums as wages; the actors were usually partners in the enterprise, managing the theatres and sharing the profits according to an accepted scale of relative importance and value.

The modern London society season was still in the future, but there seems to have been, even at that early day, some easing of work and activity during the summer months, and the various companies made journeys to the smaller towns. The records show that in successive seasons Shakespeare's company visited, among other places, Oxford, Shrewsbury, Coventry, Dover, Bristol, Bath, Rye, Folkestone. There is every reason to believe that Shakespeare travelled with his company on these tours, and that he became, in this way, personally familiar with many of the localities which are described in the plays.

The claim, more than once vigorously urged, that Shakespeare visited Scotland with his company, and breathed the air of Inverness, and felt the loneliness of the Highland heaths, which gave, by their wildness, a new note of strange and awful tragedy to the fate of Macbeth, does not rest on convincing evidence. There is more solid ground for the belief, advocated with persuasive force by Mr. George Brandes, that Shakespeare travelled in Italy and knew at first hand the background of life and landscape against which many of his most characteristic plays, both tragic and comic, are projected. Then, as now, foreign tours were sometimes made by English actors, and during the poet's life the best works of the English drama were seen in France, Germany, Holland, Denmark, and other countries; the chief patrons of the visiting artists being found at the various courts.

Italy filled a great place in the imagination of contemporary Englishmen; it was the birthplace of the Renaissance, the mother of the New Learning, the home of the young as of the older arts. Its strange and tragic history, repeated in miniature in the lives of many of its rulers, artists, poets, and men of affairs, threw a spell over the young and ardent spirit of a country just emerging into clear consciousness of its own spirit and power; while its romantic charm, its prodigal and lavish self-surrender to passion, stirred the most sensitive and gifted Englishmen of the time to the depths. What Europe is to-day, in its history,

art, literature, ripeness of landscape, and social life, to
the young American, Italy was to the young Englishman of Shakespeare's time, and for several later generations.

Chaucer had gone to Italy for some of his most
characteristic tales; Wyatt and Surrey had learned
the poetic art at the hands of Italian singers; the
immediate predecessors of Shakespeare were deeply
touched by this searching influence, and his immediate
successors, Webster and Cyril Tourneur especially, gave
dramatic form to those appalling violations of the most
sacred laws and relations of life which are the most
perplexing aspect of the psychology of the Renaissance; and it was from Italy, where his imagination was rapidly expanding in a genial air, that the
young Milton was called home when the clouds of
civil strife began to darken the close of that great
day of which Shakespeare was the master mind.

This home of beauty, history, art, romance, passion,
and tragedy must have had immense attractiveness for
Shakespeare, whose boyhood studies, earliest reading,
and first apprentice work as a playwright brought
him into close contact with it. Many men of Shakespeare's acquaintance had made the journey, and were
constantly making it; it was a difficult but not a very
expensive journey; to visit Italy must have seemed as
necessary to Shakespeare, as to visit Germany has
seemed necessary to the American student of philosophy and science, and to visit France and the Italy of
to-day to the student of art.

Mr. Brandes bases his belief that Shakespeare made

this journey on the facts that there were, in his time, none of those guide-books and manuals of various kinds which spread a foreign country as clearly before the mind of an intelligent student at home as a map spreads it before the eye; that, at the time "The Merchant of Venice" appeared, no description of the most fascinating of cities had seen the light in England; that the familiarity with localities, names, characteristics, architecture, manners, and local customs shown in "The Merchant of Venice" and in "The Taming of the Shrew" could have been gained only by personal acquaintance with the country and the people.

On the other hand, as Mr. Brandes frankly concedes, there are mistakes in "Romeo and Juliet," in "The Two Gentlemen of Verona," and in "Othello" which are not easy to reconcile with first-hand knowledge of the localities described. It must be remembered, too, that the poet had immense capacity for assimilating knowledge and making it his own; that a social or moral fact was as full of suggestion to him as a bone to a naturalist; that he lived with men whose acquaintance with other countries he was constantly drawing upon to enlarge his own information; and that he had access to books which gave the freshest and most vivid descriptions of Italian scenery, cities, and manners. Many of the striking and accurate descriptions of localites to be found in literature were written by men who never set foot in the countries with which they seem to show the utmost familiarity. One of the most charming of American pastorals describes, with complete accuracy of detail, as well as with the truest feeling for atmospheric effect, a landscape which the poet never saw. On a fortunate day he brought into his library a man who knew no other country so well. He faced his visitor to the north. "You are now," he said, "standing by the blacksmith's forge and looking to the north : tell me everything you see." The visitor closed his eyes and described with loving minuteness a country with which he had been intimate all his conscious life. When he had finished, he was turned successively to the west, the south, and the east, until his graphic vision had surveyed and reported the distant and beautiful world which was to furnish the background for the poem. The process and the result are incomprehensible to critics and students who are devoid of imagination, but perfectly credible to all who understand that such an imagination as Shakespeare possessed carries with it the power of seeing with the eyes not only of the living but even of the dead.

Shakespeare may have visited Italy during the winter of 1592 or the spring of 1593, when London was stricken with the plague and the theatres were closed as a precaution against the spread of the disease by contagion, but there is no direct evidence of such a visit ; his name does not appear on any existing list of actors who made foreign tours. It is a fact of some significance in this connection that the actors who made professional journeys to the Continent were rarely men of importance in their profession.

CHAPTER VI

APPRENTICESHIP

PROBABLY no conditions could have promised less for the production of great works of art than those which surrounded the theatre in Shakespeare's time — conditions so unpromising that the bitter antagonism of the Puritans is easily understood. It remains true, nevertheless, that in their warfare against the theatre the Puritans were not only contending with one of the deepest of human instincts, but unconsciously and unavailingly setting themselves against the freest and deepest expression of English genius and life. The story of the growth of the drama in the Elizabethan age furnishes a striking illustration of the difficulty of discerning at any given time the main currents of spiritual energy, and of separating the richest and most masterful intellectual life from the evil conditions through which it is often compelled to work its way, and from the corrupt accessories which sometimes surround it. The growth of humanity is not the unfolding of an idea in a world of pure ideality; it is something deeper and more significant : it is an outpouring of a vast energy, constantly seeking new channels of expression and new ways of action, painfully striving to find a balance between its passionate needs and desires and the conditions under which it is compelled to work, and painfully adjusting its inner ideals and spiritual necessities to outward realities.

It is this endeavour to give complete play to the force of personality, and to harmonize this incalculable spiritual energy with the conditions which limit and oppose free development, which gives the life of every age its supreme interest and tragic significance, and which often blinds the courageous and sincere, who are bent on immediate righteousness along a few lines of faith and practice, rather than on a full and final unfolding of the human spirit in accordance with its own needs and laws, to the richest and most fruitful movement of contemporary life. The attempt to destroy a new force or form in the manifold creative energy of the human spirit because it was at the start allied with evil conditions has often been made in entire honesty of purpose, but has been rarely successful; for the vital force denied one channel, finds another. The theatre in Shakespeare's time was a product of a very crude and coarse but very rich life; it served, not to create evil conditions, but to bring those already existing into clear light. The Puritans made the familiar mistake of striking at the expression rather than at the cause of social evils; they laid a heavy hand on a normal and inevitable activity instead of fastening upon and stripping away the demoralizing influences which gathered about it.

Shakespeare came at the last hour which could have made room for him; twenty-five years later he would have been denied expression, or his free and comprehensive genius would have suffered serious distortion. The loveliness of Milton's earlier lyrics reflects the joyousness and freedom of the golden age of English dramatic poetry. The Puritan temper was silently or noisily spreading through the whole period of Shakespeare's career ; within twenty-five years after his death it had closed the theatres and was making a desperate fight for the right to live according to conscience. Shakespeare arrived on the stage when the great schism which was to divide the English people had not gone beyond the stage of growing divergence of social and religious ideals ; there was still a united England.

The London theatres stood in suburbs which would to-day be called slums ; when complaint was made of the inconvenience of these outlying situations, it was promptly affirmed that "the remedy is ill-conceived to bring them into London ;" in regard to the regulation that performances should not be given during prayer-time, "it may be noted how uncomely it is for youth to run straight from prayers to plays, from God's service to the Devil's." The theatres had come into existence under the most adverse conditions, but they had established themselves because there was a genuine force behind them. They had already touched the English spirit with definite influences. In the reign of Elizabeth's reactionary sister the freedom with which the stage, the predecessor of the newspaper as a means of spreading popular opinion and discussing questions of popular interest, had spoken had brought first more rigid censorship and finally suppression of secular dramas throughout England. The court and the nobles reserved the privilege of witnessing plays in palaces and castles, but the play was too frank, in the judgment of many, to be allowed to speak to the people. The people were not, however, to be denied that which the higher classes found essential; regulations were eluded or disregarded, and plays were given secretly.

When Elizabeth came to the throne, the rules imposed on players were regulative rather than prohibitory; for Elizabeth had no mind to put under royal ban one of the chief means of easing the popular feeling by giving it expression, and of developing true English feeling by the presentation of the chief figures and the most significant events in English history. Companies were organized and licensed under the patronage of noblemen; theatres were built, and the drama became a recognized form of amusement in London. But from the beginning the theatre was opposed and denounced. Archbishop Grindall fought it vigorously, on the ground that actors were "an idle sort of people, which had been infamous in all good commonwealths," and that the crowds which attended the performances spread the plague by which London was ravaged for a number of years, and of which there was great and well-founded dread. In spite of the Queen's favour and of Leicester's patronage, theatres were compelled to take refuge in the suburbs. The struggle between the players, backed by the Queen, and the City authorities was long and bitter. The Corporation was determined to exclude players from the City, and to prevent them from giving performances during service hours, on holidays, or during the prevalence of the plague. Bitter as the struggle was, however, neither side was willing to carry it to a decisive issue. The Queen, who knew to a nicety how far she could go in asserting the royal prerogatives, had no desire to antagonize a community of growing importance and power, and exceedingly jealous of its rights and privileges; the City had no wish to set itself in final opposition to that which a powerful sovereign evidently had very much at heart. The players ceased to give regular performances within the City limits, but became, in consequence of this opposition, a permanent feature of the life of the metropolis by building permanent buildings within easy reach of the City.

And the theatre throve in the face of an opposition which ceased to be official only to become more general and passionate. The pamphlet, which was soon to come from the press in great numbers and to do the work of the newspaper, began to arraign it in no measured tones; the Puritan preachers were unsparing in their denunciations. "It is a woful sight," said one of these pamphleteers, "to see two hundred proud players jet in their silks, when five hundred poor people starve in the streets." It does not appear to have occurred to this critic of the play that whatever force his statement had, weighed equally on the court, the nobility, and the very respectable but also very prosperous burghers who jostled the same poor on their way to church. There is more point in the frank oratory of a London preacher in 1586, the year of Shake-speare's arrival in London : " Woe is me ! the play-houses are pestered, where churches are naked ; at the one it is not possible to get a place, at the other void seats are plenty. When the bell tolls to the Lec-turer, the trumpets sound to the stages."

The opposition of the City to the theatres was later merged into the opposition of the Puritan party ; and when that party became dominant, the theatre was suppressed, with all other forms of amusement and recreation which the hand of authority could touch ; for the Puritan, bent on immediate righteousness and looking with stern and searching eye at present conditions, did not discern the significance of the drama as an art, and as an expression of the genius of the English people. With the Puritan party the vital character and force of the English people for a time allied themselves, and the right to live freely and according to individual conscience was finally secured ; but, as often happens, the arts of peace, giving full play to the spiritual life in the large sense, were mis-understood, denied, and largely suppressed during the long and bitter strife of opposing parties and conflict-ing principles. The surroundings and accessories of the theatre were open to the charges brought against them and to the judgment which the Puritans pro-nounced upon them ; but it would have been an incal-culable disaster if Puritanism had come into power in time to thwart or chill the free and harmonious unfold-ing of Shakespeare's genius.

The evils which earnest-minded Englishmen saw in

the theatre were largely in its surroundings and accessories ; on the stage, life was interpreted for the most part with consistent sanity of insight and portrayal. When the appalling vices which devastated the moral life of Italy during the later Renaissance are taken into account, and the fascination of Italian scholarship and genius are recalled, it is surprising that the English drama remained essentially sound and wholesome. The English dramatists studied the tree of the knowledge of evil, of the fruit of which the Italians had partaken with an appetite sharpened by a long denial of the elemental instincts of the body and the mind, but they refused to eat of it. In Shakespeare's later years and after his death, when the sky had perceptibly darkened, the tragic genius of Webster and Tourneur seemed to turn instinctively to the crimes of the Renaissance rather than to its vivacity, variety, passionate interest in life, and vast range of spiritual activity ; and such dramas as " The Duchess of Malfi " and "The Atheist's Tragedy " record the effect on the serious English mind of the almost superhuman energy of the Renaissance when it became an assertion of absolute individualism, a passionate defiance of all law, human or divine. Italy was both the liberator and the teacher of modern Europe ; in recovering the love of beauty, the freedom of spirit, the large and noble humanity of the Greek and Roman ideals, she rendered the modern world an incalculable service ; but in the tremendous ferment through which she passed, and the radical reaction against the mediæval conceptions in which she had lived for centuries which followed, her moral life was well-nigh sacrificed. The immense resources which she recovered for mankind, the splendour of her genius, the range and depth of human experience which she made her own, and which she shared with the world in her stories and dramas, gave her an influence on the English imagination which was not diminished until long after Milton's time, and which was searching and almost overwhelming when Shakespeare began to write. The profanity, the cruelty, the excesses of passion, the use of crime, intrigue, and lust as dramatic motives, which repelled and alarmed the Puritans, were due largely to the influence and example of the Italian drama, and to the material furnished by the Italian novelle, or tales of love and intrigue; but these tragic themes, though often presented with repulsive frankness, were almost always moralized in treatment. If the crimes were appalling, the punishments were adequate; the sin was not detached from the penalty by the subtlety of a corrupt imagination, nor was the deed separated from its inevitable consequences by that dexterity, so characteristic of the Italian Renaissance, of a mind marvellously trained but smitten with ethical blindness. Compared with the contemporaneous Italian and French dramas, the early English plays show distinct moral health; they are more manly, virile, and wholesome. They are often coarse; they touch upon forbidden things at times with evident enjoyment; they occasionally show an inordinate curiosity concerning unnatural relations and offences; but they are, as a whole, morally sound in the exact sense of the words; and when the moral and intellectual conditions under which they were produced and the social influences which surrounded them are taken into account, they are remarkably clean and sane.

The English language, in which strength, beauty, and compass of expression were combined, had become a well-defined and highly developed national speech when Shakespeare began to use it, but was still the language of life rather than of literature; its freshest and most beguiling combinations of sound and sense were still to be made; it was still warm from the moulds in which it had been cast; it was still plastic to the touch of the imagination. The poet had learned its most intimate familiar symbols of homely, domestic, daily life among the people at Stratford; he had drunk of its ancient classical springs in the grammar school; and, in London, among men of gift, quality, and knowledge of the world, he came quickly to master the vocabulary of the men of action, adventure, and affairs. The drama as a literary form was at the same critical stage; it was well defined, its main lines were distinctly marked, but it had not hardened into final forms. The genius of Marlowe had brought to its development the richness of diction and the imaginative splendour of great poetry. It remained for Shakespeare to harmonize both language and art with the highest individual insight and gift of song, and to blend in forms of ultimate beauty and power the vitality of his age, the quality of his genius, a great philosophy of life, and the freedom and flexibility of a language of noble compass both of thought and music.

Apprenticeship

The stage offered both the form and the field for a great popular literature; a literature capacious enough to receive and conserve the largest thought concerning human destiny, to disclose and to employ the finest resources of poetry, and yet to use a speech which was part of every Englishman's memory and experience. The drama was the one great opportunity of expression which the age offered, and Shakespeare turned to it instinctively. The measure of his genius was the measure of his sensitiveness, and his imagination ran into dramatic channels by the spiritual gravitation of his whole nature. It is true, the drama was not yet recognized as a form of literature; and in this fortunate fact lies one of the secrets of Shakespeare's freshness and freedom; he wrote neither for the critics of his own time nor for that vague but inexorable posterity which is the final judge of the artist's work. He poured his genius, with a sublime indifference to the verdict of the future, into the nearest, the most capacious, and the most vital forms. It is doubtful if he ever differentiated in his own mind the different kinds of work which fell to his hand; he was actor, manager, and playwright, after the fashion of his time, without literary self-consciousness and without literary ambitions in the modern sense of the word; doing his work as if the eyes of the whole world were to read it, but doing it for the immediate reward of crowded audiences and the satisfaction of his own artistic conscience. Shakespeare reached London about 1586, when he was twenty-two years old; five years later, in 1591, he was revising or writing plays; and in 1612 his work was done. In about twenty years he wrote the thirty-six or thirty-seven five-act plays which bear his name; "Venus and Adonis," "The Rape of Lucrece," "A Lover's Complaint," "The Phœnix and Turtle"; the sequence of sonnets which of themselves would have put him in the front rank of lyric poets; and he made important contributions to the composite and surreptitiously printed "The Passionate Pilgrim." There is no probability that the date from which the indentures of his apprenticeship to the arts of poetry and play-writing ran will ever be known; it is known that not later than 1591 his hand was beginning to make itself felt. The time was prodigal of great men and great work. Greene, who died the following year, was starving in a garret which was in no sense traditional; Marlowe met his untimely death in 1593; the final issues of Lyly's "Euphues" were being widely read; Sidney's "Arcadia," which had been handed about in manuscript, after the fashion of a time when the publisher and the reading public were more than a century in the future, could be read from a well-printed page; the first books of the "Faerie Queene" had come out of Ireland; Sidney's "Apologie for Poetrie," written in defence of the stage, appeared in 1595, eight years after his death on the bloody field of Zutphen; Webb's "Discourse of English Poetrie" had come to light in the year of Shakespeare's introduction to London, and Puttenham's "Arte of English Poesie" had followed it three years later. Criticism did not lag behind the beautiful lyrical and rich dramatic productiveness of the age. Men of action and men of letters were equally astir, and the names of Spenser and Raleigh, of Drake and Sidney, of Granville and Marlowe, were heard on all sides among the men with whom Shakespeare lived. The Armada was fresh in the memory of a generation upon which a multitude of new and stimulating interests were playing; life was a vast ferment, and literature was on such intimate terms with experience that it became the confidant of life and the repository of all its secrets.

That Shakespeare felt the full force of the intoxicating vitality of the air in which he lived cannot be doubted; but his first attempts at play-writing were timid and tentative. The stages of the growth of his mind and art are distinctly marked in the form and substance of his work; he was in no sense a miracle, in no way an exception to the universal law of growth through experience, of spiritual ripening by the process of living, and of the development of skill through apprenticeship. He had to learn his trade as every man of parts had to learn it before him, and will have to learn it to the end of time. His first steps were uncertain; they did not lead him out of the greenroom where the stock of plays was kept. These plays were drawn from many sources; they were often composite; in many cases individual authorship had been forgotten, if it had ever been known; no sense of personal proprietorship attached to them; they belonged to the theatre; many of them had been revised so many times by so many hands that all semblance of their first forms had disappeared;

they were constantly changed by the actors themselves. These plays were, in some instances, not even printed; they existed only as unpublished manuscripts; in many cases a play did not exist as an entirety even in manuscript; it existed only in parts with cues for the different actors. The publication of a play was the very last thing desired by the writer, or by the theatre to which it was sold and to which it belonged, and every precaution was taken to prevent a publicity which was harmful to the interests of author and owner. The exclusive ownership of successful plays was a large part of the capital of the theatres. Shorthand writers often took down the speeches of actors, and in this way plays were stolen and surreptitiously printed; but they were full of all manner of inaccuracies, the verse passages readily becoming prose in the hands of unimaginative reporters, and the method was regarded as dishonourable. Reputable playwrights, having sold a work to a theatre, did not regard it as available for publication.

It is easy to understand, therefore, the uncertainty about the text of many of the Elizabethan dramas, including that of the Shakespearean plays. Having sold a play, the writer, as a rule, expected no further gain from it, and was chiefly concerned to protect it from mutilation by keeping it out of print. For this reason most of the plays acted in the reign of Elizabeth and in that of her successor are lost beyond recovery. In order to understand Shakespeare's attitude towards his work it is necessary to reverse contemporary literary conditions, under which authors are constantly urged to publish and the sense of individual ownership in literary work is intensified by all the circumstances of the literary life. Plays were sometimes published in Shakespeare's time by the consent of the theatres to which they had been sold; but the privilege was rarely applied for. When Ben Jonson treated his plays as literature by publishing them in 1616 as his "Works," he was ridiculed for his pretensions; and Webster's care to secure correctness in the printing of his tragedies laid him open to a charge of pedantry. At a later time the popular interest in plays for reading purposes opened an unsuspected source of income to play-writers, and publication became customary; of the thirty-seven plays commonly credited to Shakespeare, only sixteen were published during the life of the poet, and these were probably printed without his authorization, certainly without his revision. There was no copyright law, and the author could not protect himself against imperfect reproductions of his own works. Shakespeare's income came from the sale of plays and from the patronage by the public of the theatres in which he was interested; from every point of view he was, therefore, averse to the publication of his dramas. If he had set his heart on publicity, the theatre was the most effective form of publication which the times offered.

The prices paid for plays ranged from five to ten pounds sterling, or from twenty-five to fifty dollars, Ben Jonson receiving the larger sum as a minimum. These plays, having become the absolute property of the theatre, were treated with the utmost freedom and were made over from time to time to suit the popular taste; they were often the products of collaboration between two or more authors, and the feeling of the writer for his work was so slight that many of the plays appeared without a name.

In The Theatre or The Rose Shakespeare found a library of such plays which were the property, not of their writers, but of the owners of the theatre, and which were regarded not as literature but as the capital of the company, to be recast, rewritten, revised, and made over to fit the times and suit the audience, which was sometimes to be found at the Palace, sometimes in the Inns of Court, and regularly in the rude wooden structures in which the different group of players had finally established themselves. These plays drew freely upon history, tradition, legend, and foreign romance and tale; the soiled and tattered manuscripts bore the visible marks of the handling of many actors and prompters, and the invisible traces of a multitude of historians, poets, romancers, and dramatists whose work had been freely and frankly drawn upon; each successive playwright using what he needed, and discarding what seemed to him antiquated or ineffective. When Shakespeare became familiar with this mass of material, he found, among other themes, the story of the fall of Troy, the death of Cæsar, and various incidents in the lives of Plutarch's men, a collection of tales from Italy with the touch of the Boccaccian license and gayety on them, stories of adventure from Spanish sources, dark, half-legendary narratives from northern Europe, and a long list of plays based on English history from the days of Arthur to those of Henry VIII. and the great Cardinal. These plays were, for the most part, without order or art; they were rude in structure, crude in form, violent in expression, full of rant and excess of feeling and action, crowded with incident, and blood-curdling in their realistic presentation of savage crime; but there was immense vitality in them. They were the raw material of literature. They were as full of colour and as boldly contemporaneous as a street ballad; there was enough history in them to make them vitally representative of English life and character; but the facts were handled with such freedom as to give the widest range to the genius of the individual playwright.

This was the material which Shakespeare found ready to his hand when he began to feel the creative impulse stirring within him; and he used this material as his fellow-craftsmen used it. As an actor he knew these plays at first hand, and with a critical comprehension of their strong and weak points. He probably mended the loose and defective lines in his own rôles; all actors of any originality revised their lines freely. When he became familiar with the practical requirements of the stage, and gained confidence in his own skill and judgment, he set himself to working over some of the more popular plays which were in constant use. This was his journey-work, and in doing it he served his apprenticeship. The earlier plays which bear his name are, for this reason, his only in part.

William Shakespeare

They show his touch, as yet largely untrained, but already marvellously sure, and with something of magic in it; but they do not disclose the higher qualities of his genius, nor the large and beautiful art which he mastered after a few brief years of apprenticeship.

While it is true that the exact order in which Shakespeare wrote his plays is still uncertain, and is likely to remain undetermined, there is very little doubt regarding the general order in which they were given to the public. Evidence both external and internal has at length made possible a chronology of the plays which may be accepted as conclusive in indicating the large lines of Shakespeare's growth in thought and art. The external evidence is furnished by the dates of the earliest publication of some of the plays in quarto editions, the entries in the Register of the Stationers' Company, and the references to the plays in contemporaneous books and manuscripts; to these must be added allusions, or supposed allusions, in some of the plays to contemporaneous conditions, events, and persons. The internal evidence is derived from a critical study of Shakespeare's versification; a study which has been sufficiently fruitful to make the application of what is known as the metrical or verse-test possible.

The blank verse in the early plays conforms rigidly to the rule which required a pause at the end of each line; in the early verse rhyming couplets are in constant use. As the poet gained confidence and skill he handled his verse with increasing ease and freedom, expanding metrical usage, varying the pause, discarding rhyme and introducing prose; and there is an evident tendency to exclude the verbal conceits with which the dramatist entertained himself in his earlier work. The growing habit, revealed in the later plays, of ending a line with a preposition or conjunction furnishes material for a very minute and valuable study of what have become known as "weak endings." All these variations and peculiarities of style throw light on the chronology of the plays.

The first touches of Shakespeare's hand are found in the first part of "Henry VI.," "The Comedy of Errors," "The Two Gentlemen of Verona," "Love's Labour's Lost," and "Romeo and Juliet." The play of "Titus Andronicus" is usually included among the Shakespearean dramas, but there is little evidence of its Shakespearean authorship, and there are many reasons for doubting Shakespeare's connection with it. It was regarded as his work by some of his contemporaries, and included in the first complete edition of the plays in 1623; but sixty years after his death, Edward Ravenscroft, who edited the play in 1678, said: "I have been told by some anciently conversant with the stage that it was not originally his, but brought by a private author to be acted, and he only gave some master touches to one or two of the principal parts or characters." This tradition is probably in accord with the fact; the repulsiveness of the plot, the violence of the tragic motive, and the absence of humour from the play are essentially foreign to Shakespeare's art and mind. He may have retouched it here and there; he can hardly have done more.

And yet "Titus Andronicus," with its succession of

sanguinary scenes and massing of moral atrocities, may well find a place at the beginning of Shakespeare's work, so admirably does it illustrate the kind of tragedy which the early Elizabethan stage presented to its auditors. The theatre was then in what may be called its journalistic stage ; it was reserved for Marlowe and Shakespeare to advance it to the stage of literature. It was to the last degree sensational and sanguinary, presenting feasts of horrors to the " groundlings," as the worst sort of sensational journals of to-day spread before their readers, in crudest description, the details of the most repulsive crimes and the habits of the vilest criminals. Elizabethan audiences delighted in bloody scenes and ranting declamation, and both are still to be found in the sensational press, with this difference : the early theatre reached relatively few people, but the modern journal of the worst sort reaches an uncounted multitude. This taste for horrors and this exaggeration of speech were glorified by Marlowe's genius but remained essentially unchanged by him ; it was left for Shakespeare's serene and balanced spirit, deeper insight, and larger art to discard the repulsive elements of the tragedy without sacrificing its power. In " Lear," " Macbeth," " Hamlet," and " Othello " there are, however, traces of the older drama. Shakespeare did not wholly escape the influence of his time in this respect. " Titus Andronicus" is not without power, but it is too gross and redolent of the shambles even for Shakespeare's most immature art ; if he touched it at all, it must have been in a purely imitative way, and in the mere details of expression.

CHAPTER VII

THE FIRST FRUITS

WHETHER touched and strengthened by Shakespeare or not, " Titus Andronicus " serves as a connecting link between the drama as Shakespeare found it and his own work. It is not possible to determine the exact order in which the separate plays in the earliest group which record his period of apprenticeship appeared; but of the chronology of the group as a group there is no doubt. The first play which found its way into print appeared in 1597, when " Romeo and Juliet," " Richard II.," and " Richard III." were published; but it was not until the following year that Shakespeare's name appeared on the title-page of a drama. As early as 1592, however, lines from his hand had been heard on the stage; and he had begun the work of adaptation and revision still earlier. Among the plays which Shakespeare found in the library of The Theatre, many belonged to a class of dramas dealing with subjects and scenes in history — dramas which were probably more popular with the people who sat in the yard and in the boxes than any other plays which were presented to them. These plays appealed to the deepest instincts of men to whom the defeat of the Armada was a matter of very recent history, and in whom the race-consciousness was rapidly developing into a passionate conviction of the power and greatness of England. There was much in these plays which appealed to the imagination as well as to that thirst of action which was characteristic of the time. They brought before the eye and the mind the most commanding figures among the earlier kings and king-makers, and the most exciting and dramatic incidents in the life of the nation; there was a basis of fact ample enough to give the mimic representations that sense of reality which the English mind craves, and yet there was scope for that play of the imagination which has kept the English from the rigidity, hardness, and spiritual sterility which are the fruits of too great emphasis on the bare facts of history; there was always that touch of tragedy which invests a drama with dignity and nobility, and yet there was an abundance of that humour which is the necessity of healthy minds, because, by introducing the normal contrasts of life, it maintains that external balance which is essential to spiritual sanity.

These chronicle plays were, moreover, thoroughly representative of English society; kings, nobles, statesmen, ecclesiastics, and the lords of war were always conspicuous in the foreground, but in the middle and background there were those comic or semi-comic figures in whose boastings, blunderings, wit, and coarse vitality the common people took a perennial interest. These chronicles, crudely dramatized, were a rich mine of materials for a dramatic genius of Shakespeare's breadth and vitality, and they must

be placed, by force of the direct and indirect service
they rendered him, with the three or four chief streams
of influence which fed his creative activity. Their
direct service was rendered in the material which
they furnished him so abundantly; their indirect
service was rendered in the revelation of the possibilities for dramatic use of historical records which
they made clear to him, and which sent him, with
marvellous insight, to read the pages of Holinshed's
"Chronicles" and North's translation of Plutarch's
"Lives." In the arrangement of the thirty-seven
plays according to subject-matter and treatment,
the Histories fill a place hardly second to the Tragedies in importance. The hold which these old plays
had upon the mind of the English people was immensely deepened by Shakespeare's large and effective
handling of historical characters and situations; and he
must be regarded as one of the prime forces in the development of that intense and deeply practical patriotism which knits the widely scattered parts of the
modern empire into a vital racial unity.

It was to this rich mass of material that Shakespeare
turned at the very beginning of his career as a writer
of plays. His vocation was probably not yet clear to
him; he was groping his way toward free expression,
but he did not find it in a day. No man of genius
comes to complete self-consciousness save as the result of vital experience and a good deal of practical
experimenting with such tools as are at hand. Shakespeare began, not as a creator of individual works of
art, but as an adapter and reviser of the work of other

men, or as a collaborator with his fellow-craftsmen.
There have been a number of instances of conspicu-
ously successful collaboration among dramatists; in
Shakespeare's time, when the end in view was not the
writing of a piece of literature, but the making of a
successful acting play, coöperation among playwrights
was customary.

The three parts of "Henry VI." register Shakespeare's earliest contact with the material afforded by
the chronicles, and illustrate both the method of
using existing material in vogue at the time and
the results of collaboration on the part of two or
three contemporary writers who combined their
various gifts in order to secure higher efficiency.
Malone came to the conclusion, after long study of
this three-part play, that out of 6043 lines 1711 were
written by some author or authors preceding Shakespeare, 2373 were modified and changed by him, and
1899 written by his own hand. This mathematical
exactness is more impressive than conclusive; it has
this value, however: it brings into clear view the
composite character of the play, and shows how
Shakespeare learned his art. The poet was not bent
on creative work, but on mastering the technical part
of play-writing. Marlowe, Greene, and Peele have
been credited with participation in the authorship
of the play, but the passages assigned to them, and
to an earlier dramatist who furnished a common foundation for these later playwrights, have been selected
upon internal evidence and rest upon conjecture.
Shakespeare's connection with the play is, fortu-

The First Fruits

nately, beyond question; whether he did much or little is of small consequence so long as we have in the play the material upon which he began to work. The sources of the play are to be found in Holinshed's "Chronicles" and Hall's "Chronicle."

The presentation of "Henry VI." in its three parts at the Rose Theatre in the spring of 1592 was a notable event in the history of the early London stage. It was successful apparently, from the first performance, and the impression which it produced on men of intelligence is reflected in the words of one of Shakespeare's most successful contemporaries : "How it would have joyed brave Talbot," wrote Nash : " to thinke that after he had lyne two hundred yeares in his Tombe hee should triumphe againe on the Stage, and have his bones newe embalmed with the teares of ten thousand spectators at least (at severall times) who, in the Tragedian that represents his person, imagine they behold him fresh bleeding." It is significant that the scenes in which Talbot appears as the leading figure in the first part are now assigned to Shakespeare by common consent. It is as difficult to doubt the hand of the coming master in the powerful delineation of this great English soldier and his sturdy son as it is to find that hand in the cheap and coarse presentation of Joan of Arc. In the most immature stage of his development as an artist Shakespeare was incapable of so vulgar a misreading of a great career ; his insight would have saved him from so gross a blunder. In the heroic figure of Talbot the typical Englishman of action, with his superb energy, his dauntless courage, and his imperturbable poise, appears for the first time on Shakespeare's stage and predicts a long line of passionate, daring, and effective leaders. The scene in the Temple Garden, where the red and white roses are plucked from their fragrant seclusion to become the symbols of contending factions on bloody fields, is unmistakably Shakespearean ; and so also are some of the scenes in which Jack Cade and his mob appear.

Shakespeare's part in "Henry VI." brought him immediate recognition. He was twenty-seven years old, and had been in London six years. His competitors remembered that a very little time before he had been holding horses outside the theatres or performing the very humble duties of a call-boy. He had come up from Stratford without influential friends, a university education, or technical training for playwriting, at a time when all the successful dramatists were university-bred, scholars, wits, and men whose social advantages, however lost or misused, had been considerable. A small group of these writers were in possession of the craft and business of supplying the stage with plays. To men of the experience and temper of Marlowe, Greene, Nash, Peele, and Lodge, the sudden popular success of a youth with so little to aid and so much to retard him in external conditions must have seemed like an intrusion. They were men of loose lives, irregular habits, and broken fortunes.

Robert Greene, the son of a well-to-do citizen of Norwich, was then in his forty-third year. When he left the university in 1578, he went abroad. "For

The First Fruits

being at the University of Cambridge," he wrote toward the close of his ill-spent life, "I light among wags as lewd as myself, with whom I consumed the flower of my youth; who drew me to travel into Italy and Spain, in which places I saw and practised such villainy as is abominable to declare." The story of his later life, as told by himself, is pitiful in its moral degradation. On his death-bed — friendless, deserted, penniless, and consumed with remorse — he wrote an appeal to his old associates, full of bitterness, sound advice, and malice. "A Groats-worth of Wit bought with a Million of Repentance," written in 1592 after the striking success of "Henry VI.," urges Marlowe, Peele, and Nash or Lodge to give up vice, blasphemy, and bitterness of speech. "Base-minded men all three of you," he writes, "if by my misery ye be not warned; for unto none of you, like me, sought those burrs to cleave — those puppets, I mean, that speak from our mouths, those antics garnished in our colours. . . . There is an upstart Crow, beautiful with our feathers, that with his Tygers heart wrapt up in a players hide supposes he is as well able to bumbast out a blanke verse as the best of you; and being an absolute *Johannes factotum* is, in his own conceit, the only shake-scene in a countrie. O that I might intreate your rare wits to be imployed in more profitable courses: and let these Apes imitate your past excellence and never more aquaint them with your admired inventions."

This tirade against Shakespeare brings into clear relief the curious blending of remorse and jealousy which, even on his death-bed, was characteristic of Greene. Having wasted great talents and an adequate opportunity, he turned, with the hand of death upon him, with a malignant thrust upon the young poet who was already making friends by the charm of his temperament, as he was putting new dramatic value into old and conventionally treated material by sheer force of genius. Mr. Symonds interprets this onslaught upon the rising playwright in this fashion : " We, gentlemen and scholars, have founded the Drama in England, and have hitherto held a monopoly of the theatres. Those puppets, antics, base grooms, buckram gentlemen, peasants, painted monsters — for he calls the players by these names in succession — have now learned, not only how to act their scenes, but how to imitate them, and there is one among them, Shakespeare, who will drive us all to penury."

The fight against the new order which Shakespeare represented was useless, as such fights always are ; but Greene had very little insight into the nature of his art and its relation to the age, and he had already suffered one notable defeat. When he came to London, fresh from his university studies and his foreign travel, plays written in rhyme held the stage and were the special delight of theatre-goers, and Greene soon developed marked skill and facility in giving the public precisely what it liked. When he had gained the public and felt that the stage was practically in his hands, Marlowe brought out the tremendous drama of " Tamburlaine," written in blank verse, and effected a sudden and decisive revolution in public taste.

The First Fruits

Greene broke out into violent abuse of dramatists who were willing to stoop so low as to use blank verse; and three years before the appearance of "Henry VI.," Nash, who had been drawn into the fight by Greene, poured out his contempt on the "idiot art-masters, that intrude themselves as the alchemists of eloquence, and think to outbrave better pens with the swelling bombast of bragging blank verse, . . . the spacious volubility of a drumming decasyllabon."

It was not long before Greene was trying to make peace with the public by imitating the new style which Marlowe had brought into vogue. He made a truce with the author of "Tamburlaine," and the little group of scholar-dramatists controlled the business of play-writing. At the moment when their hold seemed most secure, Shakespeare appeared as a competitor. As Greene had fought Marlowe, so he fought Shakespeare; but in the case of Shakespeare there must have been something more than professional jealousy; men on their death-beds, as a rule, are not concerned to protect from fresh competition a business in which they have lost interest; they are often eager, however, to pay off a grudge. The cause of Greene's hatred is to be found, probably, in the perception of the contrast between his wild and wasted youth and the singular promise and sanity of Shakespeare's early career. There is abundant evidence that there was something winning in the young poet's personality, as there was something compelling in his genius. Men were drawn to him by the irresistible attraction of his radiant and lovable temperament, with its magical range of sympathetic expression. Penniless, deserted, and smitten with a remorse which tortured without purifying him, Greene shot his last arrow of malicious satire at the rising reputation of his youngest competitor, and shot in vain.

Henry Chettle, who published his rancorous attack, followed it in December, 1592, three months after Greene's death, with a public apology which contains a few words of great value as indicating the feeling Shakespeare was evoking from his fellow-workers: "Myself have seen his demeanour no less civil than he excellent in the quality he professes; besides, divers of worship have reported his uprightness of dealing which argues his honesty, and his facetious grace in writing that approves his art."

The sensitive mind of Shakespeare felt keenly the dominant influences of his time, and his earlier work reflects those influences. Brilliant as that work is, it is mainly, with touches of imitation, tentative, registering the response of the poet's imagination to the different masters of his art. "Titus Andronicus," if it came from Shakespeare's hand, betrays the influence of Marlowe; if this sanguinary drama is excluded from the canon of Shakespeare's dramas, then the reflection of Marlowe's powerful genius is to be found in "Richard II." and "Richard III." These plays were written a little later in time, but they belong within the first period of the poet's creative activity. Marlowe was then at the height of his fame and popularity, and Shakespeare could no more have escaped the spell of his splendid genius than a sensitive young poet of romantic temper in the decade between 1820 and 1830 could have escaped the influence of Byron. The three parts of "Henry VI.," with their series of pictorial tableaux, disclose the hold which the chronicle plays had taken upon Shakespeare's imagination.

The comedy "Love's Labour's Lost" betrays the influence of John Lyly, and of his famous "Euphues, the Anatomy of Wit," which appeared in London about the time Shakespeare left the Grammar School at Stratford. The writer was a young man of twenty-six years, a member of Magdalen College, Oxford, and extremely sensitive to the subtleties and refinements of sentiment and language. His talent was neither deep nor vital, but he was one of those fortunate men who arrive on the scene at the very moment when their gifts receive the most liberal reënforcement from the passion, the conviction, or the taste of the hour. Lyly had little to say, but he was a sensitive instrument ready to the hand of his time, and his time made the most of him. He made himself the fashion of the decade by fastening as if by instinct on its affectations, excesses, and eccentricities of taste. The Renaissance had made Europe, in intellectual interests at least, a community; and intellectual impulses passed rapidly from one country to another. By virtue of her recovery of classical literature and of her creative energy, Italy was the leader of culture, the exponent of the new freedom and the higher taste. To Italy men turned for the models and standards of literary art, as later they turned to France for manners and dress. The Italians were still near enough to mediæval ways and habits to find delight in wire-drawn definitions, in distinctions so fine that they were almost invisible, and in allegories and symbolism. The schoolmen were quibblers by tradition and training, and quibbling passed on into polite society when the New Learning came, and became the pastime and amusement of the cultivated and fashionable. Directness of speech went out of fashion; affectation of the most extreme type marked the man of superior refinement. Pedantry, quibbling, verbal juggling, the use of far-fetched similes and classical allusions, allegories and conceits, became the marks of elegance and culture. England, Spain, and France, eager to emulate the Italians in the newly opened field of scholarship and art, fastened, after the manner of imitators, upon the worst mannerisms of the Italians, imported them, and made them, if possible, more artificial and extravagant.

In every age, from the time of Surrey to that of Pater, English literature has shown the presence of a tendency to preciosity — an overcurious study of words and a skill in using them somewhat too esoteric. In Shakespeare's youth this tendency was both a fashion and a passion, and John Lyly was its most successful exponent. He caught the rising tide, and was carried to a great height of popularity. "Euphues" was a romance with a minimum of story interest and a maximum of reflections on love, manners, and morals, written in a style which was in the last degree ornate, elaborate, high-flown, and affected. There were no libraries or newspapers; books were few; the modern journal of fashion and well-diluted romance had not been born; time hung heavily on the hands of many women. Lyly knew his audience, and wrote for it with singular success. " Euphues," he wrote, " had rather lie shut in a lady's casket than open in a scholar's study." It found its way into a prodigious number of such caskets. The first part, originally published in 1579, was reprinted nine times in fifty years. The word Euphuism remains a lasting memorial of a tendency which was felt by nearly all the writers of Shakespeare's time, and which has left traces in all our later literature.

The Court found in this fastidious and extravagant style a highly developed language of homage and flattery, and men of affairs used it freely as poets. When Sir Walter Raleigh was forty years old and Queen Elizabeth sixty, the brilliant but unfortunate gentleman wrote these words from his cell in the Tower to Sir Robert Cecil: "While she was yet nigher at hand, that I might hear of her once in two or three days, my sorrows were the less; but even now my heart is cast into the depth of all misery. I that was wont to behold her riding like Alexander, hunting like Diana, walking like Venus, the gentle wind blowing her fair hair about her pure cheeks like a nymph; sometime sitting in the shade like a goddess; sometime singing like an angel; sometime playing like Orpheus. Behold the sorrow of this world! Once amiss, hath bereaved me of all."

There was much in Shakespeare's mind which not only made him sensitive to the attractions of Euphuism

in certain of its aspects, but stimulated the play of his
own ingenuity. When he gave free rein to his fancy,
no writer surpassed him in quips, quibbles, conceits,
puns, the use of images, allusions, and comparisons.
He could be as whimsical, fantastic, and affected as
the greatest literary fop of his time, and this not by
the way of satire but for his own pleasure. His
earlier plays are often disfigured by this vicious
verbal dexterity; mere jugglery with words, which
has no relation to art. " Love's Labour's Lost" was
first published in Quarto form in 1598, with this title-
page: "A Pleasant Conceited Comedy called Loues
Labors Lost." Shakespeare's name appears for the
first time on this title-page. The play was probably
written several years earlier. It was played before
the Queen during the Christmas festivities of 1597.
It is a very characteristic piece of apprentice work;
full of prophecy of the method of the mature dramatist, but full also of evidences of immaturity. The
young poet was trying his hand at comedy for the first
time, and his keen perception of the extravagances,
affectations, and foibles of London life had already
supplied him with a fund of material for satiric portrayal of contemporary manners. The wealth of
vitality and achievement which was characteristic of
the age ran to all manner of excess and eccentricity
of dress and speech. These were the most obvious
aspects of the life he saw about him; its deeper issues
were still beyond his experience. The quick eye of
the young observer took in at a glance the brilliance
and show of the age, the dress of which was rich and

elaborate to the last degree. "We use many more colours than are in the rainbow," says a contemporary English writer; "all the most light, garish, and unseemly colours that are in the world. . . . We wear more fantastical fashions than any nation under the sun doth, the French only excepted."

The passion for travel was general among men of fashion, and western Europe was laid under contribution for novelties in manners, dress, and speech. "Farewell, monsieur traveller," writes Shakespeare; "look you lisp, and wear strange suits; disable all the benefits of your own country; be out of love with your nativity, and almost chide God for making you that countenance you are, or I will scarce think you have swam in a gondola." The language of the day was as ornate and composite as the dress; men spoke to one another in the most flowery speech, and the language was strained to furnish compliments for women. The allusions to the Queen read like fulsome flattery, but women of lesser rank received the same homage of exaggerated and high-flown tribute. This splendour of bearing, often forced and unnatural, marked the endeavour of the age to live on a level with the greatness of life as it was brought home to the imagination by heroic and romantic achievements. When she had become a wrinkled old woman, the Queen was discovered practising a new dance-step in the solitude of her closet!

The plot of "Love's Labour's Lost" is slight and of minor importance; its sources have not been discovered; the play lives in its dialogue and satire.

William Shakespeare

The influence of Lyly is apparent not only in the extravagance and fastidiousness of speech which are satirized with ready skill, but in the give and take of the conversation and the quickness of repartee which first appeared in the English drama in Lyly's court plays.

In this comedy of manners Shakespeare makes admirable sport of the high-flown speech of the time, touching with a light but sure hand its ambitious pedantry in Holofernes, the fantastic excesses of the latest fashion in learning in Armado, and the perils of Euphuism, as he recognized them in his own art, in Biron, who probably speaks the poet's mind when he puts by forever

> Taffeta phrases, silken terms precise,
> Three-piled hyperboles, spruce affectation,
> Figures pedantical.

The youthfulness of the writer of the play is shown by the great preponderance of lines that rhyme, and by its marked lyrical character, which stamps it as the work of a brilliant poet rather than of an experienced dramatist. Three sonnets and a song are introduced, not because they are necessary parts of the drama, but because they are the natural forms of expression for a young poet; and Mr. Pater has called attention to the fact that the opening speech on the immortality of fame, spoken by the King, and the more striking passages spoken by Biron, have " something of the monumental style of Shakespeare's Sonnets, and are not without their conceits of thought and expression."

The First Fruits

The stock figures with which the stage was familiar are prominent in the play; the chief actors are sketched with a free hand rather than carefully drawn and strongly individualized after the poet's later manner; and the play contains several characters which, in the light of later plays, are seen to be first studies of some of the most notable portraits of riper years. The note of youthfulness is distinct also in the extravagance of speech which runs through it, and which was not only satirical but full of attractiveness for the poet. Indeed, the comedy may be regarded as an attempt on the poet's part to free himself from artistic peril by giving his mind, on its dexterous side, full play. The early ripening of artistic instinct into artistic knowledge is evidenced by the discernment of the danger and the well-devised remedy. Biron interprets the young poet's self-consciousness as an artist clearly and decisively; he shows us Shakespeare's insight into the methods and means of securing the freest expression of his thought, and his deliberate selection of right approaches to his art and his deliberate rejection of the most seductive errors of his time. In this comedy his mind was at play; its natural agility, alertness, keenness, love of paradox, delight in the dexterous handling of words, were allowed full scope, and the disease of his time came fully to the surface and never again seriously attacked him. With his magical quickness of mental action and command of language, he might have succumbed to the temptation to be a marvellously keen and adroit manipulator of words instead of a great creative artist; he might easily have been a fastidious writer for experts in the bizarre, the curious, and the esoteric in style, instead of becoming the full-voiced, large-minded, deep-hearted poet of humanity. This peril he escaped by discerning it and, in the very act of satirizing it, giving his mind opportunity to indulge a passion which all men of artistic feeling shared. The play dealt more freely with contemporaneous events and was more deeply embedded in contemporary conditions than any other of his dramas; for this reason it became very popular with Elizabethan audiences, but is the least interesting of Shakespeare's works to modern readers. There is in it a preponderance of the local and a minimum of the universal elements.

But Shakespeare could not satirize the extravagances and follies of his time without suggesting the larger view of life which was always in his thought; he could not touch the smallest detail of manners without bringing the man into view. In this early and sportive work, with its incessant and often metallic fence of words, the young poet disclosed his resolute grasp of the realities of life as opposed to passing theories and individual experiments. The artificial asceticism to which the King commits himself and his court, with its fasts, vigils, studies, and exclusion of women, is a gay but futile attempt to interfere with normal human emotions, needs, and habits; it breaks down under the first strain to which it is subjected, and is driven out of beclouded minds with the gayest of womanly laughter and the keenest of womanly wit. The satire

of the play assails false ideas of the place of knowledge,
false uses of speech, and false conceptions of life; it
discloses the mind of the poet already at work on the
problem which engaged him during the whole of his
productive life, and in the working out of which all
the plays are involved : the problem of the right relation of the individual to the moral order, to the family,
and to the State. The breadth of view and sanity of
temper which are at once the most striking characteristics of Shakespeare's mind and the secret of the
reality and range of his art find in " Love's Labour's
Lost " their earliest illustration. And in this play are
to be found also the earliest examples of his free and
expressive character-drawing; for Biron and Rosaline are preliminary studies for Benedict and Beatrice ; the play of wit throughout the drama predicts
" Much Ado About Nothing "; the love-making of
Armado and Jaquenetta is the earliest example of a
by-play of comedy which reaches perfection in " As
You Like It." As a piece of apprentice work " Love's
Labour's Lost " is quite invaluable ; so clearly does it
reveal the early processes of the poet's mind and his
first selection of themes, motives, human interests, and
artistic methods.

" The Comedy of Errors " belongs to this period of
tentative work, and is interesting as showing Shakespeare's familiarity with the traditional form of comedy
and as marking the point of his departure from it. It
was first published in the Folio of 1623, but it was
presented as early as the Christmas season of 1594, in
the hall of Gray's Inn ; and its production was accom-

panied by considerable disorder in the audience, which must have been composed chiefly of benchers and their guests. This disturbance is mentioned by a chronicler in the same year in these words : " After much sport, a Comedy of Errors was played by the players ; so that night began and continued to the end, in nothing but confusion and errors ; whereupon it was ever afterwards called the ' Night of Errors.' " The main, although not the only, source of the plot was the Menæchmi of Plautus, in which the Latin comedian develops the almost unlimited possibility of blunders which lies in mistakes of identity — then as now a popular device with playwrights and story tellers. Shakespeare may have read the comedy in the original, or in a translation by William Warner, which was not published until the year following the presentation of "The Comedy of Errors," but which was probably in existence in manuscript much earlier. In this form many pieces of prose and verse which later became famous were passed from hand to hand ; writing was practised chiefly for the pleasure of the writer and his friends, and publication was secondary, and usually an afterthought.

In turning to Plautus, Shakespeare paid tribute to the classical tradition which dominated Italy and was never without witnesses in England ; a tradition which cannot be disregarded without serious loss of artistic education, nor accepted without sacrifice of original power. Whenever the classical tradition has secured complete possession of the stage, a new and vital drama has been impossible ; whenever it has been entirely discarded, unregulated individualism has degenerated into all manner of eccentricities of plot and form. With characteristic insight, Shakespeare escaped both dangers ; he knew the classical manner, and was not unresponsive to its order, balance, and genius for proportion, but he refused to be enslaved or hampered by it. English tragedy had secured complete freedom, and was fast becoming the richest and most adequate expression of the English genius ; English comedy had been fighting the same battle, and "The Comedy of Errors " marks the decisive triumph of the national genius. In this play Shakespeare conformed to the ancient requirements that the action should take place in a single day and within the limits of a single locality — the time-honoured unities ; but he changed the classical into the romantic spirit by the introduction of greater complexity of characters and therefore of greater perplexity of plot, and by the infusion of a vein of pathos which is alien to the Latin comedy.

The ease with which the difficult plot is handled shows that Shakespeare had already gone far in his education as a playwright. A comparison with Plautus's play brings out his essential and fundamental cleanness of imagination. He was a man of his time, and his time was incredibly frank and coarse of speech ; but whenever he could escape into a purer speech he rarely lost the opportunity. The coarseness and occasional obscenity in his work were the dust of the road along which he travelled ; among the men of his age and vocation he was singularly refined in taste and clean in speech. Moral sanity is one of Shakespeare's most characteristic qualities; he is ethically sound throughout the entire body of his work. His insight holds him true at all points to the inexorable play of law. He offends the taste of a more fastidious age, but he is far more wholesome than many modern writers of irreproachable vocabulary. On this whole matter Coleridge has spoken the final word:

" Shakespeare has no innocent adulteries, no interesting incests, no virtuous vice; he never renders that amiable which religion and reason alike teach us to detest, or clothes impurity in the garb of virtue like Beaumont and Fletcher, the Kotzebues of the day. Shakespeare's fathers are roused by ingratitude, his husbands stung by unfaithfulness; in him, in short, the affections are wounded in those points in which all may, nay, must, feel. Let the morality of Shakespeare be contrasted with that of the writers of his own or the succeeding age, or of those of the present day who boast of their superiority in this respect. No one can dispute that the result of such a comparison is altogether in favour of Shakespeare; even the letters of women of high rank in his age were often coarser than his own writings. If he occasionally disgusts a keen sense of delicacy, he never injures the mind; he neither excites nor flatters passion, in order to degrade the subject of it; he does not use the faulty thing for a faulty purpose, nor carry on warfare against virtue, by causing wickedness to appear as no wickedness, through the medium of a morbid sympathy with the unfortunate. In Shakespeare vice never walks as in twilight; nothing is purposely out of its place; he inverts not the order of nature and propriety — does not make every magistrate a drunkard or a glutton, nor every poor man meek, humane, and temperate."

In " The Two Gentlemen of Verona " another tie with the past and another point of departure are

The First Fruits

discovered. The play seems to have been derived mainly from the Portuguese novelist and poet Montemayor, whose " Story of the Shepherdess Filismena " was well known in English through various translations of the pastoral romance of which it was part, and is reminiscent of the plays based chiefly on Italian love-stories which were popular before Shakespeare's time. This comedy of love and friendship, conceived in the romantic spirit, is slight and ineffective in construction, but full of beauty in detail. It is the work of a poet who was not yet a dramatist. There are lines in it which predict the magical verses of the later plays ; Julia and Lucetta are hasty, preliminary studies of Portia and Nerissa ; while Launce and Speed are the forerunners of a long succession of serving-men whose conceits, drolleries, whims, and far-fetched similes place them among the most original of the poet's creations.

Shakespeare's apprentice work, even when it was limited to adaptation or recasting of existing materials, is clearly discriminated from his more mature work both by its structure and its style : but it is tentative rather than imitative, and full of germs which were to find perfection of growth in the dramas of a later period.

CHAPTER VIII

THE POETIC PERIOD

During the decade between 1590 and 1600 Shakespeare's productivity was continuous, and covered a wide field of poetic expression; the nineteen or twenty plays which were written during this period included eight or nine comedies, one tragedy, and a group of historical dramas. To these must be added the two long lyrical pieces which bear his name, the few short pieces incorporated in "The Passionate Pilgrim," "A Lover's Complaint," "The Phœnix and the Turtle," and the lyrical poem on friendship and love which took the form of a sequence of one hundred and fifty-four sonnets. The apprentice work of the young dramatist may be said to end with the creation of the "Midsummer Night's Dream" and "Romeo and Juliet," though in neither of these beautiful dramas does his genius reach full maturity. At the end of six or seven years after his arrival in London he had become sufficiently known and successful to awaken envy; he had tried various dramatic forms with success; he had learned the practical side of playwriting, and he had gone a long way towards mastering its theory; he had become an actor of intelligence, if not of marked gifts; and he had established himself in his profession.

The Poetic Period

It must have been a period of deep and eager spiritual striving and unfolding. Some of the poet's devout students in Germany, to whom his fame owes much, and who have enriched Shakespearean scholarship for all time with the fruits of loving study and of fruitful insight, find evidence that during this time the poet passed through a storm-and-stress period. There are many indications, however, that this phase of the dramatist's spiritual life came later, and was coincident with tragic events which touched him to the quick. His earlier work shows a sunny nature, a sensitive mind, a gay and eager interest in many forms of experience and art.

If " Titus Andronicus " was written by Shakespeare, and at the beginning of his career, it was so purely external and imitative, so evidently outside the dramatist's life, that it does not count as a document in his spiritual history. The extraordinary accuracy of description, the resolute and unfailing grasp of the concrete, which stamp the very earliest work from his hand, show him at the start more absorbed in seeing than in meditating, more engrossed by the marvellous spectacle of the world than concerned with its spiritual order. It is true, he could not see without thinking, and Shakespeare was always of a meditative temper; but his first contact with the world called forth his full power of observation, and the emphasis of his thought fell, for a time, outside his own personality.

As he saw many sides of experience, so he felt the charm of various masters, and was drawn toward Lyly, Peele, and Marlowe; he came under the Italian influence, and he was not indifferent to classical models and imagery. Neither in his work nor in his consciousness had he come into full possession of himself.

The poet in him took precedence, in the order of development, of the dramatist; and it is as a poet that his earliest artistic successes were secured. From the beginning he had that freshness of feeling which is the peculiar and characteristic quality of the artist of every kind; he had also the sensitive imagination and the ear for melody. The world was reflected in his mind as in a magical mirror; its large outlines and its more delicate shadings lying clear and luminous before him. But he did not fully discern as yet the interior relations of spirit and form, the interdependence of individuality and the institutional order, the reaction of the act upon the actor, the unfolding of personality through action, the inevitable infolding of the tragic temperament by the tragic circumstance, and the final identification of character with destiny. The deeper insights, the creative grasp of the forces of life, and the masterful revelation of the laws which govern them through all the processes of history, which were to make him the first of dramatists, were growing within him, but they were not yet in possession of his spirit and his art; he was still primarily a poet.

The earlier plays do not reveal the evolution of character, the action and reaction of circumstances and forces within the circle of movement, the subordination of incident to action, and the husbanding of action in character, which give the dramas of his maturity their reality and authority. The poet was concerned chiefly with the beauty, the variety, and the humour of the spectacle. He was full of the charm of the show of things and of pleasure in the action of his own mind. He delighted in rhyme for its own sake; in classical allusions, not because, like torches held in the air, they illumine the path of his thought, but because they please his fancy; he gave his mind license in the use of puns, conceits, verbal dexterities of every kind; he pushed wit to the very limits of its rational meaning, and sometimes beyond; he exhausted imagery in the endeavour to drain it of its suggestiveness instead of leaving it to do its own work with the imagination. He kept comedy and tragedy apart, and simplified the drama at the expense of its manifold and deeper meaning. His eye was marvellously keen and his hand magically skilful, but he was not yet the master of the secrets of art and life; he was an ardent and impressionable young poet, playing with the problems of experience rather than closing with them in a life-and-death struggle, presenting their lighter aspects externally rather than penetrating to their heart and laying bare the fates which sleep in motive and passion.

It is easy to imagine the eager joy of the young playwright when he became conscious of the possession of the poet's insight and faculty. In his ardent imagination the great new world of the Renaissance, with the recovery of classical art in one hemisphere and the discovery of America in the other, lay in all its splendour of spiritual and material suggestiveness;

and in this vast territory, in which the human spirit seemed to have acquired a new freedom as well as an enlarged authority, he came swiftly to feel at home. He had the consciousness of great powers ; the sonnets show that clearly enough. A member of a profession which was under the ban not only of institutional religion but of society, and excluded from the chief paths of preferment and fame, he had, nevertheless, the supreme joy of discovering the beauty of the world and the infinite variety of human experience and fate, and of giving this manifold loveliness and moving show of life order, consistency, and form.

The consciousness of the possession of creative power is never born in an hour; it comes like the breaking of the day ; but, from the first gleam of light on the horizon, it stirs all the sleeping forces of the nature, and the adolescence of genius breeds an exaltation, an enthusiasm, a glow along the horizons of the future, born of a sudden awakening of passion, imagination, thought, and physical energy. To the young poet the world is as full of gods as it was to the mythmakers, and light flashes from it as if the order and splendour of the universe were being disclosed for the first time. For adolescence is the individual and personal discovery of life and the world ; the young explorer is as much alone in his experience and exaltation of spirit as if a thousand thousand earlier discoverers had not traversed the same seas and made the same journeys before him.

In " Henry VI." and " Titus Andronicus," if he did more than touch the latter play in the most perfunc-

The Poetic Period

tory way, Shakespeare was doing purely experimental apprentice work; in "The Comedy of Errors" he indulged his exuberant humour to the full; in "Love's Labour's Lost" he lightly but keenly satirized the foibles and extravagances of his time in learning, speech, and style; in "The Two Gentlemen of Verona" he made a slender plot bear the weight of his dawning imagination in image and phrase; in "Venus and Adonis" and "The Rape of Lucrece" he surrendered himself to the lyric impulse; and in the "Midsummer Night's Dream" and "Romeo and Juliet" his poetic genius rose to its full height. In these two dramas, which belong in the front rank of English poetry, fancy and imagination are seen in that creative play with the materials of experience and of ideality which fashions worlds as substantial as that on which we live, and yet touched with a beauty of form and a lucidity of meaning which we search for in vain in the world of reality.

The stages of Shakespeare's growth as a poet are as clearly marked as the stages of his growth as a dramatist. Between "Venus and Adonis" and "Romeo and Juliet" there intervened several years of experience, observation, experimentation, and unfolding. The freedom of movement, the fulness of imagination, the firm grasp of subject, and the masterly handling of material of all kinds which are characteristic of the later work did not come at call in Shakespeare's case; he was subject to the law of development and dependent upon education for the full possession of himself and the free use of his powers. In the earlier poems there are passages of unsurpassed beauty, but in construction and style the hand of the apprentice is manifest. As he had gone to school to the older playwrights when he set about the business of writing plays, so he went to school to the older poets when he began to write poetry. The spell of the classical ideal of beauty was on all sensitive minds when Shakespeare was young ; those who emancipated themselves from the classical tradition of poetic and dramatic form did not detach themselves from the poetic conceptions and the beautiful world of imagery which Europe recovered in the Renaissance. The joy of release from mediæval rigidity and repression found its natural expression in reverence for the models and standards of classical art. Man had been born again into conscious freedom ; personality had once more secured space and light for development ; to the monotony of the type in the arts had succeeded the range and variety of individuality ; love of nature and joy in her presence had returned ; confidence in the human spirit had been restored when the shadows of a world lying under the ban of heaven had been banished ; an immense exhilaration of imagination, a great liberation of personal force, were the fruits of the freedom of mind and soul which the Renaissance secured. Looking back across the Middle Ages, associated in the minds of the men of the new time with spiritual repression and intellectual bondage, the classical world lay clear, beautiful, and free in a light that was almost dazzling after the long gloom of mediævalism. It is true mediævalism had its lights, its humour, its beauty of devotion, its deep-rooted and noble art ; but the men of the Renaissance were in reaction against its repression of natural instincts, its curtailment of natural activities, and they saw the classical world in the high light of sharp contrast. That world is marvellously beautiful to the imagination of the nineteenth century, which constantly recalls it in every art and strives with passionate eagerness to recover its lost perfection of taste, of order, of workmanship ; to the imagination of the sixteenth century it was the golden age of the arts and of the spirit which fashions them — a lost but immortal world of freedom, joy, beauty, and creativeness.

Shakespeare had known this older world from boyhood. He was not subjugated by it, as were many of his contemporaries, for beneath the sensitive surface of his mind there was a vigorous and self-sustaining individuality ; but he felt its spell and discerned its educational uses. He knew his Ovid early enough to people the Forest of Arden with the older dreams of poetry ; but it was characteristic of his genius that he did not confuse the one with the other. In "Venus and Adonis" the great passages are not those which describe the beautiful goddess or the shy and radiant youth, but those which describe figures, landscapes, and incidents which he must have seen or known in the country about Stratford in his youth.

His earliest poetic experiments were in the classical vein ; for he knew the classical background of modern poetry as intimately as did Keats. He began his poetic career under the tutelage of one of the most imaginative of the Roman poets. In the early summer of 1593, with the imprint of his friend and fellow-townsman, Richard Field, on the title-page, Shakespeare made his first appeal to the reading public of his time, and his first venture in what he and his contemporaries recognized as literature. He had already made some reputation as a playwright; but plays were not then regarded as literature. Columbus died in ignorance that he had discovered a new world, so possessed was his mind with the conviction that he had touched the outlying islands of Asia. Shakespeare died in ignorance of the fact that he had made himself the foremost man in literature, so far apart in his thought and the thought of his time were plays and literature. The text of "Venus and Adonis" was carefully read, and is notably accurate; it was printed under the eye of the poet. The plays were either stolen or published in many cases without authorization, and are, for that reason, full of inaccuracies and difficult or questionable passages.

It is interesting to recall the fact, already reported, that four years earlier Richard Field had brought out the "Metamorphoses" of Ovid; and it is also worth recalling that in the year before the appearance of the "first heir" of Shakespeare's invention his father had made an appraisal of the goods of Field's father in Stratford.

"I know not how I shall offend," wrote Shakespeare in the dedication of the poem to the Earl of Southampton, "in dedicating my unpolished lines to your Lordship, nor how the world will censure me for choosing so strong a prop to support so weak a burden, only if your Honour seem but pleased, I account myself highly praised, and vow to take advantage of all idle hours till I have honoured you with some graver labour. But if the first heir of my invention prove deformed, I shall be sorry it had so noble a godfather." Shakespeare was twenty-nine years old, and the Earl of Southampton was in his twentieth year — a young man of brilliant parts and of striking beauty; well educated; with a fortune more than adequate to his rank; a great favourite in the Court circle; a lover of literature and of the drama; a generous and appreciative friend of men of letters; and a representative man in a great and brilliant period. The two young men had been brought together by those manifold affinities which in youth ripen casual acquaintance swiftly into devoted friendship; the glow of the time was on them both, although the dawn of the noble was to be quenched in the darkness of premature night, while that of the playwright broadened into a day which is likely to know no shadow of evening.

There has been wide difference of opinion regarding Shakespeare's meaning in describing the poem as "the first heir" of his invention. It has been urged that the words should be taken literally, and that the poem was probably composed at Stratford and carried to London, as Johnson carried, almost two centuries later, the tragedy of "Irene." Or the poet may have meant that it was his first attempt to write lyrical or narrative verse. When it appeared, no plays of his had been printed; the plague was raging in London, the theatres were closed, and the poem may have been composed at this time. It belongs, in any event, to his earliest productive period, and is the first fruit of his conscious artistic life.

"Venus and Adonis" shows plainly the influence of Ovid, as do some of the earlier plays; but it is free from mere imitation. Shakespeare felt the charm of the Latin poet, and reflected that charm, but he used his materials with freedom and individual skill. Ovid was followed only so far as Shakespeare found it profitable to follow. The older poet had told the story of the love of Venus for Adonis when Cupid's arrow pierced her by accident; how the goddess forsook all and followed him; how she warned him against his favourite pastime of hunting wild beasts; how she beguiled him in shady places with the tale of the help she gave Hippomenes when he outran Atalanta, and then, as a penalty for his ingratitude, brought bitter misfortune upon them; how the hunted boar gave Adonis his death-wound; how Venus brought the anemone — the sensitive and delicate wind-flower — from his blood.

On the framework of this classical tale the young poet wrought his careful, well-compacted, and thoroughly constructed poem. There is no reason to doubt that he had read the story without the aid of a translation, although Golding's version appeared in his childhood. The story was passionate, and the young poet did nothing to disguise or diminish the passion; on the contrary, he heightened it by setting the coldness of Adonis in sharp contrast with it. The poem is too frankly passionate and too naked for modern taste ; since it was written Puritan influence, by its tremendous emphasis on righteousness, has compelled us to strike a balance between the freedom of the Greek genius and the moral insight of the Hebrew spirit, and the problem of modern art is to harmonize freedom, beauty, and joy with moral sanity, order, and power. The love of beauty and the frank abandonment to its charms, which were characteristic of the Renaissance, are the dominant notes of this poem of a very young poet who was under the spell of the Renaissance spirit. It offends by its frankness rather than by its warmth ; for it is curiously cool and restrained in tone. It is full of striking lines, but the subject does not seem to inflame the poet's imagination ; he works as calmly as if he were not dealing with the most dangerous stuff in the world. His personality is as completely hidden as in the plays ; the treatment is wholly objective. "Venus and Adonis" belongs to the same period as Marlowe's glowing version of the memorable story of "Hero and Leander," but there could hardly be a greater contrast than that which is presented by the two poems. In Marlowe the current is deep and swift, and bears one on in a tumultuous rush of passion ; in "Venus and Adonis" the movement is deliberate and leisurely, and the genius of the poet is seen, not in his general treatment, but in the recurring pictures and descriptions with which the poem abounds. In the marvellous exactness of his drawing the accuracy of his observation is shown, and in the mellow euphony of many of its lines the magic of his later style is predicted. The hunted hare is so true to life that he must have been studied upon some hill about Stratford; and all the glimpses of nature are touches of genius. The noble realism of the dramatist is predicted again and again in lines which are not only suffused with beauty, but cut in outline as clearly as with a graver's tool.

"The Rape of Lucrece" appeared in the following year with the imprint of Richard Field, and the announcement that it was to be sold at "the sign of the White Greyhound in Paules Churchyard"; a neighbourhood which has been haunted by publishers and authors from that day until the last decade, when the makers of books have been seeking quarters in other sections of London. Ovid was still in the young poet's mind, although the pathetic story of Lucretia's fidelity had long been familiar in prose and verse. "Lucretia," Wharton tells us, "was the grand example of conjugal fidelity throughout the Gothic ages." Chaucer had set her in noble company in his "Legend of Good Women," and Sidney had recalled her in his beautiful "Apologie." Other English poets had felt the poetic power of the Roman matron's purity, and the theme had not escaped the attention of the balladists. The seven-line stanza in which the poem is written had been brought from France by Chaucer, and its capacity for serious subjects had been developed before Shakespeare used it. The Earl of Southampton's name appears on the page of dedication, as in the "Venus and Adonis" of the previous year; but the friendship between the two men had apparently ripened in the intervening months. The language of dedications is rarely to be taken literally, and in Shakespeare's time, as in Johnson's, it was more notable for adulation than for sincerity; but, although Shakespeare uses the speech of the courtier in addressing his friend, there is a note of sincerity in both dedications. The second is more intimate and affectionate than its predecessor. "The love I dedicate to your Lordship is without end," he writes; ". . . the warrant I have of your Honourable disposition, not the worth of my untutored lines, makes it assured of acceptance."

The subject would have permitted the most intense dramatic feeling, but, like the story in "Venus and Adonis," it is presented not only with entire objectivity but with a certain coolness and aloofness; as if the poet had chosen his theme rather than been chosen by it. His imagination was stimulated but not possessed by it; it is an impressive poetic exercise from the hand of a great poet rather than an original and characteristic expression of poetic genius. There are vivid impressions, scenes that stand out as if cut with the chisel, striking reflections, and, at intervals, the inimitable Shakespearean note, that magical harmony of sound and sense that rings like a bell in one's memory:

> For Sorrow, like a heavy hanging bell,
> Once set on ringing with his own weight goes.

But the poet is practising, not creating; learning his art, not enlarging it. It is in detached passages, not in the completed work, that we must look for the poet of "Romeo and Juliet." In "The Rape of Lucrece" there is, however, a distinct advance in seriousness and dignity; there is not only greater ease in the use of verse, but there is finer insight and higher ideality:

Who loves chaste life, there's Lucrece for a teacher:

Coleridge laid his finger on the characteristic quality of "Venus and Adonis" when he pointed out the fact that the reader of the poem is told nothing; he sees and hears everything. The dramatic element was too pronounced in Shakespeare's nature, even at a time when the poetic impulse was in the ascendant, to permit of the highest success in purely narrative verse; in any event, he did not stamp these poems with that finality of form which he put on many of the plays and on a large group of the sonnets. The earliest pieces of his original work betray the immaturity of his genius and art; they show him under the spell of the Renaissance spirit; they deal with passion without being passionate. Their significance in the history of his development has been discerned by Coleridge in a passage memorable in Shakespearean criticism:

"The Venus and Adonis did not perhaps allow the display of the deeper passions. But the story of Lucretia seems to favour, and even demand, their intensest workings. And yet we find in Shakespeare's management of the tale neither pathos nor any other dramatic quality. There is the same minute and faithful imagery as in the former poem, in the same vivid colours, inspired by the same impetuous vigour of thought, and diverging and contracting with the same activity of the assimilative and of the modifying faculties ; and with a yet larger display, and a wider range of knowledge and reflection : and lastly, with the same perfect dominion, often domination, over the whole world of language. What, then, shall we say ? Even this, that Shakespeare, no mere child of nature, no automaton of genius, no passive vehicle of inspiration possessed by the spirit, not possessing it, first studied patiently, meditated deeply, understood minutely, till knowledge, become habitual and intuitive, wedded itself to his habitual feelings, and at length gave birth to that stupendous power, by which he stands alone, with no equal or second in his own class ; to that power which seated him on one of the two glory-smitten summits of the poetic mountain, with Milton as his compeer, not rival."

It is impossible, even in work distinctly sensuous in imagery, not to discern the idealist in Shakespeare. Dealing with the physical aspects of beauty in " Venus and Adonis," he is bent on the ideal beauty. With Plato and Michael Angelo, he is driven by the appearance of beauty to that invisible and eternal reality which is at once the inspiration and justification of religion and poetry. In his earliest thought the future writer of the sonnets discerned the reality of which all beautiful faces, aspects, and images are the passing reflections, the fleeting remembrances and prophecies.

The publication of these poems gave Shakespeare another constituency and a new group of friends, and brought him recognition and reputation. In the eight years which followed its appearance no less than seven editions of " Venus and Adonis " were issued, and "The Rape of Lucrece" was in its fifth edition when the poet died. In exchanging the writing of plays for the writing of poems the poet passed from an occupation which shared to a considerable extent the social indifference or contempt which attached to the actor's profession to one in which gentlemen were proud to engage. He became, for the time being, a man of letters; he thought of readers rather than of hearers; he gave his work the care and finish of intentional authorship. He had become known to the theatre-going people as an actor of skill and an adapter of plays of uncommon parts; he now became known as a poet. Writing four years later, Richard Barnfield comments on "the honey-flowing vein" of Shakespeare,

> Whose "Venus" and whose "Lucrece," sweet and chaste,
> Thy name in fame's immortal book have plac't;

and in an oft-quoted passage, which appeared in the same year, Francis Meres, in his "Comparative Discourse of our English Poets with the Greek, Latin, and Italian Poets," uses these striking words, expressive at once of the impression which Shakespeare had made upon his contemporaries and of his association in their minds with the Latin poet upon whom he had drawn freely in both poems: "As the soul of Euphorbus was thought to live in Pythagoras, so the sweet witty soul of Ovid lives in mellifluous and honey-tongued Shakespeare; witness his *Venus and Adonis*, his *Lucrece*, his sugared sonnets among his private friends. . . ." A year later John Weever

The Poetic Period

calls Shakespeare "honie-tongued." At Cambridge in the same year St. John's College heard a fellow-playwright declare, "I'll worship sweet Mr. Shakespeare, and, to honour him, will lay his *Venus and Adonis* under my pillow." That Shakespeare had become so well known that the readers of his poems and the hearers of his plays were divided on the question of the relative importance of his works is shown, a little later, by these words of Gabriel Harvey written, Mr. Gollancz tells us, on the fly-leaf of a Chaucer folio: "The younger sort take much delight in Shakespeare's *Venus and Adonis;* but his *Lucrece*, and his tragedy of *Hamlet, Prince of Denmark*, have it in them to please the wiser sort." These references, and others of similar import, show the young poet with the earliest light of fame upon him. Life and art, friends and fame, opportunity and work, were already his. And he had been in London less than fourteen years.

The poets of his own time — Drayton, Brooke, Weever — were under the spell of his genius; and there is good reason to believe Spenser was thinking of him when he wrote in "Colin Clouts come home againe":

> And then, though last not least in Aetion;
> A gentler shepheard may no where be found,
> Whose muse, full of high thought's invention,
> Doth, like himselfe, heroically sound.

In the Christmas season of 1594 he acted at court before Queen Elizabeth, and the fact that his plays were repeatedly presented in her presence indicates her liking for his work and her purpose to show him favour. A playwright upon whose words crowds hung in the Rose and the Globe; whose great passages were recited again and again in the palaces at Greenwich, Richmond, and Whitechapel; whose poems, having passed from hand to hand among his friends, appeared in rapidly succeeding editions; to whom many contemporary writers paid glowing tribute; and who counted among his friends some of the most brilliant and influential men of his time, can hardly be regarded as having escaped the notice of his age, or as so obscure as to raise the question of his authorship of the work which bears his name.

The lyrical period in the growth of Shakespeare's mind and art culminated about 1597 or 1598, and bore its highest fruits in two dramas which hold a place by themselves; plays essentially poetic in quality and form, and singularly complete in their disclosure of the resources of his imagination and his art. The tragic story of Romeo and Juliet had attracted him at a very early date; there is evidence that he was brooding over this pathetic tale in 1591, although the play, in the form in which it has come down to us, probably did not appear before 1596. It was published in quarto form, probably without the dramatist's consent, in the following year, and the sub-title declared that it had been publicly played often and with great applause. The poet found the material for his first tragedy in several quarters, and drew upon these sources with the freedom characteristic of the time. The story has been traced as far back as the Greek romances of the early Christian centuries, but long before Shakespeare's imagination fastened upon it the congenial soil of Italy had given it new and more vigorous life. The tragic fate of the two lovers who were destined to become the typical lovers of Western literature was set forth at length by Luigi da Porto in a novel published about 1535; it had been sketched sixty years earlier by Masuccio, and it reappeared in later years in various forms; its popularity and its rich material tempting several succeeding story-tellers. Chief among these was Bandello, who made it the theme of a *novelle* in the decade before Shakespeare's birth. Two years before that event, an English poet, Arthur Brooke, told it in English verse, and five years later another English writer, William Painter, gave a prose version of the old story in his "Palace of Pleasure." The main line of development of the tragedy is to be found in Bandello, Brooke, and Shakespeare; the dramatist following quite closely the plot as it came to him from the English poet, but transforming and transfiguring both material and form by his insight, his dramatic skill, and, above all, by turning upon the passion of love for the first time the full splendour of his imagination.

"Romeo and Juliet" is the consummate flower of Shakespeare's poetic genius, the complete disclosure of his purely poetic gifts. The dramatic insight and skill with which the materials are rearranged; the the brilliancy of characterization, as in the splendid figure of Mercutio; the rising tide of emotion which bears the ill-fated lovers to their death, do not make us blind to the fact that this beautiful and appealing play, fragrant with the breath of the young summer, bathed in the soft radiance of the Italian night, touched with the imperishable charm of youth and passion, is primarily poetic and only secondarily dramatic. The characteristics of the early work of the poet are found in it: the frequent use of rhymes and the tendency to play with words; above all, the essentially lyrical quality of the play. Passages of pure and unsurpassed singing quality abound, and several verse-forms which were familiar to the mediæval poets and were in use in Shakespeare's time are found in perfection. The first meeting of the lovers in Capulet's house is described in sonnet form; Juliet's prayer in her father's orchard for the coming of night is reminiscent of the Evening-song, and has all the qualities of the Epithalamium; while the parting of the lovers, when

> Night's candles are burnt out, and jocund day
> Stands tiptoe on the misty mountain tops,

remains the most tender and beautiful Morning-song in the language. Caught in the tragic movement of a family feud, the lovers live out their romance in five passionate days, during which the drama steadily deepens and sweeps towards its end with tumultuous current; and at the supreme moment, with characteristic insight, death ushers in a final peace. It is this vision of reconciliation which made Shakespeare a master of human experience in its widest scope and significance. While exhibiting the fatality of individual struggle against the social order, he continually

The Poetic Period

makes us aware of the deep and radical changes which spring out of tragic resistance and defiance ; the searching reaction of the assertion of individuality on the social order.

Shakespeare's joy in the possession of the poetic gift, and his earliest delight in life, found radiant expression in " A Midsummer Night's Dream," a masterpiece of poetic fancy, and the gayest and most beautiful of poetic comedies. Rich as this drama is in humorous effects, it is so essentially lyrical in spirit that it stands alone in English poetry ; an exquisite expansion of the masque or festival poem into a drama of pure fancy and daring imagination. It was probably composed for some marriage celebration, though it has not been connected as yet with any wedding among the poet's friends or in the court circle.

Written about 1596, hints of the play appear to have been drawn from many sources. The modern reader finds such hints in Plutarch's "Life of Theseus," in Chaucer's "Knight's Tale," in Ovid's "Metamorphoses," and in the old French romance of "Huon of Bordeaux," of which an English translation appeared in the decade between 1530 and 1540. Shakespeare's real indebtedness, however, was to the poetic imagination of the Germanic race to which he belonged, which still kept alive, in folklore and fairy tale, in every hamlet in England, the magical world of fairy folk ; so near to the world of men, and so intimately associated with that world, and yet invisible to all save those who saw with the imagination. Especially were these elusive elves concerned with the mysteries of

love and marriage; and in the magic mirror in which
the poet shows them they not only associate Theseus
and Hippolyta with the sweetest traditions of English
field and fireside, but show forth, as in a parable, the
magic properties of love when love touches the whole
gamut of feeling and sets the whole nature vibrating
from the passions to the imagination.   There are evident connections in the play with the aspects of life
and character which interested the poet and with which
he had already dealt in " The Comedy of Errors," in
" Love's Labour's Lost," and in " The Two Gentlemen
of Verona," while its exquisite lyrical quality affiliates
it with " Romeo and Juliet "; but, both as regards
older sources of incident and his own earlier work,
" A Midsummer Night's Dream " stands in complete
and radiant individuality. It discloses the original
and spontaneous force of the poet's genius; his ability
to use, fuse, and recast the most diverse materials with
entire freedom and yet with unerring artistic instinct.
He is equally at home with the classical tradition
nobly presented in the figure of Theseus, with the
most extravagant rustic humour set in the mouths of
the inimitable clowns, and with the traditional lore of
childhood — the buoyant play of the popular imagination — in Titania and Oberon and Puck. His mastery of the verse-form which English tragedy has
adopted is equally clear and striking. The iambic
pentameter, with which his genius has almost identified English blank verse, finds in " A Midsummer
Night's Dream" the full development of its melodic
power. The line of five feet, each accented following an

unaccented syllable, without rhyme, is freed, in Shake-speare's hands, from the stiffness and rigidity which characterized it before Marlowe's time, and becomes soft as a flute in its lighter notes and resonant and full-toned as a bell in great passages:

> My hounds are bred out of the Spartan kind,
> So flew'd, so sanded; and their heads are hung
> With ears that sweep away the morning dew;
> Crook-kneed, and dew-lapp'd like Thessalian bulls;
> Slow in pursuit, but match'd in mouth like bells,
> Each unto each. A cry more tuneable
> Was never holla'd to, nor cheer'd with horn,
> In Crete, in Sparta, nor in Thessaly.

One hears in these lines that clear "chime of the vowels" which gives English verse its most penetrating and magical melody.

The fairies and the clowns made an irresistible appeal to the crowds in the theatre, and "A Mid-summer Night's Dream" enjoyed almost a century of popularity; it was imitated and pilfered from; when it lost its hold upon the generation of the Restoration, it reappeared as opera and operetta. In Germany its fortunes touched their highest prosperity; Wieland recalled its elves in his "Oberon," Goethe drew upon it in a striking scene in "Faust," and Mendelssohn, in song and overture, interpreted it with delicate insight and sympathy. It is the supreme masterpiece in the world of fairy lore.

CHAPTER IX

THE SONNETS

THE poetic period in Shakespeare's development coincided with a devotion to sonnet-writing which rose to the height of a passion from which few English poets escaped during the closing decade of the sixteenth century. The sonnet was the favourite verse-form for the expression of friendship, love, personal devotion, admiration of beauty ; it engaged the interest of the greatest poets and of the most mechanical and commonplace verse-makers ; it was the chosen instrument for the most delicate and poetic worship of individual women or of abstract virtues, and for the grossest and most obvious flattery.

At a time when an author had practically no ownership in his own work and when the business of publishing was carried on largely in defiance of or complete indifference to his wishes, and generally to his harm, a great mass of literary work was circulated in manuscript, and a goodly number of people found occupation in multiplying copies of these unpublished pieces for private circulation among the friends and admirers of authors. During the decade between 1590 and 1600 thousands of sonnets of every degree of merit passed from hand to hand, and were read, known, and talked

The Sonnets

about almost as widely, in some cases, as printed books. The reputation of certain groups of sonnets soon extended beyond the circle of the writer's friends, and general interest and curiosity made it worth while for some printer or publisher to secure copies of the poems and publish them, not only without the consent and revision of the writer, but often without his knowledge.

This appears to have been the case with a group of sonnets written by Shakespeare between 1593 and 1598, when the lyrical mood was dominant. The Sonnets were published in May, 1609, by Thomas Thorpe, who appears to have turned the absence of protection to authors to his own profit by obtaining and printing unpublished works which had secured wide reading in manuscript form. The popularity of Shakespeare's Sonnets doubtless attracted his attention, and, having secured copies of them, he sent them to the press without the poet's consent and probably without his knowledge. That many of these poems had been in existence more than ten years before the publication by Thorpe is proven by the fact that two of them appeared in "The Passionate Pilgrim," published in 1599, and that Meres, in the "Palladio Tamia," published a year earlier, referred to Shakespeare's "sug'r'd Sonnets among his private friends." Allusions and lines in the Sonnets made it possible to assign them at least proximate dates. They can hardly have been written before 1594 nor later than 1598. They belong, therefore, to the period of "Romeo and Juliet" and the "Midsummer Night's Dream," and, with "Venus and Adonis" and the

"Rape of Lucrece," which they followed at a short interval, they constitute Shakespeare's contribution to lyrical poetry. Their extraordinary beauty of thought, sentiment, and form has given them a foremost place in English poetry, while their possible significance as a record of the poet's experience or an expression of his emotions has evoked an immense body of comment.

Surrey and Wyatt brought the sonnet as a literary form from Italy, where Petrarch was its acknowledged master; but they did not slavishly reproduce the Petrarchian model; they followed a sound instinct in giving the sonnet greater simplicity. The Italian sonnet consists of an octave and sestet — a group of eight decasyllabic lines followed by a group of six decasyllabic lines; the sonnet of Shakespeare consists of three quatrains, or groups of four lines, with a concluding couplet. Precisians have held that the Shakespearean Sonnets are not sonnets, but fourteen-line poems. But Shakespeare did not originate the sonnet-structure which he used; it had been made ready to his hand by a long line of English poets. His supreme skill gave final authority to what had hitherto been an experiment.

Fifty-two years before the publication of Shakespeare's Sonnets, a group of sonnets by Surrey and another group by Wyatt had been published, many of them being translations from Petrarch. The volume containing these sonnets was reprinted six or seven times before Shakespeare left Stratford. It was followed in 1582 by Watson's "Centurie of Love"; in 1591 by Sidney's "Astrophel and Stella"; in 1592 by Daniel's "Delia" and Constable's "Diana"; in 1593 by

The Sonnets

Fletcher's "Licia," Barnes's "Parthenophil," and Lodge's "Phillis"; in 1594 by Spenser's "Amoretti" and Drayton's "Idea." To these collections of sonnets must be added probably as many more, the impulse expending itself apparently about 1597. The culminating point of this passion for sonnet-writing was probably reached about 1594, and its highest point of achievement was attained by Shakespeare. While there is much that is interesting and even important, from the standpoint not only of literary development but artistic excellence, in the work of this large group of sonneteers, Shakespeare alone gave his work universal significance and original and enduring beauty.

He did not originate a new form of sonnet, as he did not originate a new form of drama; he took the form which he found ready to his hand and gave it freedom, flexibility, a new compass, and a capacity for musical expression which the earlier English poets had predicted but had not unfolded. He continued and completed the modification of the sonnet as Petrarch left it which had been effected by the English sonneteers since the time of Surrey and Wyatt; surrendering something of the sustained fulness of tone of the Italian sonnet, but securing a sweetness, a flow of pure melody, which were beyond the compass of the earlier English sonneteers. The decasyllabic lines in groups of four, the alternate lines rhyming, and closing with a couplet, imposed rigid limitations on the poet but did not prevent him from securing some noble melodic effects.

William Shakespeare

The one hundred and fifty-four poems which make up the " Book Called Shakespeare's Sonnettes " form a sonnet-sequence, as clearly as do Mrs. Browning's " Sonnets from the Portuguese," or Dante Gabriel Rossetti's " House of Life " ; they deal with two leading themes in an order which is not necessarily historical, but which discloses an interior principle of arrangement ; to borrow a comparison from music, they consist of variations on two dominating motives or themes. The order in which they were presented in the edition of 1609 has been generally accepted, although nothing is known with regard to the principle or method of arrangement followed by the publisher. This order has been accepted because it has, in the judgment of a majority of students, the justification of a logical and intelligible grouping. In the poet's time, sonnets were often written in sequence ; the separate poems presenting, when read as a whole, a many-sided but connected treatment of a single theme or of a group of relating themes. The separate sonnets, written from time to time as expressions of diverse moods, as Tennyson wrote " In Memoriam," disclosed, when brought together, a unity, not only of manner, but of theme or thought. There is every reason to believe that Shakespeare wrote the Sonnets at intervals during a period of four or five years ; the Sonnets show that during this period his mind was constantly reverting to two kinds of emotional experience, which he approached from many different points of view and in many diverse moods, but which held a first place in his interest and moved him to expression.

The Sonnets

The one hundred and fifty-four poems in Shake-speare's sonnet-sequence have for their general themes a deep and highly idealized love of friendship for a young man of extraordinary beauty and charm of nature, and a passionate love for a "dark woman." These two unknown persons and the poet are the actors in a drama which may have been subjective in its origin, but which is definitely objective in its pres-entation. The spiritual motive is suggested in the one hundred and forty-fourth sonnet :

> Two loves I have of comfort and despair,
>   Which like two spirits do suggest me still ;
> The better angel is a man right fair,
>   The worser spirit a woman colour'd ill.

The friend to whom the first one hundred and twenty-six sonnets are addressed was noble in nature, station, and fortune, endowed with all manly qualities, and possessed of a winning beauty of feature and charm of manner ; the remaining twenty-eight are addressed to or describe relations with a woman who was plain of feature, pale, dark, treacherous, and stained, but the mistress of a potent fascination. If the sonnets are read in their present order as forming a connected poem, the poet, his friend, and the dark woman enact a drama of love, the acts of which are recorded in the emotions and meditations of the poet. The entire sequence may be broken into smaller groups, each of which conveys with more or less definiteness and com-pleteness some phase of the drama or some aspect of the poet's experience.

William Shakespeare

The sonnet-sequence opens with a celebration of the beauty and perfections of the noble youth whom the poet loves, dwelling with an idealizing delicacy and subtlety, after the manner of the Elizabethan sonneteer, on his separate and numerable charms, and urging him to marry in order that the marvellous beauty which has been given him may be reproduced in his children. Failing to secure for posterity copies of his friend's beauty by marriage, the poet offers to give it immortality in his verse. With the twenty-seventh sonnet a note of sadness and pain, foreshadowing a change in the harmony between the poet and his friend, is sounded; and the thoughts which come in absence and separation rise in the poet's mind and are set in exquisite form before the imagination in "sessions of sweet silent thought." The modulations of this theme are marvellously varied and beautiful, covering the whole range of sadness, longing, regret, loneliness, misgiving, foreboding, and despair.

So far no shadow save that of separation has rested upon the friendship between the two men, but now the dark woman enters. The poet in the forty-second sonnet describes himself as her lover, and his sorrow gets its deepest pang from the fact that his friend has robbed him of his mistress:

> If I lose thee, my loss is my love's gain,
>   And losing her, my friend hath found that loss ;
> Both find each other, and I lose both twain
>   And both for my sake lay on me this cross:
> But here's the joy: my friend and I are one;
> Sweet flattery! then she loves but me alone.

The Sonnets

Loneliness, disillusion, pain, self-denial, renunciation, and forgiveness are the notes of this phase of the poet's experience, rationalized and illuminated by meditation. There is no bitterness in his thought of his friend, estranged from him by the woman he loves and thus bringing him a double loss; his love and admiration triumph over his sense of injustice and injury. This feeling gives the episode of shattered friendship its tenderest note, and has left its record in a sonnet which registers Shakespeare's highest achievement in the field of lyric poetry:

That time of year thou mayst in me behold
    When yellow leaves, or none, or few, do hang
Upon those boughs which shake against the cold
    Bare ruin'd choirs, where late the sweet birds sang.
In me thou seest the twilight of such day
    As after sunset fadeth in the west;
Which by and by black night doth take away,
    Death's second self, that seals up all in rest.
In me thou seest the glowing of such fire,
    That on the ashes of his youth doth lie,
As the death-bed whereon it must expire,
    Consumed with that which it was nourish'd by.
This thou perceivest, which makes thy love more strong,
To love that well which thou must leave ere long.

In the forty-eighth sonnet the entrance of a rival poet is recorded, and the charms which have hitherto been celebrated by the writer of the Sonnets inspire "the travail of a mightier pen." The rival singer, whose advent gives a wound to the sonneteer's self-love, has been identified by different students of the

William Shakespeare

Sonnets with Chapman, Marlowe, Drayton, and Daniel. In the light of rejection and disillusion the poet comments with unflinching frankness on the meanness of the player's occupation, the lowliness of his own station in life, and the frequent supremacy of evil in the world. Through all these phases of his humiliation and sorrow his love for his friend remains unmoved, and he finds a deep consolation in the sense of power which his art gives him. Through art the beauty of his friend shall be the joy of posterity, as it has been the poet's inspiration.

There is a touching cry of farewell in the eighty-seventh sonnet; but after an interval of silence the poet takes up again the old themes, with more assurance and with a new note of hope and faith. This note becomes dominant in the one hundred and sixteenth sonnet, which may be regarded as the highest point of vision attained in the sequence :

> Let me not to the marriage of true minds
>   Admit impediments.   Love is not love
> Which alters when it alteration finds,
>   Or bends with the remover to remove :
> Oh, no ! it is an ever-fixed mark,
>   That looks on tempests and is never shaken;
> It is the star to every wandering bark,
>   Whose worth's unknown, although his height be taken.
> Love's not Time's fool, though rosy lips and cheeks
>   Within his bending sickle's compass come;
> Love alters not with his brief hours and weeks,
>   But bears it out even to the edge of doom.
> If this be error and upon me proved,
> I never writ, nor no man ever loved.

The Sonnets

Of the second general group of the Sonnets, beginning with the one hundred and twenty-seventh, seventeen are addressed to the woman whose dark fascinations have woven a spell over the poet's senses without beguiling his intellect, and have estranged his friend; while of the remaining eleven sonnets, nine are given up, for the most part, to the regret, repentance, and humiliation which his fatuous passion has brought to him. There is neither evasion nor self-deception in these striking confessions; they are charged with the bitterness of sincere and unflinching self-discovery and self-revelation:

> What potions have I drunk of Siren tears,
>   Distill'd from limbecks foul as hell within,
> Applying fears to hopes and hopes to fears,
>   Still losing when I saw myself to win!

The two concluding sonnets serve as a postlude to the group, and at the very end of the sequence touch with the glow and heat of " love's fire " the long story of the poem.

For many years the Sonnets shared the general indifference to Shakespeare which, perhaps as distinctly as any other sign of the times, measured the distance in taste and feeling between the age of Elizabeth and that of Queen Anne and her immediate successors. During the century now closing no part of Shakespeare's work has been more patiently or eagerly studied, and concerning none has there been greater divergence of opinion.

It has been held by some students that the Sonnets

are to be regarded chiefly as poetic exercises, and Mr. Sidney Lee has not only reënforced this view, but made a substantial contribution to literary scholarship by a thorough examination of the attitude and methods of English sonneteers in Shakespeare's time and of sonnet-writing on the Continent. Whatever interpretation is put upon the Sonnets, the background of poetic habit and convention which Mr. Lee has put behind sonnet-writing at the close of the sixteenth century must be taken into account; for Shakespeare was preëminently an opportunist so far as the use of materials and methods were concerned; with his poetic sensitiveness and thrift in invention he could not have failed to share the passion for sonnet-writing and the conventional attitude toward the art as a highly specialized form of lyric poetry.

This means that it would have been a natural exercise of Shakespeare's poetic faculty to idealize a patron; to give to a friendship for a man of great station the warmth and emotion of a deep personal love; to comment upon the frailty of women, the treachery of friends, and the hardness of the world as if these things had come within the compass of the poet's experience; to address elaborate apostrophes to abstract virtues; to make an imaginary woman the object of a passion and the shaping spirit of an intrigue which should have the semblance of reality without having any more substantial basis than the fancy of an Elizabethan sonneteer.

This is what Shakespeare may have done; but it is highly improbable that the key to the Sonnets is to

The Sonnets

be found in a comparative study of sonnet-writing in Shakespeare's time. The great majority of students have been forced to the conclusion that, while the conventional spirit and method of contemporary sonneteers had a distinct influence upon the poet so far as form and manner were concerned, the content of the Sonnets had a vital relation to his own experience. This conclusion is based upon the fact that a note of reality seems to be distinctly sounded in the series; that they tell a story or reveal an experience which is definitely outlined notwithstanding the mask of conventional imagery and phraseology which the poet employed; that throughout the entire body of his dramatic work he uniformly and consistently keeps in touch with reality, using historic material whenever he can find it adaptable for his purpose, and allying himself, apparently by instinct as well as by intention, with the force which resides in real things or in the deep and rich deposit of the imagination dealing, as in such figures as Hamlet or Prospero, with the greatest realities of experience; that in the sensitiveness, the capacity for devotion, the power of passion, which the Sonnets reveal they so entirely express the nature of Shakespeare that they must be accepted as, in a true sense, autobiographic.

Those who regard the Sonnets as pure and deliberate autobiography, containing a definite confession to be literally interpreted, probably stray as far from the truth as those who dissociate the poet entirely from his work and regard the Sonnets as technical exercises only. The habit of the age and the marked and consistent objectivity of Shakespeare's mode of expression make it highly improbable that he laid his heart bare by putting in historic order and with entire fidelity of detail a passional experience which had searched his spirit as with a lighted torch held aloft in the darkest recesses of his nature.

The truth probably lies between these two extremes of interpretation; it seems probable that the Sonnets are disclosures of the poet's experience without being transcriptive of his actual history; that they embody the fruits of a great experience without revealing that experience in its historic order. Literal, consecutive recitals of fact the Sonnets are not, but they are auto-biographic in the only way in which a poet of Shakespeare's spirit and training, living in his period, could make his art the vehicle of autobiography: they use the material which experience had deposited in Shakespeare's nature, but they hide the actual happenings in his life behind the veil of an elaborate art and of a philosophy with which the thought of western Europe was saturated in his time. The Sonnets may be read as the poetic record of an emotional experience which left lasting traces behind it, and as a disclosure of the mind of the poet; but they cannot be safely read as an exact record of fact. The poet, as Shelley suggests, was willing to intrust his secret to those who had the wit to understand it.

The dedication of the Sonnets was written, not by their author, but by their publisher, and has furnished material for one of the most extensive of the many controversies which have centred about Shakespeare:

The Sonnets

In these words Thomas Thorpe, not Shakespeare, addressed a patron whom the research and acumen of many decades of investigation and speculation have not been able to identify to the satisfaction of a majority of students. For many years the claims of William Herbert, Earl of Pembroke, were urged with great ingenuity and with considerable success. This young nobleman was a representative man of the close of the Elizabethan epoch. Clarendon describes him as "very well bred, and of excellent parts, and a graceful speaker upon any subject, having a good proportion of Learning, and a ready Wit to apply it and enlarge upon it; of a pleasant and facetious humour, and a disposition affable, generous, and magnificent." The "dark lady" was identified with Mary Fitton, who was a Maid of Honour to the Queen, of a gay and pleasure-loving disposition, on very friendly terms with some of the players of Shakespeare's company, of free manners and easy morals, who was finally

175

driven from the Court by the results of her intimacy with the Earl of Pembroke. The claims of Henry Wriothesley, Earl of Southampton, the brilliant and popular courtier, scholar, soldier, and patron of the theatre, to whom Shakespeare dedicated "Venus and Adonis" and "The Rape of Lucrece," have been presented with much force. Many facts in the careers of the Earl of Southampton and of the Earl of Pembroke meet the requirements of the few and uncertain biographical data furnished by the Sonnets; but the acceptance of either of these noblemen as the "W. H." of the dedication raises almost as many questions as it answers.

It is highly improbable that a dedication written by the publisher of a collection of poems, which he was about to issue without authorization, would disclose the identity of the chief figure in the drama of passion guarded in its record by the most highly conventionalized poetic form of the age. It is more probable that such a dedication would be addressed to a possible patron of the volume or to a personal friend of the publisher — some such person as the printer, William Hall, whose claims to the mysterious initials "W. H." Mr. Lee has brought forward as the most recent contribution to a discussion which will never, in all probability, be finally settled, and which turns, in any event, upon a matter which is solely one of intelligent curiosity.

The supreme value of the Sonnets lies in their beauty and completeness as works of art. They disclose marked inequalities of inspiration and of workmanship; in some cases they are prime examples of the strained imagery, the forced fancy, the artificial style, of the Elizabethan sonneteer; but again and again in the noble sequence the poet blends experience, philosophy, and the most sorely over-used poetic form of his time in a harmonious whole which appeals with equal power to the intellect and to the sense of beauty. The artificial frame of fourteen lines becomes fluid in his hand; the emotion which penetrates and irradiates it rises out of the depths of his nature; and both are touched with the inimitable magic of the poet's imagination.

The volume in which the Sonnets were published in 1609 contained a detached poem of forty-nine stanzas in the metre of "The Rape of Lucrece," in which the sorrows of a young girl, betrayed and deserted by her lover, are set forth in the gentle, tender, melodious manner of Spenser. Of "A Lover's Complaint" nothing further is known than this fact. It has no relationship with the Sonnets, and is in a wholly different key; but there is no reason why Shakespeare should not have written it in the early lyrical period. Its appearance with the Sonnets makes it highly probable that it was in circulation among Shakespeare's friends in manuscript and was secured by Thorpe in the same way in which copies of the Sonnets were obtained. The poem is in the manner of the conventional pastoral so popular at the same time, and is pervaded by an air of quiet melancholy and gentle beauty. Complaints were sung in many keys by the Elizabethan poets, and "A Lover's Complaint" was probably an early experiment in an imitative mood.

Robert Chester's "Love's Martyr; or, Rosalin's Complaint," published in 1601, contained, according to the preface, "diverse poetical essays on . . . the Turtle and Phœnix, done by the best and chiefest of our modern writers." Shakespeare's contribution to this collection of verse was "The Phœnix and the Turtle," the most enigmatical of his works. This poem of thirteen stanzas of four lines each, concluding with a Threnos in five stanzas of three lines each, is a poetical requiem for the Phœnix and the Turtle, whose love "was married chastity." Among the contributors to the collection were Shakespeare's great contemporaries, Jonson, Chapman, Marston; but neither the purpose nor the occasion of the publication has yet been discovered, nor has any light been shed from any quarter on the allegory whose meaning Shakespeare seems to have hidden from posterity in this baffling poem. Emerson suggested that a prize be offered for an essay which "should explain, by a historical research into the poetic myths and tendencies of the age in which it was written, the frame and allusions of the poem ; " but although much research has been devoted to this object and many metaphysical, political, ecclesiastical, and historical interpretations have been suggested, "The Phœnix and the Turtle" remains an unsolved enigma.

In 1599 William Jaggard, who, like Thorpe, laid hands upon any unpublished writing which had secured popularity and promised success to a venturesome publisher, issued a small anthology of contemporary verse under the title of "The Passionate Pilgrim. By W. Shakespeare." The first two selections were Sonnets by Shakespeare hitherto unpublished, and there were three poems taken from "Love's Labour's Lost," which appeared in 1591. The collection was reprinted in 1671 with the addition of two poems by Thomas Heywood. Shakespeare appears to have borne the affront in silence, but Heywood protested, in a dedicatory epistle which appeared in that year, against the injury done him, and declared that Shakespeare was much offended "with Mr. Jaggard that (altogether unknown to him) presumed to make so bold with his name." This protest was not without effect, for a new title-page was issued from which Shakespeare's name was omitted. Of the twenty-one pieces which make up "The Passionate Pilgrim," only five can be ascribed to Shakespeare. The collection was a miscellany, "a rag-picker's bag of stolen goods," put together without authority from the poets whose work was stolen, and the use of Shakespeare's name is one evidence of its weight with readers.

CHAPTER X

THE HISTORICAL PLAYS

THE period of Shakespeare's apprenticeship ended about 1596; the succeeding four or five years show him in full possession of his art and his material, though the deeper phases of experience were still before him and the full maturity of his genius was to be coincident with the searching of his spirit in the period of the Tragedies. The last half-decade of the sixteenth century were golden years in the life of the rising dramatist. He had made his place in the world; he had learned his craft; he had come to clear self-consciousness; the intoxication of the possession of the poetic imagination and the gift of poetic expression was upon him; he had immense zest in life, and life was at full-tide in his veins and in the world about him. The Queen was at the height of her splendid career; the country had grown into clear perception of its vital force and the possible greatness of its fortunes; English energy and courage were preparing the new soil of the new world for the seeds of a greater England at the ends of the earth; London was full of brilliant and powerful personalities, touched with the vital impulse of the age, and alive in emotion, imagination, and will. It was a time of great works of art and of action; in the two worlds of thought and of affairs the tide of creative energy was at the flood.

The genius of Spenser bore its ripest fruit in "Colin Clout," the "Epithalamium," and the concluding books of the "Faerie Queene." Sidney's noble "Apologie for Poesie," which was in the key not only of the occupations and resources of his mind but of his life, appeared in 1595, and a group of Bacon's earlier essays in 1597. Chapman's "Homer" and Fairfax's "Tasso" enriched the English language with two masterpieces of translation. Hooker and Hakluyt were writing and publishing. Among the playwrights are to be found the great names of Dekker, Jonson, Middleton, Heywood, Marston, and Chapman. The men who had possession of the stage when the poet came up from Stratford — Marlowe, Peele, Greene, Lodge, Nash, Kyd, and Lyly — had been succeeded by Shakespeare's generation. That he should have detached himself from this great group and made a distinct impression on his contemporaries is not the least among the many evidences of his extraordinary power. English literature was in one of its noblest periods, and Shakespeare shared an impulse which, like a great tide, carried men of every kind of power to the furthest limits of their possible achievement.

At no period of his life was Shakespeare more keenly observant, more intellectually alert, more inventive, more joyous in spirit, more spontaneous and poetic. He had solved the problem of his relation to his time by discovering his gift, acquiring his tools, and discerning his opportunity; he had ease of mind and openness of imagination. He gave himself up to the joy of life, and lived in its full tide with immense delight. He was not only in the world but of it. Even in this eager and golden period so meditative a mind could not escape those previsions of tragedy and fate which are never far off; and sorrow did not pass by the household at Stratford, for in August, 1596, according to the parish record, Hamnet, Shakespeare's only son, was buried. In this year "King John" was written, and it has been surmised that in the pathetic and beautiful character of Arthur, which is essentially unhistoric, the poet was portraying his own son, and in the touching lament of Constance giving voice to his own sorrow. This loss, which must have been poignant, was apparently the only shadow on these prosperous years when the poet was in his earliest prime.

History and comedy absorbed the imagination and divided the creative energy of Shakespeare from 1596 to 1600. Of the ten plays founded on English history, "King John" serves as a prelude, with "Richard II.," the two parts of "Henry IV.," "Henry V.," the three parts of "Henry VI.," and "Richard III." as a chronicle play on a great scale; while "Henry VIII." may be taken as an epilogue. The plays were not, however, written in historical sequence, nor did Shakespeare have any intention at the start of making a connected treatment of a stirring and dramatic period in English history. He found the old plays dealing with Henry VI. ready to his hand, as has been noted, and used them as material, touching "Henry VI." very lightly and probably only in the way of adaptation and revision, and the interpolation of a few characteristic scenes and passages. "Richard III." came a little later in time, and is so evidently modelled after Marlowe that its Shakespearean authorship has been questioned by very competent critics. It is full of echoes and reminiscences of Marlowe's manner; it is tempestuous, turbulent, and violent; it is history dramatized rather than a true historical drama; but the figure of Richard, which dominates the play and charges it with vitality, is as clearly realized and as superbly drawn as any character in the whole range of the plays. The lack of artistic coherence in the play is due to the inharmonious elements in it — the attempt to combine the method of Marlowe and the spirit of Shakespeare. The framework of the play was conventional even in Shakespeare's time; the manner is so lyrical that it is a tragic poem rather than a dramatic tragedy; nevertheless, Richard is drawn with a hand so firm, a realism so modern, that a play of very inferior construction becomes immensely effective for stage purposes, and has been almost continuously popular from its first representation. Shakespeare followed Holinshed and Marlowe in writing "Richard III."; but he put into the play that element of ethical purpose which stamps all his work and separates it in fundamental conception from the work of Marlowe.

The parallelisms between "Richard II." and Marlowe's "Edward II." are so obvious that it is impossible to escape the inference that Shakespeare was still under the spell of the tremendous personality of the author of "Tamburlaine"; but there are signs of liberation. There is a change of subject from the fortunes of the House of York to those of the House of Lancaster; blank verse, to which Marlowe rigidly adhered, gives place to frequent use of rhyme; and the atmosphere in which the action takes place is softened and clarified. The weak king's eloquence often betrays Shakespeare's inimitable touch, and the superb eulogy on England spoken by John of Gaunt is a perfect example of Shakespeare's use of the grand manner. Still following Holinshed, and under the influence of Marlowe, the dramatist was swiftly working out his artistic emancipation.

To this period belongs "King John," which was probably completed about 1595, and which was a recast of the older play of "The Troublesome Raigne of John, King of England," published in 1591. The conventional construction was not greatly modified by Shakespeare, but the play marks the transition from the chronicle play to the true drama; in which incidents and characters are selected for their dramatic significance, a dramatic motive introduced, dramatic movement traced, and a climax reached. The older playwrights, dealing with the events of a whole reign, would have given the play an epical or narrative quality; Shakespeare selected, compressed, foreshortened, and grouped events and figures in such a way as to secure connected action, the development of character, and a final catastrophe which is impressive, if not intrinsically dramatic. He instinctively omitted certain coarse scenes which were in the older play; he brought into clear light and consistency certain characters which were roughly sketched in the earlier work; in the scene between Hubert and Arthur he struck a new note of tenderness and pathos; while in giving marked prominence to the humour of Faulconbridge he opened the way for that blending of comedy with tragedy and history which is one of the marks, not only of his maturity, but of his greatness. The play has no hero, and is not free from the faults of the long line of dramas from which it descended and to which it belongs, but Shakespeare's creative energy is distinctly at work in it.

The growth of the poet's mind and art was rapid, and, in its large lines, is readily followed; but it was a vital, not a logical, development, and it was not, therefore, entirely orderly and harmonious. In his later work he sometimes returned to his earlier manner; at his maturity he more than once took up existing material, and was content to retouch without reconstructing it. The plays vary greatly in quality and insight; it would not be easy to find in the work of any other poet of the first rank more marked inequalities. Many of the sonnets touch the very limits of perfection; others are halting, artificial, full of the conceits and forced imagery of the day. The early historical plays are often panoramic rather than dramatic; " Henry IV.," on the other hand, is sustained throughout its wide range of interest and action by the full force of Shakespeare's genius. This inequality in the plays, the irregularities of growth which often present themselves, and the occasional reversions to the conventional construction which Shakespeare inherited from his predecessors or to his own earlier manner, humanize the poet, bring his work well within the range of the literary evolution of his time, and, while leaving the miracle of his genius unexplained, make his career and his achievement intelligible and explicable.

The brilliant years between 1596 and 1600 or 1601 were divided between history and comedy; between the splendid show and pageant of society as illustrated in the story of the English kings, and the variety, the humour, the inconsistency of men, as these qualities are brought out in social life. The "Taming of the Shrew," and the "Merchant of Venice," in which the genius of the dramatist shines in full splendour, probably antedated by a few months the writing of the two parts of "Henry IV." and of "Henry V.," but these plays are so nearly contemporaneous that their exact order of production is unimportant. The historical plays may be grouped together for convenience, keeping in mind the fact that the dramatist was apparently finding relief from dealing with great matters of state and great historical personages by turning from time to time to comedy, and perhaps by writing comedy simultaneously with history.

The first part of "Henry IV." was written not later than 1597; the second part followed it after an interval of not more than two years. The sources of the play are to be found in Holinshed and an earlier chronicle play of little merit but marked popularity, "The Famous Victories of Henry V." The play fol-

The Historical Plays

lows history with deviations, the most important being the bold stroke of making the Prince and Hotspur of the same age ; in the earlier drama the hints of the rich humour, the inimitable comic action of Shakespeare's work, are also found. But that which came into the hands of the dramatist as crude ore left it pure gold, stamped with ineffaceable images. In the use of this raw material, Shakespeare came to his own and made it his own by virtue of searching insight into its ethical significance and complete mastery of its artistic resources. Other plays show the poet in higher moods, but none discloses so completely the full range of his power; construction, characterization, pathos, humour, wit, dramatic energy, and the magical Shakespearean touch are found in "Henry IV." in free and harmonious unity of dramatic form. In no other play is there greater ease in dealing with apparently discordant elements ; nor is there elsewhere a firmer grasp of circumstances, events, and persons in dramatic sequence and action. The play has a noble breadth of interest and action, a freedom of movement and vitality of characterization, which give it the first place among the historical dramas.

The humour of Falstaff and the greed and vulgarity of his ragged, disreputable but immortal followers reënforce the dignity of the play, which is sustained throughout at a great height. Nothing which is human escapes the clear, piercing, kindly gaze of this young master of character and destiny ; he sees so broadly and deeply that nothing repels him which has any touch of reality or soundness in it. In his hands, and preëminently in this play, the drama broadens to compass the full range of humour and character and experience; and the tragic and humorous are blended, as in life, without incongruity or violation of the essential unities of human action and knowledge. Henry IV. and Hotspur are not blurred in outline, nor is the significance of their struggle obscured by the roisterers and thieves who are at the heels of Falstaff. The heroic note of the old ideals of chivalry is sounded as distinctly as if the broad, rollicking humour of Falstaff had no existence. Falstaff is one of the most marvellous of Shakespeare's creations; a gross braggart, without conscience, and as simply and naturally unmoral as if there were no morals, Shakespeare has drawn him with such matchless vitality that, although the stage is crowded with great figures, he holds it as if it were his own. Sir John Oldcastle, whose character undoubtedly gave Shakespeare a rough sketch of Falstaff, and whose name was originally used by Shakespeare, appears in the earlier play which the poet had before him; in deference to the objections of the descendants of Sir John, the name was changed in the printed play, and became Falstaff, but there is reason to believe that the earlier name was retained in the acting play. There was ground for the objection to its use, for Sir John Oldcastle was a Lollard and a martyr.

Shakespeare created a kind of English Bacchus at a time when every kind of fruit or grain that could be made into a beverage was drunk in vast quantities; and sack, which was Falstaff's native element, was both strong and sweet. Falstaff is saved by his humour and his genius; he lies, steals, boasts, and takes to his legs in time of peril, with such superb consistency and in such unfailing good spirits that we are captivated by his vitality. It would be as absurd to apply ethical standards to him as to Silenus or Bacchus; he is a creature of the elemental forces; a personification of the vitality which is in bread and wine; a satyr become human, but moving buoyantly and joyfully in an unmoral world. And yet the touch of the ethical law is on him; he is not a corrupter by intention, and he is without malice; but as old age brings its searching revelation of essential characteristics, his humour broadens into coarseness, his buoyant animalism degenerates into lust; and he is saved from contempt at the end by one of those exquisite touches with which the great-hearted poet loves to soften and humanize degeneration.

"Henry IV." is notable not only for the range and variety of types presented, but also for the freedom of manner which the poet permits himself. About half the first part is written in prose. Shakespeare was not alone among his contemporaries in breaking with the earlier tradition which imposed verse as the only form upon the drama; Jonson, Beaumont and Fletcher used both prose and verse in the same drama; but Shakespeare alone showed equal mastery over both forms. His prose is as characteristic and as perfect as his verse; he turns indifferently from one to the other and is at ease with either. He makes the transition in many places for the sake of securing variety and heightening certain effects which he wishes to produce, as he often introduces humorous passages into the most tragic episodes.

Mr. Sill makes the interesting suggestion that, verse being the natural form of expression for emotion, Shakespeare instinctively turned to prose when he was presenting ideas detached from emotion, when he wished to be logical rather than moving, and practical or jocular rather than philosophical or serious ; and, verse being essentially based on order and regularity, the poet turned to prose whenever he wished to give expression to frenzy or madness. There would have been essential incongruity in putting blank verse into the mouths of clowns, fools, drunkards, and madmen. These suggestions are of special interest when they are applied to " Hamlet."

In " Henry IV.," as in "The Merry Wives of Windsor " and " The Taming of the Shrew," the references to Warwickshire are unmistakable ; the dramatist was still too near his youth to have forgotten persons and localities known in his boyhood.

" Henry V.," drawn from the same sources, is a continuation of " Henry IV.," and presents in the splendid maturity of the king one of Shakespeare's great men of action ; a type in which his own time was rich, and in the delineation of which, being himself a man of reflection and expression, the poet found infinite satisfaction. In this play the events of a reign are grouped for dramatic effectiveness, and war is dramatized on a great scale. The material is essentially epical, but the treatment is so vigorous that the play, while not dramatic in the deepest sense, has the dignity and interest of a drama. The introduction of the Chorus, in which the dramatist speaks in person, shows how deeply he had meditated on his art, and how deliberately he had rejected the conventional unities of time, place, and action for the sake of the higher and more inclusive unity of vital experience. No other play so nobly expresses the deepening of the national consciousness at the end of the sixteenth century, and the rising tide of national feeling. The play is a great national epic; and the secret of the expansion and authority of the English race is to be found in it. It was presented in the last year of the century, and probably in the Globe Theatre, then recently opened.

"King Henry VIII." was written at least ten years later, and is distinctly inferior to the historical plays of the decade which closed with the production of "Henry V.," and is generally regarded as a piece of composite work, Fletcher probably completing that which Shakespeare had planned, but of which he had written only the first two acts.

The historical plays belong, as a whole, to Shakespeare's earliest period of productiveness; they keep the record of his apprenticeship; they find their place in the first stage of his development. This was due only in a subordinate way to accident; there was reason for it in the psychology of his art. The material for these plays was ready to his hand in the earlier chronicle plays in the libraries of the theatres, and in the records of Holinshed and Hall; and there was ample stimulus for their production in their popularity. But other and deeper sources of attraction are not far to seek. These plays mark the transition from the epic to the drama; from the story of events and persons as shaped by fate to the story of events and persons as they disclose the fashioning of character by action and the reaction of character on events, knitting men and actions together in a logical sequence and a dramatic order. The historical plays find their logical place in the order of development between the old plays dealing with historical subjects and the masterpieces of Shakespeare and his contemporaries; and in the unfolding of Shakespeare's art they hold the same middle place. These plays preserve the characteristics of the older plays and predict the fully developed drama; they do not reveal the full play of the poet's genius nor the perfect maturity of his art, although the plays which deal with Henry IV. and Henry V. reveal the full range of his interests and his gifts.

In these plays the young poet put himself in deepest touch with the life of his race, and, in bringing to clear consciousness the race spirit, brought out with the utmost distinctness the racial qualities of his own genius. He is preëminently the English poet, not only by virtue of his supremacy as an artist, but by virtue of the qualities of his mind; and these qualities were developed and thrown into striking relief by the historical plays. His greatest work was in other fields, but through no other work has he impressed himself so deeply on the imagination of the

men of his own race. He vitalized a great section of
English history, and has made it live before the eyes
of ten generations; he set the figures of great Englishmen on so splendid a stage that they personify finally
and for all time the characteristics of the English
race; he so exalted liberty as represented by the
English temper and institutions that, more than any
statesman, he has made patriotism the deepest passion
in the hearts of Englishmen. No other poet has
stood so close to the English people or affected them
so deeply; and from the days when the earliest popular applause welcomed "Henry VI." on the stage of
The Theatre, The Rose, and The Globe, to these
later times when Irving's Wolsey crowds the stalls of
the Lyceum, Shakespeare has been the foremost
teacher of English history. There are many who, if
they were as frank as Chatham, would confess that
they learned their history chiefly from him.

In these plays, moreover, the young poet trained
himself to be a dramatist by dealing with men under
historical conditions; with men in action. The
essence of the drama as distinguished from other
literary forms is action, and in the historical plays
action is thrown into the most striking relief; sometimes at the sacrifice of the complete development
of the actors. Before taking up the profoundest
problems of individual destiny or entering into the
world of pure ideality, Shakespeare studied well the
world of actuality. On a narrower stage, but in a
higher light, he dealt with the relation of the individual
to the political order, and showed on a great scale the

development of character in relation to practical ends. The depths of his spiritual insight and the heights of his art are to be found in the Tragedies; but the breadth, comprehensiveness, and full human sympathy of his genius are to be found in the historical plays; and in these plays, at the very beginning of his career, appeared that marvellous sanity which kept him poised in essential harmony between the divergent activities and aspects of life, gave him clearness of vision and steadiness of will, and made him the master of the secrets of character and destiny. The play of the divine law, which binds the deed to the doer, and so moralizes experience and makes it significant, is nowhere more clearly exhibited than in these many-sided dramas, with their rich diversity of character and their wide range of action. Shakespeare is one of the greatest of ethical teachers, not by intention, but by virtue of the depth and clearness of his vision. The historical plays reveal the justice of God working itself out through historical events and in the lives of historical persons; with the constant perception that no man is wholly good or evil; that out of things evil good often flows; that sin turns often, through the penitence of humility and service, into blessedness; and that about the certain and evident play of the divine justice there is a mercy which is a constant mediation, and hints, at times, at a redemption as inclusive as humanity.

Schlegel has well said of the historical plays that they are "a mirror for kings." In no other literature is there so complete a portraiture of the grandeur of the kingly office and the uncertainty of the kingly character; the pathos of the contrast between the weak man and the great place is often searching to the verge of irony. Shakespeare never permits his kings to forget that they are men, and the splendour of their fortunes sometimes serves to bring into ruthless light the inadequacy of their natural gifts for the great responsibilities laid upon them. The trappings of royalty heighten the criminality of John and Richard III.; the eloquent sentimentality of Richard II. and the ineffective saintlessness of Henry VI. are thrown into high relief by the background of royal position; the well-conceived and resolute policy of Henry IV. and the noble energy and decision of Henry V. — Shakespeare's typical king and the personification of the heroic, virile, executive qualities of the English nature — take on epical proportions from the vantage-ground of the throne.

The contrast between the man and the king sometimes deepens into tragedy when the desires and passions of the man are brought into collision with the duties of the king; for the king is always conceived as the incarnation of the State, the personification of society. His deed reacts, not only upon himself, but upon the community of which he is the head, and whose fortunes are inextricably bound up with his fortunes. In the plays dealing with historical subjects Shakespeare exhibits the divine order as that order is embodied in the State, and the tragedies which occupy the great stage of public life arise from the collision of the individual with the State, of the family with the State, and of the Church with the State. The political insight and wisdom shown in this comprehensive ethical grasp of the relation of the individual to society in institutional life are quite beyond the achievements of any statesman in the range of English history; for statecraft is everywhere in the exposition of the dramatist, the application of universal principles of right and wise living to the affairs of State. Thus, on the great stage of history, Shakespeare, in the spirit of the poet and in the manner of the dramatist, dramatized the spirit of man working out its destiny under historic conditions.

CHAPTER XI

DURING these prosperous five or six years Shake-speare's hand turned readily from history to comedy and from comedy to history; the exact order in which the plays of the period were written is unimportant so long as we are able to identify the group as a whole. The rising tide of creative energy, his mounting fortunes, and the deep fascination of the spectacle of life evoked his humour and gave free play to the gayety of his nature and the buoyancy of a mind which played like lambent lightning over the whole surface of experience and knowledge. It is probable that he was at work on several plays at the same time; taking up history or comedy as it suited his mood, and giving himself the rest and refreshment which come from change of work. It is certain that some of the greater Tragedies were slowly shaping themselves in his imagination from the earliest working years. "Romeo and Juliet" and "Hamlet" had taken root in his mind while he was yet an unknown apprentice in his craft; during these fertile years the germinal ideas which were to take shape in the entire body of his work were clarifying themselves in his consciousness; while his hand was engaged with one subject his mind was dealing with many. He had already used the comedy form in "The Two Gentlemen of Verona," "The Comedy of Errors," and "Love's Labour's Lost," and had made it clear to his contemporaries that he possessed the genius of comedy — that rare, penetrating, radiant, sane genius which was also the possession of Homer and Cervantes, and, later, of Molière and Goethe — the genius which not only looks into human experience deeply, but sees it broadly and in true perspective. It was Shakespeare's ease of mind, derived from the largeness and deep humaneness of his view, which kept him sane during the years when he was living in the heart of tragedy; and this ease of mind found expression in the comedy. The Shakespearean comedy is a comedy of life rather than of manners — a gay, sweet, high-spirited play with the weaknesses, follies, incongruities of men as these are projected against the great background of the spiritual kinship and destiny of humanity. There is no touch in Shakespeare of that scorn which is the mood of those lesser men who see the details of human character but not the totality of its experience. Shakespeare was equally at home with the tragic and comic elements in human nature, because both spring from the same root. In dealing with the tragic forces he is always superior to them; at their worst they are rigidly limited in their destructive force; he is not the victim of their apparent finality; he sees through and beyond them to the immovable order of the world, as one sees through the brief fury of the storm to the untouched sun and unmoved earth which are hidden

The Comedies

for a moment by the cloud. In like manner and for the same reason he laughs with men, but is saved from the cheapness of the sneer and the hard blindness of scorn. In his wide, clear, dispassionate vision he sees the contrast between the greatness of man's fortunes and the occasional littleness of his aims, the incongruities of his occupations, the exaggerations and eccentricities of his manners. He is mirthful because he loves men; it is only those who love us who can really laugh at and with us, and it is only men of great heart who have the gift of humour on a great scale. For humour, Dr. Bushnell says, " is the soul reeking with its own moisture, laughing because it is full of laughter, as ready to weep as to laugh ; for the copious shower it holds is good for either. And then, when it has set the tree a-dripping,

> And hung a pearl in every cowslip's ear,

the pure sun shining after will reveal no colour of intention in the sparkling drop, but will leave you doubting still whether it be a drop let fall by laughter or a tear."

Later in life, for a brief period, Shakespeare's laughter lost its ring of tenderness, its overflowing kindness; but his vision became clear again, and, although the spirit of mirth never regained its ascendency, the old sweetness returned. " Shakespeare is a well-spring of characters which are saturated with the comic spirit," writes George Meredith ; " with more of what we will call blood-life than is to be found anywhere out of Shakespeare ; and they are of this world,

William Shakespeare

but they are of the world enlarged to our embrace by
imagination, and by great poetic imagination. They
are, as it were — I put it to suit my present comparison — creatures of the woods and wilds, not in walled
towns, not grouped and toned to pursue a comic
exhibition of the narrower world of society. Jaques,
Falstaff and his regiment, the varied troop of Clowns,
Malvolio, Sir Hugh Evans and Fluellen — marvellous
Welshmen ! — Benedict and Beatrice, Dogberry and
the rest, are subjects of a special study in the poeti-
cally comic."

In "The Merchant of Venice" the poet finally
emancipated himself from the influence of Marlowe,
and struck his own note with perfect distinctness.
There is a suggestion of the "Jew of Malta" in Shylock, but the tragic figure about whom the play moves
bears on every feature the stamp of Shakespeare's
humanizing spirit. The embodiment of his race and
the product of centuries of cruel exclusion from the
larger opportunities of life, Shylock appeals to us the
more deeply because he makes us feel our kinship
with him. Marlowe's Jew is a monster ; Shakespeare's
Jew is a man misshapen by the hands of those who
feed his avarice.

The comedy was produced about 1596; it was
entered in the Stationers' Register two years later,
and was twice published in 1600. The dramatist
drew freely upon several sources. There are evidences of the existence of an earlier play ; the two
stories of the bond, with its penalty of a pound of
flesh, and of the three caskets were already known in

The Comedies

English literature, and had been interwoven to form a single plot. A collection of Italian novels of the fourteenth century and the well-known " Gesta Romanorum " contributed to the drama as it left Shakespeare's hands. As a play, it has obvious defects; the story is highly improbable, and, as in at least three other plays, the plot involves bad law; for the poet, although sharing the familiarity of the dramatists generally with legal terms and phrases, shows that his knowledge was second-hand, or acquired for the occasion, by his misuse of well-known words of legal import. In invention in the matter of plots and situations Shakespeare was inferior to several of his contemporaries; and he was content, therefore, to take such material as came to his hand with as much freedom as did Molière. In this case, as in every other, he at once put his private mark on the general property and made it his own. He purified the material, he put a third of the play into prose, and he imparted to the verse a beauty, a vigour, and a freedom from mannerisms which separate it at once from work of the apprentice period. He freely and boldly harmonized the tragic and comic elements; in Portia he created the first of those enchanting women for whom no adjective has yet been found save the word Shakespearean, for they are a group by themselves; and he set on the stage the first of his great tragic figures. In 1596 the Jew was contemptible in the mind of western Europe; he was the personification of greed and subtlety, and he was under suspicion of deeds of fiendish cruelty. He was robbed upon the slightest pretext, stoned on the streets, and jeered at on the stage. His sufferings were food for mirth. In 1594, a Jew, who was acting as physician to the Queen, had been accused of attempting to poison Elizabeth, and had been hanged at Tyburn, and popular hate against the race was at fever-heat when Shakespeare put on the stage the Jew who has since been accepted as typical of his race. It is not probable that the dramatist definitely undertook to modify the popular conception of the Jew; his attention may have been directed to the dramatic possibilities of the character by the trial and execution of Dr. Lopez; and when he dealt with the material at hand, he recast it in the light of his marvellous imagination, and humanized the central figure. Shylock was a new type, and he was not understood at first. For many years the part was played in a spirit of broad and boisterous farce, and the audiences jeered at the lonely and tragic figure. At every point in "The Merchant of Venice" the poet shows clearer insight than in his earlier work, deeper wisdom, greater freedom in the use of his material, and fuller command of his art.

Shakespeare had an older play before him when he wrote "The Taming of the Shrew," and he followed its main lines of story so closely that the play as we now have it is an adaptation rather than an original work. That the dramatist was thinking of the theatre and not of the public or of posterity is shown by the readiness with which he passed from the noblest creative work to the work of revision and adaptation. The earlier play gave him the idea of the Induction and

The Comedies

the characteristic passages between Petruchio and Catharine, but was an inferior piece of work, full of rant, bathos, and obvious imitation of Marlowe; the plot was followed, but the construction and style are new; the story of Bianca and her lovers was worked in as a subsidiary plot, and, although the play sometimes passes over into the region of farce, it is charged with the comedy spirit.

This comedy carries the reader back to the poet's youth, to Stratford and to Warwickshire. It is rich in local allusions, as are also "The Merry Wives of Windsor" and the second part of "Henry IV." There is no reason to doubt that Shakespeare's intercourse with Stratford was unbroken through these earlier years, though the difficulties and expense of travel may have prevented frequent visits. Now that prosperity and reputation were bringing him ease and means, his relations with his old home became more intimate and active. There are many evidences of his interest in Stratford and in his father's affairs, and it is evident that the son shared his rising fortunes with his father. The latter had known all the penalties of business failure; he was often before the local courts as a debtor. He seems to have had a fondness for litigation, which was shared by his son. In the dramatist's time the knowledge of legal phrases among intelligent men outside the legal profession was much more general than it has been at any later time, but there is reason to believe that Shakespeare knew many legal processes at first hand. He bought and sold land, brought various actions for the recovery of debts, filed bills in chancery, made leases, and was engaged in a number of litigations.

In 1596, after an absence of ten years from Stratford, the poet reappears in his native place as a purchaser of valuable lands and a rebuilder of his father's shattered fortune. In that year his only son, Hamnet, a boy of eleven, died and was buried in Holy Trinity Churchyard. In the same year John Shakespeare made application to the College of Heralds for the privilege of using a coat of arms. The claim was based on certain services which the ancestors of the claimant were declared to have rendered "the most prudent prince King Henry the Seventh of famous memorie." The ancestral distinction put forward on behalf of John Shakespeare was not more apocryphal than the services set forth in many similar romances formally presented to the College of Arms as records of fact. The statement that the applicant's wife, Mary, heiress of Robert Arden, of Wilmcote, was the daughter of a gentleman has not been verified. The application was granted three years later, and the Garter King of Arms assigned to John Shakespeare a shield : "gold, on a bend sable, a spear of the first, and for his crest or cognizance a falcon, his wings displayed argent, standing on a wreath of his colours, supporting a spear gold steeled as aforesaid." The motto, "Non Sans Droict," appears in a sketch or draft of the crest. Two years later the dramatist was styled "gentleman" in a legal document.

This effort to rehabilitate his father was followed, a year later, by the purchase of New Place — a con-

spicuous property at the northeast corner of Chapel
Street and Chapel Lane, opposite the Guild Chapel, in
Stratford, upon which stood what was propably the
largest house in the town. This substantial house, built
of timber and brick by Sir Hugh Clopton in the previous
century, had probably been long neglected, and was
fast going to decay.

No clear account of the appearance of the house
has been preserved; but enough remains to show its
considerable size and substantial structure. The walls
of the larger rooms and probably the ceilings were
covered with sunken panels of oak, some of which
have been preserved. Nothing else now remains of
the building save a few timbers which projected into
the adjoining house, now used as a residence for the
custodian of the Shakespeare properties, a fragment
of the north wall, the well, pieces of the foundation,
which are guarded by screens, the lintel, and an ar-
morial stone.

Shakespeare restored New Place, and enlarged its
grounds by considerable purchases of land. At his
death it passed into the possession of his daughter,
Susannah, the wife of Dr. John Hall, and in July, 1643,
Queen Henrietta Maria was entertained for three days
under its roof. Upon the death of Mrs. Hall, six years
later, New Place became the property of her only
child, Elizabeth, at that time the wife of Thomas
Nashe, later the wife of Sir John Barnard, of Abingdon.
Lady Barnard was the last of Shakespeare's direct
descendants.

At a later period the property came once more into

the hands of the Clopton family, and was subsequently sold to the Rev. Francis Gastrell, a vicar in Cheshire, who appears to have been a person of considerable fortune, dull perception, and irritable temper. He resented the interest which visitors were beginning to show in the place; in order to break up the growing habit of sitting under the mulberry tree, which was intimately associated with the dramatist, he cut the tree to the ground in 1756. This attitude towards the one great tradition of the town brought the owner of New Place into a disfavour with his fellow-townsmen which took on aggressive forms. The Stratford officials charged with the laying and collection of taxes made use of their power to secure the utmost farthing from Mr. Gastrell, and that gentleman, in order to relieve himself of further taxes, pulled down the house, sold the materials, and left Stratford amid execrations which have been echoed in every succeeding generation. The house adjoining New Place was the property of one of the poet's friends, and now serves as a residence for the custodian and as a museum of Shakespearean relics. The adjoining house was the home of Shakespeare's friend, Julius Shaw, who was one of the witnesses to his will; and, after various changes, it is still standing. New Place is to-day a green and fragrant garden; the fragments of the original foundation are infolded in a lawn of velvet-like texture; the mulberry tree has survived the vandalism of a hundred and fifty years ago; behind the old site there is a small but perfectly kept park where many flowers of Shakespearean association may be found, where the air

The Comedies

seems always fragrant and the place touched with abiding peace. The tower of Guild Chapel rises close at hand; in the near distance is the spire of Holy Trinity; the Avon is almost within sight; the earlier and the later associations of Shakespeare's life cluster about the place which he saw every day as a schoolboy, to which he returned in his prime, where he gathered his friends about him, and where he found reconciliation and, at last, peace.

The purchase and restoration of New Place made Shakespeare a man of consequence among neighbours who could understand the value of property, however they might miss the significance of literature. In a letter, still extant, dated October 25, 1598, Richard Quiney, whose son Thomas subsequently married Judith Shakespeare, appealed to the poet for a loan; and there are other evidences that he was regarded as a man whose income afforded a margin beyond his own needs.

The poet's acquaintance with country life in its humblest forms; with rural speech, customs, and festivals; with sports and games; with village taverns and their frequenters, was so intimate and extensive that he used it with unconscious freedom and ease. No other contemporary dramatist shows the same familiarity with manners, habits, and people; an intimacy which must have been formed by a boy who made his first acquaintance with life in Warwickshire. These reminiscences of boyhood, reënforced by the later and deliberate attention of a trained observer, continually crop out in many of the plays, as the formations of an earlier geologic period often show themselves through the structure of a later period.

The fertility of resource which gives the two parts of " Henry IV." such overflowing vitality made the writing of " The Merry Wives of Windsor " inevitable. It was quite impossible for the dramatist to leave a character so rich in the elements of comedy as Falstaff without further development under wholly different conditions. In the Epilogue to "Henry IV." the dramatist promised to " continue the story with Sir John in it, and make you merry with fair Katharine of France " ; but " Henry V." contained no reference to the old knight save the brief but inimitable account of his death. Almost a century after the death of the Queen three writers reported almost simultaneously the tradition, apparently current at the time and probably of long standing, that Elizabeth was so delighted with the humour of Falstaff in " Henry IV." that she commanded Shakespeare to continue the story and show Falstaff in love. " I knew very well," wrote Dennis, by way of introducing an adaptation of the play in 1702, " that it had pleas'd one of the greatest queens that ever was in the world. . . . This comedy was written at her command and by her direction, and she was so eager to see it acted that she commanded it to be finished in fourteen days." Seven years later Rowe added the further information that " she was so well pleased with the admirable character of Falstaff in the two parts of ' Henry IV.' that she commanded him to continue it for one play more, and to show him in love." The tradition apparently has

been long accepted, and there are intrinsic evidences
which make it credible. "The Merry Wives of
Windsor" is the kind of play which such a command
would have secured. It is a comedy which continually
runs into broad farce ; there is no touch of pathos in
it ; it deals with contemporaneous middle-class people,
in whom the dramatist shows very little interest ; it is
laid in Windsor, and contains references to the castle
which must have been very acceptable to the Queen.
The ground was evidently familiar to the dramatist,
and there are references of a realistic character, not
only to Windsor, but to Stratford. Moreover, the
play, although admirable in construction, is below the
level of Shakespeare's work of this period in intellectual quality, and lacks those inimitable touches
of humour and poetry which are the ineffaceable
marks of his genius when it is working freely and
spontaneously.

The play owes little in the way of direct contribution to earlier sources, though various incidents used
in it are to be found in Italian and other stories. It
was probably written about 1599, and the Queen, according to tradition, was "very well pleased with the
representation." The plot is essentially Italian ; the
introduction of the fairies was a revival of the masque ;
but the atmosphere of the play is entirely English ; it
reflects the hearty, healthy, bluff spirit and manner of
middle-class life in an English village. It is the only
play dealing with the English life of his own time which
Shakespeare wrote, and it undoubtedly reproduces conditions, manners, and habits which he had known at

first hand in Stratford. Falstaff shows a great decline in spontaneity, freshness, and humour ; he has become gross, heavy, and dull ; he easily falls a victim to very obvious devices against his dignity ; he has sunk so low that he has become the butt of practical jokers. It is probable that this particular development of Falstaff was suggested to Shakespeare by Elizabeth rather than forced upon him by the expansive vitality of the character. As a whole, the play shows breadth of characterization and genuine humour, while Windsor and the country about it are sketched with unusual fidelity to detail, but with characteristic freshness of feeling for fields and woods.

This homely comedy of middle-class English country life, with its boisterous fun, its broad humour, and its realistic descriptive passages, was probably written not long before " Much Ado About Nothing," but the two plays present the most striking contrasts of method and manner. The Italian play is in an entirely different key ; it is brilliant, spirited, charged with vivacity, and sparkling with wit ; it is a masterpiece of keen characterization, of flashing conversation, of striking contrasts of type, and of intellectual energy, playing freely and buoyantly against a background of exquisite beauty. The dramatist was now completely emancipated from his earlier teachers, and had secured entire command of his own genius and of the resources of comedy as a literary form. In this splendid creation of his happiest mood in his most fortunate years, the prophecy of sustained and flashing interchange of wit in Lyly's court plays is amply fulfilled, and the

The Comedies

promise of individual power of characterization clearly discerned in Biron and Rosaline is perfectly realized in Benedict and Beatrice ; while Dogberry and Verges mark the perfection of Shakespeare's skill in drawing blundering clowns. In this play the blending of the tragic and humorous or comic is so happily accomplished that the two contrasting elements flow together in a vital and exquisite harmony of experience, full of tenderness, loyalty, audacity, and brilliancy ; the most comprehensive contrast of character is secured in Hero and Claudio, Benedict and Beatrice, as chief actors in the drama, with Dogberry and Verges as centres of interest in the minor or subsidiary plot. Hazlitt declares with reference to this play that perhaps "the middle point of comedy was never more nicely hit, in which the ludicrous blends with the tender, and our follies, turning round against themselves in support of our affections, retain nothing but their humanity." In "The Merry Wives of Windsor" Shakespeare drew with a free hand the large and rather coarse qualities of English middle-class life ; in "Much Ado About Nothing" he presented a study of life in the highest stage of the social order, touched at all points with distinction of insight, characterization, and taste. The gayety and brilliancy of the great world as contrasted with the little world of rural and provincial society are expressed with a confidence and consistency which indicate that the poet must have known something of the court circle and of the accomplished women who moved in it.

Written probably about 1599, and drawing appar-

William Shakespeare

ently for some features of the plot and comic incidents upon the inexhaustible Bandello and upon one of the greatest works of Italian genius, the " Orlando Furioso " of Ariosto, " Much Ado About Nothing " marks the highest point of Shakespeare's creative activity in comedy, and perhaps the most brilliant and prosperous hour in this prolific and fortunate period of his life.

In the same year Shakespeare created his masterpiece of poetic pastoral drama, " As You Like It." He was still in the sunlight, but the shadows were approaching; his mood was still gay and his spirits buoyant, but the one was touched with premonitions of sadness and the other tempered by a deepening sense of the complexity of life and its mystery of good and evil. In the form and background of the play he was in touch with the love of pastoral life shared by many of the poets of his time ; by Lodge and Greene, by Spenser and Sidney. The Arcadia of literature was in his imagination, but the deep shadows and wide spaces of the Forest of Arden in Warwickshire were before his eye ; he knew the affected passion for flowering meads and gentle shepherds which were the stock-in-trade of many contemporaries, but he also felt that fresh and unforced delight in nature which brings him in touch with the modern poets. He knew how to use the conventional poetic speech about nature, but he saw nature with his own eyes as clearly as Burns and Wordsworth saw her two centuries later. The plot of " As You Like It " was probably taken from Lodge's " Rosalynde, Euphues' Golden Legacie,"

an old-fashioned, artificial, pastoral romance, full of
affectations and unrealities, based upon the much older
"Tale of Gamelyn," which appeared in the fourteenth
century and was handed down in several manuscripts
of Chaucer's "Canterbury Tales," and was probably
intended for use in a tale which the poet left unwrit-
ten. This old story belongs to the cycle of the Robin
Hood ballads; and Shakespeare had this origin of the
story in mind when he wrote: "They say he is already
in the Forest of Arden, and a many merry men with
him; and there they live like the old Robin Hood of
England."

The woodland world of Arden, in which sonnets are
affixed to ancient trees, and lovers, courtiers, and
moralists live at ease, has much in common with the
pastoral backgrounds of Spenser and Lodge; but its
artificiality is redeemed by its freshness of spirit, its
out-of-door freedom, and its enchanting society. Rosalind and Orlando are the successors of a long line of
pastoral lovers, but they, alone among their kind,
really live. In Rosalind purity, passion, and freedom
are harmonized in one of the most enchanting women
in literature. In her speech love finds a new language,
which is continually saved from extravagance by its
vivacity and humour. In Audrey and Corin the passion of Orlando and Rosalind is gently parodied; in
Touchstone the melancholy humour of Jaques is set
out in more effective relief. There are threatenings
of tragedy in the beginning of the play, but they are
dissolved in an air in which purity and truth and
health serve to resolve the baser designs of men into

harmless fantasies. In Jaques, however, there appears for the first time the student of his kind who has pierced the illusions of place and power and passion, and touched the underlying contradiction between the greatness of man's desires and the uncertainty and inadequacy of his achievements. This sadness is touched with a not unkindly irony; for Shakespeare's vision was so wide that he was rarely able to look at life from a single point; its magnitude, its complexity, the rigour of its law, and at the same time the apparent caprice with which its diverse fortunes were bestowed, were always within his view. At the best, we seem to hear him say in this mood:

> All the world's a stage,
> And all the men and women merely players.

Jaques must not be taken too seriously, but there are hints of Hamlet's mood in his brooding meditation; and through the whole play there is a vein of sadness which, mingled with its gayety and poetic loveliness, gives it a deep and searching beauty.

In the Christmas season of 1601 "Twelfth Night" was presented in the noble hall of the Middle Temple. "At our feast," writes John Manningham, a member, in his diary, "we had a play called 'Twelfth Night; or, What You Will.' Much like the 'Comedy of Errors' or 'Menæchmi' in Plautus; but most like and near to that in Italian called 'Inganni.' A good practise in it to make the steward believe his lady widowe was in love with him, by counterfeiting as from his lady in general terms, telling him what she liked best in him, and prescribing his gesture in smiling, his apparel, etc., and then when he came to practise making him believe they took him to be mad." This charming comedy, so characteristic of Shakespeare's genius at play, was probably acted by the Lord Chamberlain's servants, the company with which Shakespeare was associated, before the Court in the old palace at Whitehall during the same season.

The ultimate source of the play was probably Bandello's "Novelle," though the Italian plays to which Manningham refers (there were several plays with the title Inganni) may have furnished incidents ; but Malvolio, Sir Toby Belch, Sir Andrew Aguecheek, Maria, and, above all, Viola, as they live in the comedy are Shakespearean to the heart. The framework of the play is essentially serious, a beautiful vein of poetic feeling runs through it, and, intermingled with these, the most unforced and uproarious fun. In inventiveness in the comic type and in freedom in handling it, as well as in grouping of diverse materials and fusing them into a harmonious and captivating whole, this comedy was never surpassed by the dramatist. He parted with the muse of comedy at the very moment when he had mastered the art of touching the weaknesses, follies, and minor sins of men with a touch which was keen with the wisdom of a great knowledge of the world, and gentle with the kindness of one who loved his kind for what they had lost rather than for what they had won.

CHAPTER XII

THE APPROACH OF TRAGEDY

WITH the advent of the seventeenth century, Shakespeare entered the greatest period of his life as an artist — the period of the Tragedies. During eight eventful years he was brooding over the deepest problems of human experience, and facing, with searching and unfaltering gaze, the darkest aspects of life. That this absorption in themes which bore their fruit in the Tragedies was due primarily to a prolonged crisis in his own spiritual life is rendered practically certain by the persistence of the sombre mood, by the poet's evident sensitiveness to and dependence upon conditions and experience, and by a series of facts of tragical import in the lives of some of his friends. His development in thought and art was so evidently one of definite progression, of the deepening of feeling and broadening of vision through the unfolding of his nature, that it is impossible to dissociate the marked change of mood which came over him about 1600 from events which touched and searched his own spirit.

Until about 1595 Shakespeare had been serving his apprenticeship by doing work which was to a considerable extent imitative, and to a larger extent experimental; he had tried his hand at several kinds of

writing, and had revealed unusual power of observation, astonishing dexterity of mind, and signal skill in
making the traditional characters of the drama live
before the eyes and in the imagination of the theatre-
goers who made up his earliest constituency. From
about 1594 to 1600 he had grown into harmonious
and vital relations with his age, he had disclosed poetic
genius of a very high order, and he had gone far in his
education as a dramatist. He had written the Sonnets, and he had created Portia, Beatrice, Rosalind,
Juliet, Romeo, Mercutio, Benedict, Henry V., Falstaff,
Shylock, Hotspur, and Dogberry. If he had died in
1600, his place would have been secure. His reputation was firmly established, and he had won the hearts
of his contemporaries by the charm of his nature no
less than by the fascination of his genius.

His serenity, poise, and sweetness are evidenced
not only by his work but by the representations of
his face which remain. Of these the bust in the chancel of Holy Trinity Church at Stratford, made by
Gerard Jonson, a native of Amsterdam, and a stone-
mason of Southwark in the poet's time, and the Droeshout portrait, which appeared on the title-page of the
First Folio edition of the poet's works, issued in 1623,
were accepted by his friends and contemporaries, and
must present at least a general resemblance to the
poet's features. They are so crude in execution that
they cannot do justice to the finer lines of structure or
to the delicacy of colouring of Shakespeare's face and
head, but they make the type sufficiently clear. They
represent a face of singular harmony and regularity of

feature, crowned by a noble and finely proportioned head. The eyes were hazel in colour, the hair auburn ; the expression, deeply meditative and kindly, was that of a man of thoughtful temper, genial nature, and thorough self-control. In figure Shakespeare was of medium stature and compactly built.

It is significant that, after the first outburst of jealousy of the young dramatist's growing popularity in Greene's "A Groatsworth of Wit Bought with a Million of Repentance," the expressions of Shakespeare's contemporaries indicate unusual warmth of personal regard, culminating in a magnificent eulogy from his greatest rival, and one who had reason to fear him most.

That he was of a social disposition, and met men easily and on pleasant terms, is evident from the extraordinary range of his knowledge of men and manners in the taverns of his time — those predecessors of the modern club. That he enjoyed the society of men of his own craft is evident both from his own disposition and from the fact that he stood so distinctly outside the literary and theatrical quarrels of his time. The tradition which associates him with the Mermaid Tavern which stood in Bread Street, not far from Milton's birthplace, is entirely credible. There he would have found many of the most brilliant men of his time. Beaumont's well-known description inclines one to believe that under no roof in England has better talk been heard :

> What things have we seen
> Done at the Mermaid ? heard words that have been

The Approach of Tragedy

So nimble and so full of subtle flame,
As if that every one from whence they came
Had meant to put his whole wit in a jest,
And had resolved to live a fool the rest
Of his dull life.

The age was eminently social in instinct and habit; society, in the modern sense of the word, was taking shape; and men found great attraction in the easy intercourse and frank speech of tavern meetings. Writing much later, but undoubtedly reporting the impression of Shakespeare's contemporaries, Thomas Fuller says, in his "Worthies": "Which two I beheld like a Spanish great gallion and an English man-of-war: Master Jonson (like the former) was built far higher up in learning; solid, but slow in his performances. Shake-spear, with the English man-of-war, lesser in bulk, but lighter in sailing, could turn with all tides, tack about, and take advantage of all winds, by the quickness of his wit and invention."

At the end of the sixteenth century Shakespeare was on the flood-tide of a prosperous life; at the very beginning of the seventeenth century a deep and significant change came over his spirit. In external affairs his fortunes rose steadily until his death; but in his spiritual life momentous experiences changed for a time the current of his thought, and clouded the serene skies in the light of which nature had been so radiant and life so absorbingly interesting to him. While it is highly improbable that the Sonnets record in chronological order two deep and searching emotional experiences, the autobiographic note in them is unmistakable; it is impossible to avoid the conclusion that they express, if they do not literally report, a prolonged emotional experience culminating in a crisis which shook the very bases of his nature; which brought him in the beginning an intense and passionate joy, slowly dissolving into a great and bitter agony of spirit; and issuing at last, through the moralization of a searching insight, in a larger and deeper harmony with the order of life. This experience, in which friendship and love contended for supremacy in his soul; in which he entered into a new and humiliating consciousness of weakness in his own spirit, and in which he knew, apparently for the first time, that bitterness of disenchantment and disillusion which to a nature of such sensitiveness and emotional capacity as his is the bitterest cup ever held to the lips, found him gay, light-hearted, buoyant, full of creative energy, and radiant with the charm and the dreams of youth; it left him saddened in spirit, burdened with the consciousness of weakness, face to face with those tragic collisions which seem at times to disclose the play of the irony of fate, but out of which, in agony and apparent defeat, the larger and more inclusive harmony of the individual with the divine and the human order of society is secured and disclosed.

Shakespeare drank deep of the cup of suffering before he set in the order of art, with a hand at once stern and tender, the colossal sorrows of his kind. Like all artists of the deepest insight, the keenest sensitiveness to beauty, and that subtle and elusive but magical spiritual sympathy which we call genius,

The Approach of Tragedy

which puts its possessor in command of the secret experience of his kind, Shakespeare's art waited upon his experience for its full capacity of thought and feeling, and touched its highest points of achievement only when his own spirit had sounded the depths of self-knowledge and of self-surrender. In the great Tragedies life and art are so completely merged that they are no longer separable in thought; these dramas disclose the ultimate harmony between spirit and form.

This searching inward experience was contemporaneous in Shakespeare's life at the beginning of the seventeenth century with fierce dissensions between his personal friends in his own profession, with growing bitterness of feeling and sharper antagonism between the two great parties in England, and with a gradual but unmistakable overshadowing of the splendours of the "spacious days of great Elizabeth." What is known as "The War of the Theatres" was at its height between 1598 and 1602; the chief combatants being Ben Jonson on one side, and Dekker and Marston on the other; the weapons of warfare, satirical plays. Thirteen or fourteen dramas are enumerated as having their origin in the antagonism between the rival playwrights, the best known and most important of these plays being Jonson's striking and characteristic comedy "Every Man in His Humour," and his "Poetaster." Dekker's "Satiromastrix" and Marston's "What You Will" are chiefly interesting as forming part of the record of this vociferous war, and "The Return from Parnassus" on account of one interesting but obscure reference to Shakespeare which it contains: "Few of the University pen plaies well, they smell too much of that writer *Ovid*, and that writer *Metamorphosis*, and talke too much of *Proserpina* and *Juppiter*. Why, heres our fellow *Shakespeare* puts them all downe, I and *Ben Jonson* too. O, that *Ben Jonson* is a pestilent fellow, he brought up *Horace* giving the Poets a pill, but our fellow *Shakespeare* hath given him a purge that made him betray his credit." These words were put into the mouth of the actor Kempe and spoken to the well-known actor Burbage, and Mr. Ward suggests that their meaning may be put into plain speech: "Our fellow, Shakespeare, ay, and Ben Jonson, too, puts down all the university play-writers."

The reference to a purge administered by Shakespeare to Jonson has led to much speculation regarding Shakespeare's part in this professional quarrel, and "Troilus and Cressida" has sometimes been placed among the plays which contributed either light or heat to the discussion; many of Shakespeare's characters have been identified by different critics with the leading combatants and with others among his contemporaries; in no case, however, has any speculation in this field secured a proper basis of proof. This very fact, taken in connection with Shakespeare's long and cordial relations with Jonson, make it more than probable that the dramatist stood outside the arena, maintaining a friendly attitude toward both parties to the strife.

The relations between Jonson and Shakespeare are in the highest degree creditable to both; but it is probable that Shakespeare's sweetness of nature was the chief element in holding them on so high a plane. By gifts, temperament, difference of early opportunity, methods of work, conceptions of art, the two were for many years rivals for supremacy in the playwright's field. The contrast between them could hardly have been more marked. Jonson was nine years the junior of Shakespeare, having been born in 1573. His grandfather had been a clergyman, and he was the descendant of men of gentle blood. He was city born and bred ; at Westminster he came under the teaching of a man of great learning, William Camden, who made him a student and put the stamp of the scholar on his mind. He became a devout lover of the classics and a patient and thorough intellectual worker. Poverty forced him to work with his hands for a time, and when the War of the Theatres was at its height, his antagonists did not hesitate to remind him that he had been a bricklayer in his stepfather's employ. From this uncongenial occupation he found escape by taking service in the Netherlands, where he proved his courage by at least one notable exploit. He returned to London, and married at about the age at which Shakespeare took the same important step. He was a loyal and affectionate father, and a constant if not an adoring husband ; he described his wife many years after his marriage as " a shrew, yet honest."

Like Shakespeare, he turned to the theatre as a means of support ; appeared as an actor ; revised and, in part, rewrote older plays ; collaborated with other playwrights. He lacked the faculty of adaptation, the capacity for practical affairs, and the personal charm which made Shakespeare successful as a man of business; but, through persistent and intelligent work, he placed himself at the head of his profession.

He was of massive build; his face strong rather than sensitive or expressive; his mind vigorous, orderly, and logical, rather than creative, vital, and spontaneous; he was, by instinct, habit, and conviction, a scholar; saturated with the classical spirit, absolutely convinced of the fixed and final value of the classical conceptions and methods in art; with a touch of the scholar's contempt for inaccuracy, grace, ease, flexibility. He was a poet by intention, as Shakespeare was a poet by nature; a follower and expounder of the classic tradition, as Shakespeare was essentially a romanticist; he achieved with labour what Shakespeare seemed to accomplish by magic; he wrought out his plots with the most scrupulous care for unity and consistency, while Shakespeare appeared to take whatever material came to hand with easy-going indifference to the niceties of craftsmanship. To a man of Jonson's rugged and somewhat sombre temper, the success and love which Shakespeare evoked with such ease must have seemed out of proportion to his desert; while Shakespeare's methods of work must have seemed to him fundamentally defective and superficial. It was a case of great dramatic intelligence matched against great dramatic genius. When it is remembered that the two men were working in the same field and for the same audience, the intensity of their rivalry, and the provocations to jealousy and ill feeling which would naturally rise out of it, become very clear.

Shakespeare's generous nature, reënforced by his breadth of vision, apparently kept him free all his life from any touch of professional jealousy or animosity. Jonson saw his rival pass him in the race for popular favour, and could hardly have been blind to the fact that Shakespeare distinctly distanced him in artistic achievement. He was a conscientious man, standing loyally for the ideals of his art; he was a scholar, to whom accuracy in every detail was a matter of artistic morals; but as the immense vitality of the age seemed to penetrate to the very source of his massive intellect and lift it above its laborious methods of work into the region of art, and to turn its painstaking patience into lyrical ease and grace, so Jonson's essential integrity of nature and largeness of mind forced upon him a recognition of his rival's greatness. It is true he sometimes criticised Shakespeare; he commented sharply on certain passages in "Julius Cæsar," where Shakespeare was on his own ground; he declared that Shakespeare had "small Latine and less Greek"; that he "wanted art"; that he ought to have "blotted a thousand" lines; that he "had an excellent fancy; brave notions and gentle expressions; wherein he flowed with that facility that sometimes it was necessary he should be stopped;" but all these adverse opinions, for which there was, from Jonson's point of view, substantial ground, fall into true perspective and are evidences of discriminating judgment rather than uncritical eulogy when the passage in

William Shakespeare

which they stand is taken in its entirety, to say nothing of the noble lines which appear in the First Folio. "I loved the man," wrote Jonson, "and do honour his memory, on this side idolatry, as much as any. He was indeed honest, and of an open and free nature; had an excellent fancy; brave notions and gentle expressions. . . . There was more in him to be praised than pardoned."

That there were occasional outbursts of impatience with Shakespeare's ease, spontaneity, and indifference to the taste and standards of men who were primarily scholars and only secondarily poets, is highly probable; it could hardly have been otherwise. To men of plodding temper, of methodical habits of work, of trained faculties rather than of force and freedom of imagination, the facility of the man of genius often seems not quite normal and sound; it is incomprehensible to them, and therefore they regard it with a certain suspicion. It is greatly to Jonson's credit, when his temper and circumstances are taken into account, that he judged Shakespeare so fairly and recognized his genius so frankly.

There is good reason to believe that Shakespeare kept aloof from the professional quarrels of his time among his fellow-craftsmen, and that he was a kind of peacemaker among them; his kindliness went far to disarm the hostility of those who differed with him most widely on fundamental questions of art. It is an open question, which has been discussed with ability on both sides, whether Jonson had Shakespeare in mind in a striking passage in "The Poetaster"; it is

quite certain that he could hardly have described
Shakespeare's genius more aptly:

> His learning labours not the school-like gloss
> That most consists of echoing words and terms, ·
> And soonest wins a man an empty name;
> Nor any long or far-fetch'd circumstance
> Wrapp'd in the curious generalities of arts,
> By a direct and analytic sum
> Of all the worth and first effects of art.
> And for his poesy, 'tis so ramm'd with life,
> That it shall gather strength of life with being,
> And live hereafter more admired than now.

Deeper matters than occasional references to his
lack of scholarship, and sharp antagonisms among the
men with whom he worked and among whom he
lived, pressed on Shakespeare's mind and heart in the
opening years of the seventeenth century. The reign
of Elizabeth was drawing to its close, under a sky full
of ominous signs. The splendour of the earlier years,
which has given the reign a place among the most
magnificent epochs in the annals of royalty, had suffered, not an eclipse, but a slow clouding of the sky,
a visible fading of the day. The Queen had become
an old and exacting woman, craving a love which she
knew was not given her, and an admiration which she
could no longer evoke. She still held her place, but
she understood how eagerly many who surrounded her
with service and protestations of devotion were wait-
ing for the end and the chances of promotion in a
new court. While they were praising her immortal
youth, they were writing to James in Scotland that she

was aging rapidly and that the end was at hand. There were faces, too, that must have been missed by the lonely sovereign as she looked about her. When she signed the death-warrant of Essex, she ended the career of one of the most brilliant men of the age, and one of her most devoted servants. Southampton was sentenced to death at the same time, but his sentence was commuted to imprisonment for life. The people firmly believed in Essex's innocence of any designs upon the Queen, and her haughty refusal to listen to the pleas made in his behalf turned their hearts against her. The Earl of Southampton was not a man of sound judgment or of cool temper; but there were in him a generosity of spirit, a loyalty to his friends, and a charm of temper and manners which bound men to his person and his fortunes.

Through him there is every reason to believe that Shakespeare was drawn into close relations with Essex, who was, like Southampton, a man who lacked the qualities of character necessary for success in a period of conflicting movements and sharp antagonistic influences, but who had a winning personality. In the prologue to the fifth act of "Henry V." Shakespeare made an unmistakable allusion to Essex, and one which showed how near Southampton's friend was to his heart:

> Were now the general of our gracious empress,
> As in the good time he may, from Ireland coming,
> Bringing rebellion broached on his sword,
> How many would the peaceful city quit
> To welcome him!

The Approach of Tragedy

Later, when the plot against the ruling party at the court was on the point of execution, the play of "Richard II." was put on the stage of the Globe Theatre and elsewhere for the purpose of awakening and giving direction to popular indignation against the men about the Queen. It is probable that the play produced under these circumstances, and at the instigation of the organizers of the ill-fated enterprise, was Shakespeare's well-known drama. This play never had the approval of the Queen, who disliked its theme. There is no evidence beyond this fact to connect Shakespeare with the plot which sent Essex to the block. It is highly improbable that so rash an enterprise would have secured his support. It was not necessary that he should follow Essex's fortunes in order to love him.

Deficient in strength and ability both as a soldier and a politician, Essex knew how to charm not only the crowd but those who stood near him. His face has that touch of distinction which is far more captivating than many more solid qualities. He had the gracious air of a benefactor; there was an atmosphere of romance and adventure about him; he was a lover of the arts and the friend and patron of writers, who recognized and rewarded his generosity in a flood of dedications full of melodious praise. The temper of the age was personified in these two ardent, passionate, adventurous, brilliant personalities far more truly than in many men of cooler temper and more calculating spirit. It is significant that the representative men of the Elizabethan period rarely husbanded the fruits of their genius and perils; they lived too much in the imagination to secure those substantial gains which men of lesser ability but greater prudence laid up for themselves. Drake, Raleigh, Sidney, Essex, Spenser, were splendid spenders of energy, time, genius, and opportunity, rather than hoarders of money, influence, and power. Shakespeare gave full value to sagacity, prudence, and poise of character, but he loved the adventurers because the light of the imagination was on their careers and the touch of tragedy on their fortunes.

It is easy to understand, therefore, how deeply the fate of Essex and Southampton weighed upon his heart. In their downfall the iron entered his own soul. When Elizabeth died in 1603, he remained silent while the chorus of poets filled the air with plaintive eulogy. Chettle complained that " the silver-tongued Melicert," as he called Shakespeare, did not "drop from his honied muse one sable tear."

The temper of the time had changed, and there were unmistakable signs of the approaching storm. The deep cleavage which was to divide the English people for many decades began to be visible. The Puritan spirit was steadily rising under the pressure of restriction and persecution ; the deep springs of gayety in the English nature, which ran to the surface in all manner of festivals and merry-making, in a passion for music and an almost universal knowledge of the art, in the habit of improvising songs and a general appreciation of the singing quality which gave English literature almost a century of spontaneous and captivating song-writing, were beginning to flow less freely and with diminished volume.

The Approach of Tragedy

It was not, therefore, a matter of accident, or as a result of deliberate artistic prevision, that, about 1601, Shakespeare began to write tragedies, and continued for seven or eight years to deal with the most perplexing and sombre problems of character and of life. He had passed through an emotional experience which had evidently stirred his spirit to the depths; the atmosphere in which he lived was disturbed by bitter controversies; men whom he honoured and loved had become the victims of a tragic fate; and the age was troubled with forebodings of coming strife. The poet was entering into the anguish of suffering and sharing the universal experience of loss, surrender, denial, and death. He had buried his only son, Hamnet, in the summer of 1596; in the autumn of 1601 his father, in whose fortunes he had manifested a deep interest, died at Stratford, and was buried in the quiet churchyard beside the Avon. The poet had learned much of life; he was now to learn much of death also.

CHAPTER XIII

THE EARLIER TRAGEDIES

THE order of the appearance of the Tragedies has not been definitely settled; they were written, however, in the same period, and that period began about 1601 and ended about 1609. The poet was at work on these masterpieces during the closing years of the reign of Elizabeth and the early years of the reign of James First. While he was meditating upon or writing "Julius Cæsar," Essex and Southampton had embarked upon their ill-planned conspiracy, and one had gone to the block and the other was lying in the Tower; soon after finishing "Coriolanus," the poet left London and returned to Stratford. The first decade of the seventeenth century was, therefore, his "storm and stress" period. Its chief interest lies in its artistic product, but the possible and probable relations of his artistic activity to his personal experience have been indicated. Those relations must not be insisted upon too strenuously; in a sense they are unimportant; the important aspect of the work of this decade lies in the continuity of mood and of themes which it represents, and in the mastery of the dramatic art which it illustrates.

During these days Shakespeare dealt continuously with the deepest problems of character with the clearest insight and the most complete command of the resources of the dramatic art. It is significant of the marvellous harmony of the expert craftsman with the poet of superb imagination that the plays of this period have been at the same time the most popular of all the Shakespearean dramas with theatre-goers and the most deeply studied by critical lovers of the poet in all parts of the world.

Shakespeare had read Holinshed and Hall with an insight into historic incident and character quite as marvellous in its power of laying bare the sources of action and of vitalizing half-forgotten actors in the drama of life as the play of the faculty of invention, and far more fruitful; he now opened the pages of one of the most fascinating and stimulating biographers in the whole range of literature. It is doubtful if any other recorder of men's lives has touched the imagination and influenced the character of so many readers as Plutarch, to whom the modern world owes much of its intimate and vital knowledge of the men who not only shaped the destinies of Greece and Rome, but created the traditions of culture which influenced Shakespeare's age and contemporaries so deeply. Part of Plutarch's extraordinary influence has been due to the inexhaustible interest of his material and part to the charm of his personality. He was and will remain one of the great interpreters of the classical to the modern world; a biographer who breathed the life of feeling and infused the insight of the imagination into his compact narratives. It has well been said of his work that it has been "most sovereign in its dominion over the minds of great men in all ages"; and the same thought has been suggested in another form in the description of that work as "the pasturage of great minds."

Sir Thomas North's English version of "The Lives of the Noble Grecians, compared together by that grave learned philosopher and historiographer Plutarke, of Chæronia, translated out of Greek into French by James Amyot, Abbot of Belloxane, Bishop of Auxerre, one of the King's Privy Council, and great Amner of France, and now out of French into English by Thomas North," was published in 1579, while Shakespeare was coming to the end of his school days in the Grammar School at Stratford; and it forms one of that group of translations, including Chapman's "Homer," Florio's "Montaigne," and Fairfax's "Tasso," which, in their influence, must be ranked as original contributions to Elizabethan literature. Plutarch is not only the foremost biographer in the history of Letters, he had the further good fortune to attract a reader who, more than any other, has disclosed the faculty of grasping the potential content of a narrative, as well as mastering its record of fact. It is one of Plutarch's greatest honours that he was the chief feeder of Shakespeare's imagination during the period when his genius touched his highest mark of achievement; for it was in Plutarch that the poet found the material for three of the greatest of the Tragedies, " Julius Cæsar," " Antony and Cleopatra," and "Coriolanus," and, in part, for "Timon of Athens." Not only did he find his material in Plutarch, but he found passages so nobly phrased, whole dialogues sustained at such a height of dignity, force, or eloquence, that he incorporated them into his work with essentially minor changes. Holinshed furnished only the bare outlines of movement for "Richard II." and "Richard III.," but Plutarch supplied traits, hints, suggestions, phrases, and actions so complete in themselves that the poet needed to do little but turn upon the biographer's prose his vitalizing and organizing imagination. The difference between the prose biographer and the dramatist remains, however, a difference of quality so radical as to constitute a difference of kind. The nature and extent of Shakespeare's indebtedness to the works upon which he drew for material may be most clearly shown by placing in juxtaposition Mark Antony's famous oration over Cæsar's body as Shakespeare found it and as he left it : " When Cæsar's body," writes Plutarch, " was brought into the market-place, Antonius making his funeral-oration in praise of the dead, according to the ancient custom of Rome, and perceiving that his words moved the common people to compassion, he framed his eloquence to make their hearts yearn the more, and taking Cæsar's gown all bloudy in his hand, he layed it open to the sight of them all, shewing what a number of cuts and holes it had in it. Therewith all the people fell presently into such a rage and mutinie that there was no more order kept among the common people."

A magical change has been wrought in this narrative when it reappears in Shakespeare's verse in one of his noblest passages :

William Shakespeare

You all do know this mantle: I remember
The first time ever Cæsar put it on;
'Twas on a summer's evening, in his tent,
That day he overcame the Nervii:
Look, in this place ran Cassius' dagger through;
See what a rent the envious Casca made;
Through this the well-beloved Brutus stabb'd;
And as he pluck'd his cursed steel away,
Mark how the blood of Cæsar follow'd it,
As rushing out of doors, to be resolved
If Brutus so unkindly knock'd, or no;
For Brutus, as you know, was Cæsar's angel:
Judge, O you gods, how dearly Cæsar loved him!
This was the most unkindest cut of all;
For when the noble Cæsar saw him stab,
Ingratitude, more strong than traitor's arms,
Quite vanquish'd him: then burst his mighty heart:
And, in his mantle muffling up his face,
Even at the base of Pompey's statua,
Which all the while ran blood, great Cæsar fell.

"Julius Cæsar" probably appeared in 1601. Many
facts point to this date, among them the oft-quoted
passage from Weever's "Mirror of Martyrs," which
was printed in that year:

The many-headed multitude were drawn
    By Brutus' speech, that Cæsar was ambitious.
When eloquent Mark Antonie had shewn
    His virtues, who but Brutus then was vicious?

A little later, in a still greater play, Polonius, recalling
his life at the University, said:

I did enact Julius Cæsar: I was killed i' the Capitol:
Brutus killed me.

The Earlier Tragedies

The story, like many others with which Shakespeare dealt, was popular, and had been presented on the stage at an earlier date. Shakespeare's rendering was so obviously superior to all its predecessors that it practically put an end to further experiments with the same theme.

In the English historical plays the dramatist never entirely broke with the traditional form and spirit of the Chronicle play; in his first dealing with a Roman subject he took the final step from the earlier drama to the tragedy. "Julius Cæsar" is not, it is true, dominated by a single great character, as are the later Tragedies, but it reveals a rigorous selection of incidents with reference to their dramatic value, and a masterly unfolding of their significance in the story. The drama was not misnamed; although Cæsar dies at the beginning of the dramatic movement, his spirit dominates it to the very end. At every turn he confronts the conspirators in the new order which he personified, and of which he was the organizing genius. Cassius dies with this recognition on his lips:

> Cæsar, thou art revenged,
> Even with the sword that kill'd thee.

And when Brutus looks on the face of the dead Cassius he, too, bears testimony to a spirit which was more potent than the arms of Octavius and Antony:

> O Julius Cæsar, thou art mighty yet!
> Thy spirit walks abroad, and turns our swords
> In our own proper entrails.

William Shakespeare

This new order in the Roman world, personified by Cæsar, is the shaping force of the tragedy; Octavius represents without fully understanding it, and Brutus and Cassius array themselves against it without recognizing that they are contending with the inevitable and the irresistible. At a later day, the eloquent and captivating Antony, a man of genius, enthusiasm, and personal devotion, but without the coördinating power of character, flings himself against this new order in the same blank inability to recognize a new force in the world, and dies as much a victim of his lack of vision as Brutus and Cassius. Nowhere else is Shakespeare's sense of reality, his ability to give facts their full weight, more clearly revealed than in "Julius Cæsar." Brutus is one of the noblest and most consistent of Shakespearean creations; a man far above all self-seeking and capable of the loftiest patriotism; in whose whole bearing, as in his deepest nature, virtue wears her noblest aspect. But Brutus is an idealist, with a touch of the doctrinaire; his purposes are of the highest, but the means he employs to give those purposes effect are utterly inadequate; in a lofty spirit he embarks on an enterprise doomed to failure by the very temper and pressure of the age. "Julius Cæsar" is the tragedy of the conflict between a great nature, denied the sense of reality, and the world-spirit. Brutus is not only crushed, but recognizes that there was no other issue of his untimely endeavour.

The affinity between Hamlet and Brutus has often been pointed out. The poet was brooding over the story of the Danish prince probably before he became interested in Roman history; certainly before he wrote the Roman plays. The chief actors in both dramas were men upon whom was laid the same fatal necessity; both were idealists forced to act in great crises, when issues of appalling magnitude hung on their actions. Their circumstances were widely different, but a common doom was on both; they were driven to do that which was against their natures.

In point of style "Julius Cæsar" marks the culmination of Shakespeare's art as a dramatic writer. The ingenuity of the earlier plays ripened in a rich and pellucid flexibility; the excess of imagery gave place to a noble richness of speech; there is deep-going coherence of structure and illustration; constructive instinct has passed on into the ultimate skill which is born of complete identification of thought with speech, of passion with utterance, of action with character. The long popularity of the play was predicted by Shakespeare in the words of Cassius:

> How many ages hence
> Shall this, our lofty scene, be acted over
> In States unborn and accents yet unknown.

The great impression made by "Julius Cæsar" in a field which Jonson regarded as his own probably led to the writing of "Sejanus," which appeared two years later, and of "Catiline," which was produced in 1611. A comparison of these plays dealing with Roman history brings into clear relief the vitalizing power of Shakespeare's imagination in contrast with the conscientious and scholarly craftsmanship of Jonson. In " Sejanus " almost every incident and speech, as Mr. Knight has pointed out, is derived from ancient authorities, and the dramatist's own edition of the play was packed with references like a text-book. The characters speak with admirable correctness after the manner of their time ; but they do not live. Brutus, Cassius, Antony, Portia, on the other hand, talk and act like living creatures, and the play is saturated with the spirit and enveloped in the atmosphere of Rome.

The story of Hamlet, Prince of Denmark, like that of Dr. Faustus, had a long and wide popularity before it found place among the classics. There was much in both tales which appealed to the popular imagination ; there was a touch of the supernatural in both, and the Renaissance mind still loved the supernatural ; there was in both an abundance of horrors, and the age of Shakespeare craved strong incitements of the imagination ; and in both there was a combination of story and psychologic interest which appealed from the beginning to the crowds who frequented the theatres, and, later, to the greatest of modern poets. In this fusion of immediate human interest with the very highest and most complex problems of character and destiny these two stories are unique ; and it is due to the presence of these qualities that, in their final versions, these stories hold the first place among those dramas which deal with the ultimate questions of life.

Saxo Grammaticus, who lived about the year 1200, midway between the earliest crusades and the discovery of America, was, as his name suggests, a man of unusual learning. He was the earliest Danish writer of importance, and his Latin style evoked the admiration of so competent an authority as Erasmus, who expressed his surprise that a Dane of that age should be able to command such a " force of eloquence." The great work of this brilliant Latinist was the *Historia Danica*, or " History of the Danes " ; written, there is reason to believe, with Livy as a model. This history, like all other histories of that age, was largely made up of mythical and legendary tales chiefly illustrative of heroic persons and incidents. One of the most striking of these hero stories is that which relates the tragical experiences of Hamlet ; in his origin possibly one of those mythical figures who typified the forces of nature in the Norse mythology. The roots of great works of art are sunk deep in the soil of human life ; and a creation of the magnitude of the Hamlet of Shakespeare always rests on a broad, solid foundation of prehistoric myth, or legend, or semi-historic tradition. Characters of such world-wide significance and such typical experience as Hamlet and Faust are, in a sense, the children of the race and are born in those fertile ages when the imagination plays freely and creatively upon the external world and upon the facts of human experience. In the pages of Saxo Grammaticus, Hamlet is a veritable man, caught in a network of tragical circumstances, feigning madness to protect himself from an uncle who has killed his father, seized the throne, and married Hamlet's mother, and who seeks to entrap Hamlet by many ingenious devices. A crafty old courtier plays the eavesdropper; a young girl is put forward as part of the plot against Hamlet; he is sent to England and secret orders to put him to death are sent with him. In the end Hamlet's feigning saves him; he kills the usurper, explains his deed in an address to the people, and is made king.

This group of incidents constitutes the story of Hamlet in its earliest recorded form, which was probably the survival of earlier and mythical forms. In the fifteenth century the story was widely known throughout northern Europe, where it had the currency of a popular folk-tale. About 1570 it was told in French in Belleforest's *Histoires Tragique*. That there was an English play dealing with Hamlet as early as 1589 is now generally believed. In that year Greene made an unmistakable reference to such a play; and seven years later Lodge wrote of "the wisard of a ghost, which cried so miserably at the theatre, like an oyster-wife, *Hamlet revenge*." That startling cry of the ghost appears to have made a deep impression on the imagination of the time, and was heard on the stage again and again in later plays.

This earlier English version of Hamlet has disappeared, but the probabilities point to Thomas Kyd, whose "Spanish Tragedy" was one of the most popular plays of the age, as its author; there are obvious similarities between the plays. The introduction of the ghost was in keeping with the traditions of the English stage and the temper of the time. This earlier version of the tragedy was probably a very rough study, so far as action was concerned, of Shakespeare's work; some fragments of it may have been used by the dramatist in the earlier sketches of his own version; and some remnants of it are to be found, perhaps, in a German version, which is probably a copy of a translation used in that country by English actors not much later than Shakespeare's time. It is probable that both the author of the lost version and Shakespeare read the story in Belleforest's French version.

There are very perplexing questions connected with the text of "Hamlet" as it is found in different editions; the probability is that Shakespeare worked his material over more than once, revising and, in part, recasting it. There is reason to believe also that the story found a lodgement in his imagination at an early day, and that it slowly took shape, widening in its significance with his experience, and striking deeper root in the psychology of the human spirit as his insight into life deepened. This was the history of the growth of the Faust idea in Goethe's mind. The play probably appeared in 1602. In that year the edition known as the First Quarto was published, with the announcement on the title-page that the piece had been "acted divers times in the city of London, as also in the two Universities of Cambridge, Oxford, and elsewhere." Although the longest of Shakespearean plays, and farthest removed from the ordinary interests of theatregoers, "Hamlet" has not only been critically studied and widely commented upon, but has been put upon the stage of every civilized country and has awakened an unfailing popular interest. The dramatic move-

William Shakespeare

ment is much slower than in most of the dramas; the plot unfolds very gradually; there are a number of scenes in which the interest is almost wholly psychological; but the spell of the play has been felt as keenly by the unlearned as by the cultivated, and the story has appealed as directly to the crowds before the footlights as to students and critics. There is no higher evidence of Shakespeare's genius than this presentation of a great spiritual problem in a form so concrete and with such marvellous distinctness of characterization that "Hamlet" as a great world-drama and "Hamlet" as an engrossing stage play may be seen on the same stage on the same night.

The rough sketch upon which Shakespeare worked had all the characteristics of the Elizabethan play; it was sanguinary, noisy, full of movement, action, crime; it was written for the groundlings. Upon this elemental basis, with its primary and immediate elements of human interest, Shakespeare built up a drama of the soul, which never for a moment loses touch with reality, and never for a moment loses its universal significance. In the pathetic figure of Hamlet, with his gifts of genius and personal charm, every generation has recognized the protagonist of humanity. The concentration of interest, the intensity of feeling, the hushed passion, which characterize the play, make us feel that it had some exceptionally close relation to the poet's experience, and that in an unusual degree his personality pervades it. There is nothing to connect it with the happenings of his own life and the development of his own spirit save the fact that it falls within the tragic period and that it immediately precedes two of his most sombre dramas. The authenticity of an autograph of Shakespeare, on a fly-leaf of a copy of Florio's Montaigne in the British Museum, is doubted, but there are passages in " Hamlet " which are reminiscent of Montaigne's speculations and reflections. It was in his own nature, however, that Shakespeare found the questionings, the perplexities, the deep and almost insoluble contradictions, which are presented with such subtle suggestiveness in " Hamlet."

No play has called forth so vast a literature or has been the subject of so much criticism and interpretation. The problem presented by Hamlet is so many-sided that it will evoke the thought and ingenuity of every successive generation of students. Much has been done, however, in removing obscurities, and discussion has cleared the air of some confusing mists. That Hamlet was sane is the conviction of the great majority of the students of the play ; an insane Hamlet would rob the drama of its spiritual significance and destroy its authority as a work of art. That in his long feigning Hamlet sometimes lost for the time the clear perception of the difference between reality and his own fancies is probable ; but he is at all times a responsible actor in the drama of which he is the central figure. Goethe's exposition of his nature and his fate remains one of the classics of Shakespearean criticism, so clear and definite is its insight into one aspect of Hamlet's character.

> "The time is out of joint ; O cursed spite,
> That ever I was born to set it right !

William Shakespeare

"In these words, I imagine, is the key to Hamlet's whole procedure, and to me it is clear that Shakespeare sought to depict a great deed laid upon a soul unequal to the performance of it. In this view I find the piece composed throughout. Here is an oak tree planted in a costly vase, which should have received into its bosom only lovely flowers; the roots spread out, the vase is shivered to pieces.

"A beautiful, pure, and most moral nature, without the strength of nerve which makes the hero, sinks beneath a burden which it can neither bear nor throw off; every duty is holy to him — this too hard. The impossible is required of him — not the impossible in itself, but the impossible to him. How he winds, turns, agonizes, advances, and recoils, ever reminded, ever reminding himself, and at last almost loses his purpose from his thoughts, without ever again recovering his peace of mind. . . .

"It pleases, it flatters us greatly, to see a hero who acts of himself, who loves and hates us as his heart prompts, undertaking and executing, thrusting aside all hinderances, and accomplishing a great purpose. Historians and poets would fain persuade us that so proud a lot may fall to man. In 'Hamlet' we are taught otherwise; the hero has no plan, but the piece is full of plan. . . .

"Hamlet is endowed more properly with sentiment than with a character; it is events alone that push him on; and accordingly the piece has somewhat the amplification of a novel. But as it is Fate that draws the plan, as the piece proceeds from a deed of terror, and the hero is steadily driven on to a deed of terror, the work is tragic in its highest sense, and admits of no other than a tragic end."

This interpretation leaves other aspects of Hamlet unexplained. This subjective condition must be supplemented by taking into account the objective world in which Hamlet found himself. Sensitive alike in intellect and in his moral nature, he was placed in a corrupt society, in which every relation was tainted. The thought of his mother, which ought to have been a spring of sweetness and strength, was unendurable. He was surrounded by false friends and paid spies. Upon him was laid the appalling task of reasserting moral order in a loathsome household and a demoralized kingdom ; and the only way open to him was by the perpetration of a deed of vengeance from which his whole nature drew back in revolt. The tragic situation was created by the conflict against the State and the family to which he was committed by the knowledge of his father's death, his uncle's crime, and his mother's lust, and the conflict within himself between the duty of revenge and the horror of blood-shedding. If to these considerations is added the fact that he was an idealist, with a deep and irresistible tendency to the meditation and subtle speculation which feel in advance all the possible results of action so keenly that the responsibility for acting becomes almost unbearable, the character of Hamlet becomes intelligible, if not entirely explicable.

The weight of evidence shows, as has been suggested, that in the " war of the theatres " which raged at the end of the sixteenth and the beginning of the seventeenth century Shakespeare took no active part ; he was by nature free from the narrowness of partisanship, and there are indications that he was on friendly terms with men of all shades of literary opinion. In " Hamlet," however, he distinctly takes sides with the adult actors against the growing prominence of boys on the stage. The relation of boy choirs, and especially that of the Chapel Royal, to the theatre in Shakespeare's time was pointed out in an earlier chapter. These choirs were, in an informal way, training schools for the stage at a time when all women's parts were taken by boys, and there was, in consequence, constant need of their services. About the time of the appearance of "Julius Cæsar" there was a sharp rivalry between adult and boy actors, the public espousing warmly the performances of the boys. The development of this rivalry cannot be traced, but in 1601 the theatre-going public had become partisans of the boys and were deserting the theatres in which adults held the stage. This preference had become so pronounced that Shakespeare's company was driven into the provinces. In their travels the members of the company appeared at Cambridge, and it was probably on this visit that the new play of "Hamlet" was presented. The popularity of the boys not only jeopardized the fortunes of the regular companies, but seriously impaired the quality of the performances. When the Children of the Chapel were able to secure for their own use the new theatre in Blackfriars, which Burbage had recently built, the Globe company began to feel the competition very keenly ; and, for a time, so marked was the popularity of the boys, their prospects and those of the art of acting were dark indeed.

Shakespeare was at work on "Hamlet" in this crisis in his own fortunes and those of the theatre, and stated his position in the controversy with entire clearness.

The Earlier Tragedies

In answer to Hamlet's question why the tragedians travel when it was better both for reputation and profit that they should stay in the city, Rosencrantz replies that their retirement into the provinces has been caused by the " late innovation " :

" Do they hold the same estimation they did when I was in the city? Are they so followed?

" No, indeed, are they not.

" How comes it? [continues Hamlet] ; do they grow rusty?

" Nay, their endeavour keeps in the wonted pace ; but there is, sir, an aery of children, little eyases, that cry out on the top of the question, and are most tyrannically clapped for't : these are now the fashion, and so berattle the common stages — so they call them — that many wearing rapiers are afraid of goose-quills and dare scarce come thither.

" What, are they children? who maintains 'em? how are they escoted? Will they pursue the quality no longer than they can sing? will they not say afterwards, if they should grow themselves to common players — as is most like, if their means are no better — their writers do them wrong, to make them exclaim against their own succession?

" 'Faith, there has been much to do on both sides ; and the nation holds it no sin to tarre them to controversy ; there was, for a while, no money bid for argument, unless the poet and the player went to cuffs in the question.

" Is't possible?

" O, there has been much throwing about of brains.

" Do the boys carry it away?

" Ay, that they do, my lord ; Hercules and his load too."

This conversation between Hamlet and Rosencrantz is significant of the close touch with the realities of life which Shakespeare never lost for a moment, even when dealing with the greatest themes or creating works of pure imagination.

To this period, in its final form, at least, belongs the play of "All's Well that Ends Well," to which Meres, in his "Palladio Tamia," probably refers when he includes among the plays ascribed to Shakespeare "Love's Labour's Won." It was probably sketched and perhaps fully written at a much earlier date than its final revision. The plot is derived from a group of stories in Boccaccio's "Decameron," which narrate the fortunes of lovers who surmount obstacles and gain the rewards of love only after great or persistent effort; a phase of experience which is beyond doubt the key-note of the play. The story was translated by Paynter and appeared in English in "The Palace of Pleasure" in 1566 or 1567. Shakespeare departed widely from the story in its earlier form by the greater prominence given to the part of Helena and the singular sweetness and devotion which irradiate her whole course. Coleridge thought her Shakespeare's loveliest creation. The portraiture of her character is touched throughout with exquisite delicacy and skill. Helena suffers, however, from the atmosphere of the play, which is distinctly repellent; it is difficult to resist the feeling that, conceding all that the play demands in concentration of interest upon the single end to be achieved, Helena cheapens the love she finally wins by a sacrifice greater than love could ask or could afford to receive. And when the sacrifice is made and the end secured, the victory of love is purely external;

there is no inward and deathless unity of passion between the lovers like that which united Posthumus
and Imogen in life and Romeo and Juliet in death.

The play must be interpreted broadly in the light
of Shakespeare's entire work; in this light it finds its
place as the expression of a passing mood of deep and
almost cynical distrust; it is full of that searching
irony which from time to time finds utterance in the
poet's work and was inevitable in a mind of such
range of vision. It is well to remember, also, that in
this play the poet, for the sake of throwing a single
quality into the highest relief, secured entire concentration of attention by disregarding or ignoring
other qualities and relations of equal importance and
authority. This was what Browning did in his much
misunderstood poem "The Statue and the Bust." It
is always a perilous experiment, because it involves so
much intelligent coöperation on the part of the reader.
It is a triumph of Shakespeare's art that Helena's
purity not only survives the dangers to which she
exposes it, but takes on a kind of saintly whiteness
in the corruption in which she plays her perilous
part.

CHAPTER XIV

THE LATER TRAGEDIES

SHAKESPEARE was now in the depths of the deep stirring of his spirit which has left its record in the Tragedies. The darkest mood was on him, apparently, when "Hamlet" and the three succeeding plays were written, — the mood in which the sense of evil in the world almost overpowered his belief in the essential soundness of life, and the mystery of evil pressed upon the imagination with such intensity that he was tempted to take refuge in fundamental cynicism. It is in the plays of this period that Shakespeare gives place to the deep-going irony which pervaded the Greek drama, and which at times obscures the essential freedom and shaping power of personality. In his darkest mood, however, the sanity and largeness of the poet's mind asserted themselves and kept the balance against the temptation to narrow the vision by tingeing the world with the colour of a mood, or by substituting for clear, direct, dispassionate play of the mind on the facts of life the easy process of reading universal history in the light of personal experience.

How completely Shakespeare escaped a danger which would have been fatal to him is seen in the changes he wrought in the story which forms the

The Later Tragedies

basis of "Measure for Measure." This play, like
"All's Well that Ends Well" and "Troilus and
Cressida," is painful and repellent; it is tinged with
an irony which has a corrosive quality; it is touched
with a bitterness of feeling which seems foreign to
Shakespeare. The evil of life was evidently pressing
upon his imagination so heavily that it had become a
burden on his heart. In "Hamlet" he had portrayed
a rotten society; in "Measure for Measure" he de-
picted a state full of iniquity and a group of men cor-
rupted by the very air they breathed; in "Troilus and
Cressida" the same vileness was personified in the
most loathsome characters.

In the great Tragedies we breathe an air which is
charged with fate, and feel ourselves involved in vast
calamities which we are powerless to control; in the
plays which have been named we breathe an atmosphere which is fetid and impure, and human nature
becomes unspeakably mean and repulsive. This is,
perhaps, the effect of the terrible strain of the tragic
mood on Shakespeare's spirit; and these plays are to
be accepted as expressions of a mood of depression
verging upon despair. They are often classed with
the Comedies, but they belong with the Tragedies,
not only in temper, but in time.

Even in this blackness of thick darkness the poet's
sanity is never lost. In a dull play by George Whetstone, published in 1587, called "Promos and Cas-
sandra" and based on an Italian novel by Cinthio,
who also worked it into a tragedy, Shakespeare found
the plot of "Measure for Measure"; the story was

253

told in prose by Whetstone four years later in a collection of tales which he called " Heptameron of Civil Discourses." In the title of the play the earlier dramatist affirmed that it showed in the first part " the unsufferable abuse of a lewd magistrate ; the virtuous behaviour of a chaste lady ; the uncontrolled lewdness of a favoured courtesan ; and the undeserved estimation of a pernicious parasite." Shakespeare's modifications of the plot are highly significant : in the older versions Isabella surrenders her virtue as the price of her brother's life ; in " Measure for Measure " her impregnable purity gives the whole play a saving sweetness. To Shakespeare's imagination is due also the romantic episode of the moated grange and the pathetic figure of Mariana. In the murky atmosphere of this painful drama Isabella's stainless and incorruptible chastity invests purity with a kind of radiancy, and she finds her place in the little company of adorable women in whom Shakespeare's creative imagination realized and personified the eternal feminine qualities.

" Measure for Measure " was probably produced about 1603, and " Troilus and Cressida " belongs, in its final form, to the same year. The problems presented by the different versions are not more difficult than those presented by the play itself, which has been described as " a history in which historical verisimilitude is openly set at naught, a comedy without genuine laughter, a tragedy without pathos." The editors of the First Folio were so uncertain about its essential character that they evaded the necessity of classifying it by placing it between the Histories and the Tragedies. In temper, spirit, and probably in time, it belongs with the Tragedies, where it is now generally printed. It is the only play in which Shakespeare drew upon the greatest stream of ancient story and the materials for which he found in many forms in the literature of his time. Chief among these was Chaucer's noble rendering of the ancient romance in the "Canterbury Tales," to which may be added Chapman's "Homer," Lydgate's "Troy Book," and probably Robert Greene's version of the story which appeared in 1587.

In this play Shakespeare was dealing with material which had generally been regarded as heroic and which was rich in heroic qualities; his treatment is, however, essentially satirical, with touches of unmistakable cynicism. This attitude was not, however, entirely new to Shakespeare's auditors; the great Homeric story had already been handled with a freedom which bordered on levity. Shakespeare shows little regard for the proprieties of classical tradition; this satirical attitude did not, however, blur his insight into the nature of the men whom he portrayed.

The drama brings into clear light the irony of human fate; but it is not a blind fate which the dramatist invokes as the shaping power in the drama; it is a fate set in motion by the fundamental qualities or defects of the chief actors. The special aspect of irony which the play presents is the confusion brought into private and public affairs by lawless or fatuous love. Thersites goes to the heart of the matter when, with brutal directness, he characterizes the struggle as a "war for a placket." Helen,   .

> A pearl,
> Whose price hath launch'd above a thousand ships,

involves Greece and Troy in measureless disaster, while Cressida's cheap duplicity makes Troilus the fool of fortune.

This play, it will be remembered, has been regarded by some critics as a contribution to the "war of the theatres," and as containing direct references, not only to the matters at issue, but to the characteristics and works of the chief combatants. Mr. Fleay has made a thorough study of the play from this point of view, and has presented his case with great acumen and skilful arrangement of facts and inferences. It is difficult to find in the play, in its present form, adequate basis for the supposition that it was written as an attack on Jonson, or that one of Shakespeare's contemporaries is portrayed in Thersites. Shakespeare may have touched humorously on some of the extravagances of that bloodless but vociferous combat; but the drama must have had a deeper root. Unsatisfactory and repellent as it is in some aspects, "Troilus and Cressida" has very great interest as a document in Shakespeare's history as a thinker and an artist. It is remarkable for its range of style, reproducing as it does his earlier manner side by side with his later manner. It is notable also for its knowledge of life, expressed in a great number of sententious and condensed phrases; for its setting aside of the dramatic mask and direct statement of the truth which the dramatist means to convey. And it is supremely interesting because in the person of Ulysses, the real hero of the drama, Shakespeare seems to present his own view of life. The ripest wisdom of the dramatist speaks through the lips of this typical man of experience, whose insight has been corrected by the widest contact with affairs, whose long familiarity with the world has made him a master of its diseases, and whose speech has the touch of universality in its dispassionateness, breadth, and clarity of vision. This tragedy of disillusion has at least the saving quality of a rich and many-sided knowledge of life.

Queen Elizabeth died in March, 1603, while Shakespeare was absorbed in the problems presented in the Tragedies. His silence when the chorus of elegies filled the air has already been noted; his friendship for Southampton and Essex had probably estranged him from the Queen. Shortly after his accession to the throne, James I. showed his favour to a group of nine actors, among whom were Shakespeare and Burbage, by granting them a special license of a very liberal character, and giving them the right to call themselves the King's Servants. The plays of Shakespeare were repeatedly presented before the King at various places; among them, Wilton House, the residence of the Earl of Pembroke, which stands in a charming country about three miles from Salisbury, and in which Sidney wrote the "Arcadia." The whole region is touched with literary associations of the most diverse kinds. The course of travel taken by Shakespeare's company makes it probable that he saw the noble Cathedral in its beautiful close as Dickens saw it when he laid the scene of " Martin Chuzzlewit " in that neighbourhood, and that he passed the little church where holy George Herbert lived five years of his beautiful life a quarter of a century later. In the following year, wearing the scarlet robe presented for the occasion, Shakespeare, in company with other actors, walked in the procession which formally welcomed the King to London. Mr. Lee agrees with Mr. Halliwell-Phillipps in the belief that Shakespeare and his fellow-actors of the King's Company were present at Somerset House by royal order, and took part in the magnificent ceremonies with which the Spanish ambassador, who came to England to ratify the treaty of peace between the two countries, was entertained at midsummer in the same year. And during the succeeding autumn and winter the records show that Shakespeare's company appeared before the King at Whitehall on at least eleven occasions. Much as the King loved the society of prelates and the amenities of theological discussion, it is clear that he was not indifferent to the charms of the stage.

One of the plays which the King saw was " Othello." In " Hamlet " Shakespeare spoke for and to the Germanic consciousness ; in " Romeo and Juliet," and still more directly in " Othello," he spoke for and to the Latin consciousness. " Othello " is one of the simplest, most direct, conventional, and objective of the plays. In its main lines it is an old-fashioned drama of blood-shedding, saved by the penetrating insight with which the motives of the chief characters are revealed, and by the vitalizing skill with which the situations are related to the plot and the plot rooted in the moral necessities of the human nature within the circle of movement. The thread of the story was clearly traced by Cinthio in the series of novels from which " Measure for Measure " was also derived. The Italian romancer furnished nearly all the incidents, but Shakespeare breathed the breath of dramatic life into them, made Othello and Desdemona the central figures, and developed the subtle deviltry of Iago.

It is Othello's open and generous nature which, like the idealism of Brutus, makes him the victim of men smaller than himself. Desdemona loves him for the dangers he has passed, and, like Helena, surrenders herself without question or hesitation to her passion. The audacity of her surrender is heightened by the difference of race between her and Othello — a difference so wide and deep that to cross it almost inevitably created a tragic situation. From the very beginning the play is touched with a certain violence of emotion and action which bears in itself the elements of disaster. Iago, keeping himself in the background and striking blow after blow, is one of the most significant and original of Shakespeare's creations — a malicious servant of a fate compounded of his devilish keenness of insight into the weaknesses of noble natures and of their unsuspicious trustfulness. The basis of tragedy in Othello was his ready belief in Iago and his quickly awakened distrust of Desdemona. In the end, Iago, after the manner of those who invoke the tragic forces for their own evil ends, is destroyed by the tempest of passion he has let loose in the world.

By reason of its simplicity, its rapidity of movement, and its dramatic interest, " Othello " has long been one of the popular Shakespearean plays on the stage. Its chief characteristic is perhaps its pathos ; the deep and penetrating appeal which the spectacle of the defeat of two noble natures by pure villany makes to the imagination. Wordsworth declared that " the tragedy of Othello, Plato's records of the last scenes in the career of Socrates, and Izaak Walton's ' Life of George Herbert ' are the most pathetic of human compositions."

Shakespeare was now swiftly mounting to the sublimest heights of dramatic creation, penetrating farther and farther into the depths of the human spirit, and steadily bringing the tragic movement home to the soul of the tragic hero. In " Romeo and Juliet " the family and social forces are more powerful than the passion and devotion of the ill-fated lovers ; in " Julius Cæsar " the interest fastens upon Brutus, while the dead Imperator remains in the background as the personification of a new order in society ; in " Hamlet " the time, which was out of joint, must be taken into account if the chief actor is to be made comprehensible. In " Othello " the essential movement is wholly within the circle of the character of the protagonist ; the tragic action springs out of Othello's nature ; the drama issues out of the heart of the hero and is centred in him. This marks the culmination of Shakespeare's art as a dramatist; every element in the play — character, action, incident, background — is strictly subordinated to the unity and totality of the movement, and the concentrated energy and vitality of the dramatist's genius bear the drama swiftly forward to the dramatic crisis.

In " Macbeth," which takes rank with " Hamlet," " Lear," and " Othello " as the dramatic masterpieces of Shakespeare, the same breadth and unity of interest are notable. It is one of the shortest of the plays; there is almost no relief from humour or a subsidiary plot; the style is broad and firm, almost sketchy in the largeness of outline and the indifference to detail. The brevity and condensation of the play have raised the question whether it is not an abridgment. There is no question, however, regarding the definiteness and completeness of impression which it conveys — an impression of massive and inevitable tragedy. The sources of " Macbeth " are to be found in Holinshed's " Chronicle of England and Scotland "; suggestions for the witch scenes may have been found in the " Discoverie of Witchcraft " which appeared not long before the poet left Stratford. The play was completed about 1606, and the Scottish background suggests that the interest of the King in the scenic and historic associations of the drama may have directed Shakespeare's attention to the subject.

" Macbeth " presented the poet with a new motive or theme of dramatic interest. Up to this point the

tragic heroes had committed deeds of violence, but
Lear spoke for them all when he said :

> I am a man more sinn'd against than sinning.

Macbeth does not belong in this company of the
children of fate ; he deliberately sets in motion the
tragic forces which sweep the stage ; he becomes a
criminal on a colossal scale ; he kills his king under
his own roof, uses murder as if it were a legitimate
political method, and converts all the opportunities
of usurpation into a consistent practice of tyranny.
He fills the stage ; the whole drama is rooted in his
nature ; and, criminal as he is, he commands unwill-
ing admiration and breathless interest by the massive
simplicity of his character, the concentration of his
purpose, and the directness of his action. The play
moves with unusual rapidity, and presents no elements
which withdraw the attention for a moment from the
central figures or the swift and definite movement.

The weird sisters on the blasted heath had long
been part of the Macbeth legend. In Shakespeare's
version of the story these supernatural beings were
neither the creations of Macbeth's brain nor the masters of his destiny ; they had objective reality, but
they were not the ministers of fate. Macbeth's fate
was in his own hands. The sisters spoke to Banquo
as directly as to Macbeth, but Banquo's clear vision
and deep integrity gave their word no lodgement.
Whether they speak truth or falsehood, they leave his
fate untouched ; in Macbeth's mind, on the other hand,
they find a quick soil for evil suggestion.

The Later Tragedies

It has been urged by several critics that some parts of " Macbeth " were interpolated at a later day by Thomas Middleton, chiefly on the ground that these passages are un-Shakespearean in character, that there are obvious resemblances between the witch scenes in the play and Middleton's play " The Witch," which appeared in 1610, and that two songs to which allusion is made in the stage-directions of " Macbeth " appear in " The Witch." Charles Lamb long ago pointed out the marked differences between the witches of Shakespeare and those of Middleton; the resemblances between the plays are most readily explained by the assumption that Middleton had Shakespeare too much in his mind. The two songs beginning " Come away, come away," and " Black spirits and white," may have been written by Middleton and interpolated in the acting version of " Macbeth " at a later date, or they may have been written by Shakespeare and revised or modified by Middleton. The scene in which the porter speaks after the murder was long regarded as questionable. Coleridge found the introduction of the comic element too abrupt, and failed to perceive the deepening of the tragic impression which the scene produces by its startling contrast with the awful atmosphere of crime which pervades the castle. This point was finally settled by the keen instinct of De Quincey, in one of the most famous passages in Shakespearean criticism :

" Another world has stept in ; and the murderers are taken out of the region of human things, human purposes,

human desires. They are transfigured: Lady Macbeth is
'unsexed'; Macbeth has forgot that he was born of a
woman; both are conformed to the image of devils; and
the world of devils is suddenly revealed. But how shall
this be conveyed and made palpable? In order that a new
world may step in, this world must for a time disappear.
The murderers and the murder must be insulated — cut
off by an immeasurable gulf from the ordinary tide and
succession of human affairs — locked up and sequestered
in some deep recess; we must be made sensible that the
world of ordinary life is suddenly arrested, laid asleep,
tranced, racked into a dread armistice; time must be anni-
hilated, relation to things abolished; and all must pass self-
withdrawn into a deep syncope and suspension of earthly
passion. Hence it is that, when the deed is done, when the
work of darkness is perfect, then the world of darkness
passes away like a pageantry in the clouds; the knocking
at the gate is heard; and it makes known audibly that the
reaction has commenced; the human has made its reflux
upon the fiendish; the pulses of life are beginning to beat
again; and the reëstablishment of the goings-on of the
world in which we live first makes us profoundly sensible
of the awful parenthesis that had suspended them."

Dr. Simon Forman has left an account of a performance of "Macbeth" which he saw at the Globe
Theatre in the spring of 1611. The play finds its
place in the front rank of tragedies ancient or modern; and its massive structure, its boldness of conception, the largeness of its outlines, have inclined
some critics to give it the first place. It is pervaded
by an atmosphere of tragedy, but it is free from the
irony of blind fate. Macbeth is not the victim of a
fate which is imposed upon him from without; he
invokes the fate which pursues him, and "life be-

comes a tale told by an idiot, full of sound and fury, signifying nothing," because he has violated its laws and wilfully evoked its possibilities of disaster.

In "Macbeth" the epic element mingled with the dramatic; in "King Lear" the tragic element is supreme and unmixed, and the tragic art of Shakespeare touches its sublimest height. There is no more tragic figure in literature than that of the old king, accustomed to rule and flung out into the night by the children among whom he has divided his power; intensely affectionate and wilfully irrational; with all the majesty of a king joined to the passionateness of a child; his illusions destroyed, his reason unseated; with no companionship save that of the Fool, wandering shelterless in the storm, symbolical of the shattering of his life in the awful tempest of passion.

This Titanic drama, which ranks with the sublimest work of Æschylus and Sophocles and stands alone in modern literature, was performed before the King at Whitehall, at Christmas-tide, 1606. The story, in a condensed form, is found in Geoffrey of Monmouth's "Historia Britonum," and was derived from an old Welsh chronicle; some of the motives introduced into the legend appear in a wide range of folk-tales. Like "Hamlet," the formative conception in "King Lear" has its foundations deep in the vital experience of the race. It is Celtic in its origin; but it found its setting in literature at the hands of the old English chroniclers, Layamon, Robert of Gloucester, Robert of Brunne, and, finally, of Holinshed, in whose pages

William Shakespeare

Shakespeare read it. The story of Cordelia was told in verse in " The Mirrour for Magistrates " and in " The Faerie Queene," and had been dramatized at least fifteen years before Shakespeare dealt with it. The poet's attention may have been definitely drawn to the dramatic possibilities of this old story by a rude play which appeared in 1605, entitled "The True Chronicle History of King Leir and His Three Daughters — Gondrill, Ragan, and Cordella " ; a version which, in the opinion of Dr. Ward, seemed only to await the touch of such a hand as Shakespeare's to become " a tragedy of sublime effectiveness." This was precisely what Shakespeare, by omitting irrelevant parts, by a free use of all the material, and by entirely reorganizing it, made of the old folk-story.

Appalling as is the presentation of the play of elemental forces and passions in " King Lear," and completely as it seems to break away from all relation to a spiritual order, and to exhibit men as the sport of fate, it is, nevertheless, rooted in the character of the men and women who are tossed about in its vast movements as by some shoreless sea. Gloucester, the putting out of whose eyes perhaps surpasses in horror any other incident in the plays, is not so blind that he cannot read the story of his own calamities in the sin of his youth. We are reminded of this relation between present misery and far-off offences when Edgar says :

> The gods are just, and of our pleasant vices
> Make instruments to plague us;
> The dark and vicious place where thee he got
> Cost him his eyes.

The Later Tragedies

The play is Titanic not only in force and grandeur, but in the elemental character of the passions and ideas which contribute to the catastrophe. Such a nature as Lear's — passionate, wilful, undisciplined, dominated by a colossal egoism — could not escape a conflict of appalling dimensions. When the world which Lear had organized about him by the supremacy of his own will was shattered, he could neither recognize nor accept a new order, but must fling himself in a blind passion of revolt against the new conditions which he had unwittingly brought into being. His madness grew out of his irrational attitude towards his family.

Lear's sufferings are heightened by interweaving with them the sufferings of Gloucester. "Were Lear alone to suffer from his daughters," wrote Schlegel, "the impression would be limited to the powerful compassion felt by us for his private misfortunes. But two such unheard-of examples taking place at the same time have the appearance of a great commotion in the moral world; the picture becomes gigantic, and fills us with such alarm as we should entertain at the idea that the heavenly bodies might one day fall from their appointed orbits." To still further deepen this impression, the Fool, the very soul of pathos in humorous disguise, strikes into clear light not only the King's misfortunes, but his faults as well.

In "King Lear," as clearly as in the other tragedies, men reap what they sow, and the deed returns to the doer with inexorable retribution; but the play is not to be explained by any easy and obvious application

267

of ethical principles. It lifts the curtain upon the most appalling facts of life, and makes no attempt to rationalize them. In this revelation of the ultimate order of life, which is inexplicable by the mind in its present stage of development, the play takes its place with the Book of Job, with the great trilogy of Æschylus, or with the sublime " Œdipus Tyrannus," of which Shelley thought it the modern equivalent. Its sublimity lies in the vastness of its presentation of the great theme of human suffering, and in the nobility of its method. Such a theme could have been touched only by a man of the first magnitude ; and such a man could not go beyond its dramatic presentation ; to have attempted the solution would have cheapened the work. The end of art is not to solve the problems of existence, but to deepen and freshen the sense of life ; when this sense is deep and fresh, these problems are so dealt with that, as in the Book of Job, their very vastness and mystery suggest the only adequate and satisfying answer. In " King Lear," the greatest dramatic achievement of our race, the poet so enlarges the field of observation and dilates the imagination of the reader that the postponement of the ultimate solution of the problem of the tragedy is not only inevitable, but is the only outcome which would be tolerated by the reader.

In " Timon of Athens," which probably followed close upon " King Lear " in point of time, the poet turned once more from the lofty severity of tragedy, full of pity and of terror, to the easier, narrower, and less noble attitude of the satirist, in whose comment there is a touch of corrosive bitterness. In style, in treatment, and in attitude this play is so full of inconsistencies and, in parts, so essentially un-Shakespearean, that it is now generally regarded as a sketch made by the poet, but elaborated and put into its present form by other and later hands. This conclusion seems more probable than the hypothesis that it is an old drama worked over by Shakespeare, or that it was the product of collaboration with another playwright. It is not certain that any play on the subject was known to Shakespeare, who found the story of Timon in Plutarch's "Life of Antonius," and also in the version of the story in that repository of old stories, Paynter's "Palace of Pleasure." It seems probable that the author of the play was familiar with Lucian's dialogue on Timon.

The character of Timon relates itself in various ways to that of Lear. Both confided blindly; both were generous without measure or reason; there was in both an element of irrationality; and in both the reaction was excessive and akin to madness. There were in both the elements of simple and kindly goodness; and both were lacking in perception and penetration. In both the seeds of tragic calamity lay very near the surface. The irony of Timon lies not so much in the reaction of his irrational prodigality upon his fortunes and character as in the fierce light thrown upon those who had benefited by his lavish mood. Timon hates mankind upon a very narrow basis of personal experience; Apemantus hates mankind because he is a cynic by nature. Timon is blind alike to the good and the evil in mankind ; he fails to recognize the loyal devotion of his steward Flavius, after misfortunes have overtaken him, as he failed to heed his warnings in the days of prodigality. In this blindness his calamities are rooted ; it is this which turns all the sweetness of his nature into acid when the world forsakes him; and it is this which makes his judgment of that world valueless save as an expression of his own mood. "Timon" is a study of temperament, not a judgment upon life.

There could hardly have been a greater contrast of subject and material than that which Shakespeare found when he turned from "King Lear" or "Timon" to "Antony and Cleopatra"; a tragedy almost incredibly rich in variety and range of character and in splendour of setting. He had recourse again to Plutarch's "Life of Antonius," fastening this time not upon an episode, but upon the nature and fate of one of the most fascinating figures on the stage of the antique world. That world he re-created in its strength and weakness, in its luxury and magnificence, in a drama which brought before the imagination with equal firmness of touch the power of Rome, personified in the disciplined and far-seeing Octavius, the voluptuous temperament of the East in Cleopatra, and the tragic collision of two great opposing conceptions of life in Mark Antony — a man born with the Roman capacity for action and the Eastern passion for pleasure. In Cæsar's house in Rome, in newly contracted alliance with Octavius, Antony's heart is in Egypt :

I' the East my pleasure lies.

The Later Tragedies

The style marks the transition to the poet's latest manner; rhyme almost disappears, and " weak endings," or the use of weak monosyllables at the end of the lines, become very numerous. The poet had secured such conscious mastery of his art that he trusted entirely to his instinct and taste. The story in Plutarch's hands has a noble breadth and beauty, and is full of insight into the ethical relations of the chief actors in this world-drama. The full splendour of Shakespeare's genius has hardly done more than bring out dramatically the significance of these great words of the Greek biographer:

" Antonius being thus inclined, the last and extremest mischief of all other (to wit, the love of Cleopatra) lighted on him, who did waken and stir up many vices yet hidden in him, and were never seen to any; and if any spark of goodness or hope of rising were left him, Cleopatra quenched it straight and made it worse than before."

Again and again Shakespeare touched upon this great theme and showed how tragic disaster issues out of unregulated passion and infects the coolest nature with madness; but nowhere else is that tragedy set on so great a stage and so magnificently enriched with splendid gifts of nature, noble possessions, and almost limitless opportunities of achievement.

It is the drama of the East and West in mortal collision of ideals and motives, and the East succumbs to the superior fibre and more highly organized character of the West. Cleopatra is the greatest of the enchantresses. She has wit, grace, humour; the intoxication of sex breathes from her; she unites the passion of a great temperament with the fathomless coquetry of a courtesan of genius. She is passionately alive, avid of sensation, consumed with love of pleasure, imperious in her demands for that absolute homage which slays honour and saps manhood at the very springs of its power. This superb embodiment of femininity, untouched by pity and untroubled by conscience, has a compelling charm, born in the mystery of passion and taking on the radiance of a thousand moods which melt into one another in endless succession, as if there were no limit to the resources of her temperament and the sorceries of her beauty. Of her alone has the greatest of poets dared to declare that "age cannot wither her, nor custom stale her infinite variety." It is this magnificence which invests Cleopatra's criminality with a kind of sublimity, so vast is the scale of her being and so tremendous the force of her passions.

The depth of Shakespeare's poetic art and the power of his imagination are displayed in their full compass in "Antony and Cleopatra." The play is vitalized as by fire, so radiant is it in energy and beauty of expression. Not only are the chief figures realized with historical fidelity, but they breathe the very atmosphere of the East.

In "Julius Cæsar" there is Roman massiveness of construction and severity of outline; "Antony and Cleopatra" is steeped in the languor and luxury of the East. The Roman play has the definiteness and solidity of sculpture; the Egyptian play has the glow and radiancy of painting.

The Later Tragedies

The study of classical subjects bore final fruit at the end of this period in Shakespeare's life as an artist in "Coriolanus," the tragedy of a great nature wrecked by pride. Written about 1609, and closely related to the magnificent drama of the East and West, the poet turned for the last time to the pages of Plutarch, who told this story, as he told the story of Antony, with a noble dignity and beauty which were not lost at the hands of the English translator. The motive of the play is so admirably set forth in a few phrases in the "Life of Coriolanus" that it is impossible to avoid quoting them:

"He was a man too full of passion and choler, and too much given over to self-will and opinion, as one of a high mind and great courage, that lacked the gravity and affability that is gotten with judgment of learning and reason, which only is to be looked for in a governor of State; and that remembered not how wilfulness is the thing of the world, which a governor of a commonwealth, for pleasing, should shun, being that which Plato called 'solitariness'; as, in the end, all men that are wilfully given to a self opinion and obstinate mind, and who will never yield to other's reason but to their own, remain without company and forsaken of all men. For a man that will live in the world must needs have patience, which lusty bloods make but a mock at. So Marcius, being a stout man of nature, that never yielded in any respect, as one thinking that to overcome always and to have the upper hand in all matters, was a token of magnanimity and of no base and faint courage, which spitteth out anger from the most weak and passioned part of the beast, much like the matter of an impostume: went home to his house, full freighted with spite and malice against the people."

William Shakespeare

The humorous scenes which give the play variety were entirely contributed by Shakespeare; and the presentation of the mob is highly characteristic. The poet hated the irrationality and violence of untrained men. Coriolanus never for a moment conceals his contempt for them:

> I heard him swear,
> Were he to stand for consul, never would he
> Appear i' the market-place, nor on him put
> The napless vesture of humility;
> Nor, showing (as the manner is) his wounds
> To the people, beg their stinking breaths.

This is quite in accord with Casca's contempt for the "rabblement" which "hooted, and clapped their chapped hands, and threw up their sweaty nightcaps, and uttered such a deal of stinking breath," because Cæsar refused the crown. This contempt finds its most satiric expression in Jack Cade's manifesto:

"Be brave then; for your captain is brave, and vows reformation. There shall be, in England, seven half-penny loaves sold for a penny; the three-hooped pot shall have ten hoops; and I will make it felony to drink small beer; all the realm shall be in common, and in Cheapside shall my palfrey go to grass."

In complete contrast with this conception of the common people as a mere rabble, full of passion and devoid of ideas, stands Coriolanus — a typical aristocrat, with the virtues of the aristocrat: courage, indifference to pain, scorn of money, independence of thought, command of eloquence, and natural aptitude for leadership. These great qualities are neutralized by colossal egotism, manifesting itself in a pride so irrational and insistent that, sooner or later, by the necessity of its nature, it must produce the tragic conflict. Coriolanus, in spite of his great faults, has heroic proportions, and fills the play with the sense of his superiority; he lives and dies like a true tragic hero.

CHAPTER XV

MR. DENTON SNIDER, who has interpreted Shakespeare with breadth of view and keenness of insight, and has brought out with convincing clearness the poet's conception of life and art from the institutional point of view, describes the Shakespearean drama as " the grand Mystery Play of humanity." The essence of the mystery play was the disclosure of a divine power at work in the world dealing directly with human affairs ; the interior union of the seen with the unseen, of the temporal with the eternal, of the human with the divine, was set out in childlike simplicity in these dramas of mediæval faith and genius. In Shakespeare this disclosure of an invisible background against which human life is set and from the order of which it cannot escape without setting tragic forces in motion, took on a new and deeper form in the Tragedies which came from his hand in uninterrupted succession after 1601. In these dramas all the elements of power and art which were present in germ in the Mystery, the Morality, and the Interlude were unfolded and harmonized in the spirit of freedom and with the feeling for beauty which were the gifts of the Renaissance to the greatest of its children.

276

Ethical Significance of the Tragedies

Shakespeare was preëminently a poet, and it is highly improbable, therefore, that he thought out in advance the philosophical bearings of his art and worked out for himself a systematized conception of life. Even Goethe, whose insight into the principles of art productivity was as clear and final as his creative genius was direct and spontaneous, was primarily a poet and secondarily a critic or philosopher. There is every reason to believe that Shakespeare's view of life came to him through the gradual disclosure of an experience which was rationalized and interpreted by habitual meditation. A nature of such sensitiveness and receptivity as his would feel the beauty of the world and the variety, the interest, and the humour of life as he felt these things in the years when he was serving his apprenticeship and, a little later, writing the Comedies. Such a nature, constantly fed by that vital sympathy with men which is part of the gift of genius, steadily deepened and clarified by experience and illumined by the insight of genius, would inevitably pass through the show of things to the moral order behind them, and discern more and more clearly the significance of character in the fortunes and fates of men, as Shakespeare did in the period of the historical and purely poetic dramas.

If at this stage a deep and searching crisis were to occur in his spiritual life, misfortune overtake the men whom he loved and who personified for him the spirit and genius of his time, and that time, so splendid in its earlier promise and performance, become over-clouded like a day fast hastening to night, his vision would insensibly widen and deepen, as did Shakespeare's when he entered upon the period of the Tragedies. Through all the earlier years in London he was steadily approaching the mystery of life; in the years of the Tragedies he entered into that mystery and was enfolded by it. He wrote the Tragedies as he had written the Comedies, because the creative impulse was on him and play-writing was his vocation; but the order of the world which comes to light in them, giving significance to human striving and suffering, was not less clearly seen nor less authoritatively revealed because Shakespeare did not definitely set it before him as the object of his artistic endeavour. The poet is a more impressive witness to the ethical order of life than the moralist, because his discovery of that order is, in a sense, incidental and unintentional; he sees it, not because he set out to discover it, but because it is there and he cannot avoid seeing it.

That Shakespeare deliberately, and in a spirit of philosophic detachment from life, studied, after the manner of a psychologist, the phenomena of experience, and formulated a system of interpreting those phenomena, is incredible in the exact degree in which one comprehends his nature; that he was blind to this great order, that he did not discern what he saw nor understand what he said, that his mind was simply a mirror in which was caught up the reflection of a world which he never realized in consciousness, is still more incredible. When he laid aside the dramatic mask, as he did at times in the Sonnets and more than once in the plays, and notably in "Troilus and Cressida," he made it plain that he understood the significance of his own thought, and that his attitude toward the great matters with which he deals was intelligent and deliberate, if not at all moments self-conscious.

It was his rare good fortune as an artist to pluck the fruits of the most searching scrutiny of the facts of life without losing that free and captivating spontaneity which is the joy of art; to command the knowledge of the psychologist without losing the magic of the poet; to be at the same time one of the most penetrating of thinkers and the most beguiling of poets, with a clear vision of the deepest realities of existence and a voice full of the careless, rapturous melody of birds under the free sky.

In the period of the Tragedies Shakespeare set forth with perfect clearness his view of a man's place and meaning in the world. His whole conception of the authority and significance of human nature rests on personality — the master word of the thought of the Western world and the source of its formative ideas of freedom, responsibility, beauty, democracy, the reality of experience, the dignity of individual effort, and personal immortality. In the Tragedies Shakespeare worked out in dramatic form this central conception about which Western thought, since Plato, has organized itself. He exhibits the individual man as shaping his destiny largely by his own will; as fashioning himself chiefly through action, by means of which ideas and emotions are transmuted into character and re-form the man. The problem of life, as it is presented in the Shakespearean dramas, is to bring the individual will into harmony with the institutional life of society, organized in the family, the Church, and the State; and to bring these institutions into harmony with the immutable principles of righteousness. This result is brought about in the Tragedies by the collision of the individual with the established order, either to his own hurt or to the betterment of the order itself; and the moment of collision is the moment of tragedy. It is at this moment, when the inner subjective force of the man sweeps into light through action, becomes objective and begins to affect others, to set in motion reactions upon himself and to change the order of things about him, that Shakespeare fastens attention upon the tragic character; and, through the collision between his will and the order of society or of life, reveals as by a lightning flash the soul of the man and the visible or invisible order in which his life is set.

As clearly as does Dante, though in a very different fashion, he shows the inevitable reaction of the deed upon the doer, and so strikes into sudden light the massive and all-embracing moral order of life. He swept away the last lingering shadows of the pagan conception of fate by showing that character is destiny, and that "character is the only definition we have of freedom and power."

In the word character — the organization of impulse, emotion, will, and deed into a permanent, self-conscious personality, which becomes a shaping force in the world — is to be found the key to Shakespeare's conception of life and of the function of dramatic art. If he made plays which were suited to the taste of his

age and were skilfully adapted to the limitations and
possibilities of the stage in his day, he also made
dramas which disclosed the most searching study of
human experience, and the most adequate and ultimate interpretation and representation of that experience in the forms of art. He was at once a trained
and practical playwright, with a first-hand knowledge
of his business and of his constituency ; and he was
also a thinker and an artist of the first order ; and
there was no contradiction between the man of skill
and the man of genius in the same personality. The
difficulty in understanding and accepting the many-
sidedness of Shakespeare and the happy balance of
spontaneity and reflection in him has its roots, not in
the limited potentialities of the human spirit, but in
the lack of imagination on the part of his readers.
The miracle of genius — that magical insight which is
apparently independent of character in its origin, but
largely dependent on character for harmonious and
adequate expression ; which never originates in any
kind of education, but is largely conditioned upon
education for its free and full development — is incredible to those who strive to reduce life and its arts
to a set of formulæ, and to divide men arbitrarily into
types which are consistent throughout. Shakespeare
is not to be explained by a formula nor to be studied
as a type of mind formed by a rigid method; he
was neither an irresponsible genius, to whom great
thoughts, unerring insights, and moments of inspired
speech came without sequence or relation to his inner
life, nor was he a systematically trained, intensely

self-conscious workman, whose happiest strokes were planned with the nicest sense of craftsmanship, and whose consistent and coherent view of life was thoroughly thought out before the first studies were put on paper.

He was primarily and always a poet; it was as a poet that he first won recognition, and it was in the poetic temper and view of things that he found refuge and peace after the period of the Tragedies was passed; and during the years when the dramatic instinct and impulse dominated him and shaped his work, his methods, his spirit, and his relations to his vocation were those of a poet. As a poet he saw with the clearness of direct vision and felt with the freshness and power of spontaneous emotion, and he instinctively passed behind the fact to the truth which it suggested or illustrated; but this spontaneous action of his nature was broadened, deepened, and brightened by quick and sensitive perception of the value and uses of methods, tools, and instruments of every kind, and by habitual meditation on the spectacle of life as it lay in his imagination. It is impossible to separate the poetic and the philosophic in his nature, to mark the points at which the process of observation ends and the free play of the imagination begins; to sever that which was acquired from that which was creative in him; to divide the conscious from the unconscious elements in his power and his life; to distinguish between the thinker and the poet in his work. His work reveals with the utmost clearness a coherent and profound view of life, consistently set forth in a long series of dramas; every page bears the unmistakable stamp of the thinker; but the mind behind this varied and splendid work is the mind of a poet, and the personality which shapes all this material into forms of beauty is that of the artist. When this point of view is taken, Shakespeare's genius does not cease to be marvellous, but it does cease to be incredible.

The fate of the critic who attempts to slip the net of logical definition over this elusive spirit was charmingly portrayed by Heine in a passage which students of the dramatist will do well to keep in mind:

"I fell asleep and dreamed," writes Heine — "dreamed that it was a starry night, and I swam in a small boat in a wide, wide sea, where all kinds of barks filled with masks, musicians, and torches gleaming, music sounding, many near or afar, rowed on. There were costumes of all countries and ages, old Greek tunics, mediæval knightly coats, Oriental turbans, shepherds' hats with fluttering ribbons, masks of beasts wild or tame — now and then I thought I saw a well-known face, sometimes I heard familiar greetings — but all passed quickly by and far away, and the merry music grew softer and fainter, when, instead of the gay fiddling, I heard near me the mysterious, melancholy tones of hunters' horns from another part. Sometimes the night wind bore the strains of both to my ear, and then the mingled melody made a happy harmony. The water echoed ineffably sweet sounds and burned as with a magical reflection of the torches, and the gayly-pennoned pleasure boats with their wondrous masquerades swam in light and music. A lovely woman, who stood by the rudder of one of the barks, cried to me in passing, 'Is it not true, friend, thou wouldst have a definition of the Shakespearean comedy?' I know not whether I answered 'Yes,' but in that instant the beautiful woman dipped her hand in the water and sprinkled the ringing sparks in my face, so that there was a general laughter, and I awoke."

Many students and critics who have forgotten that Shakespeare is first and always a poet, and have approached him as if he were primarily a philosopher, have shared Heine's disaster without the consolation of Heine's vision.

In the Tragedies Shakespeare touched the highest point of his power and his art; more adequately than the Histories, Comedies, or Romances they give that impression of final authority which issues only from the greatest work of the greatest minds, and which has its roots in the perception that in these masterpieces the study of character is most searching and its portraiture most convincing. If the view of life and art which lies at the heart of the thought and action of the Western races is sound, Shakespeare becomes, in these great plays, their foremost interpreter. It is in these dramas that the function of action is revealed in a full, clear, adequate way almost for the first time in literature, and the process of historic development is set forth not as an intellectual but as a vital evolution. The problem of existence is not to be solved by the action of the mind alone; men deal with life primarily not as thinkers but as men, with all the resources of a complex nature; with instincts, ap-

petites, passions ; with emotion, thought, and will.
By means of action, impulse and thought pass out of
the region of pure subjectivity into the world of
actuality and become definite, concrete, potential ;
through action, they react on the actor and reform or
transform existing conditions and institutions. They
create a human world against the background of the
natural world ; they exhibit the human spirit in this
world by giving external form to its inward and hidden
nature ; men cease to be mere observers and reflectors ;
they become creative, and through action they enter
into history and shape its movement. This action
may not always justify itself in its positive results, but
it always reveals man to himself and to his fellows ; it
evokes his power, liberates him from the limitations
of his own experience by setting him in a universal
order ; develops his personality ; gives, in a word, free
play to the human spirit, makes it conscious of its
place in the order of life, and provides an educational
process which makes life intelligible, gives it moral
significance, dramatic interest, and invests it with immortal hopes. In these dramas the ultimate truths of
life and the deepest secrets of experience are organized
into forms of the highest beauty, and a great light
suddenly shines in the heart of man ; for all true art
is the illumination of experience.

The vital quality of Shakespeare's work, its living
force, its convincing reality, are rooted in the closeness
of its relation to experience, in the directness with
which life fed the springs of his nature and the sources
of his art. The conception of life, as revealed in the

vast range of human action reacting on character, not only gives the ethical significance of his work convincing authority, but stretches and expands indefinitely the normal and wholesome range of human interest beyond the arbitrary and shifting limits set by different schools and successive generations of moralists. Shakespeare's ethical view of life was rooted in realities and had the large, vigorous vitality of an elemental order, spacious enough to admit of the full, free, and normal development of the human spirit on all sides. To a mind of such breadth of view and deep vitality as his any kind of asceticism was not only a violation of instinct but of the nature of man; any kind of denial of the dignity of the body was as truly atheistic as any kind of denial of the reality of the experiences of the spirit. Into the region of pure spiritual impulse and ultimate spiritual relationship Shakespeare did not penetrate; in that fact lies his limitation. If to his other gifts had been added the spiritual insight of Dante, he would have been not only the foremost but the ultimate interpreter of the life of the race. In the region of action, however, where spiritual impulses and convictions are worked into character, Shakespeare is a master of observation and of interpretation. He sees the facts, and he sets them in their ethical order. In this field, therefore, his freedom, his range, and the vast variety of his interests are significant of the breadth and compass of normal human living.

It is needless to prove that he was not a Puritan, to quote "I had as lief be a Brownist as a politician," or "Though honesty be no Puritan, yet it will be no hurt;

it will wear the surplice of humility over the black gown of a big heart;" by the very constitution of his mind Shakespeare was set apart for another service to his kind, and committed to a different view of life. The Puritan, with all his devotion and greatness of soul, was the master of a crisis, the man of a period, the representative of a phase of human development; Shakespeare was the master of the universal movement of life, the man of all time, the exponent of the full and free play of all the forces of personality. He stands, therefore, not for the occasional altitudes of human experience, but its broad, general, productive movement; for large, varied, many-sided, fertile life, with full play of instinct, passion, emotion, thought, and will; for freedom in an ordered world, in which all normal human faculties and desires are to find normal expression and use; in which, however, law and proportion and harmony between different parts of the nature are to be preserved, the lower is to be subordinated to the higher, the individual kept in his place in the social order, and the institutional life of society sustained at any private cost.

In such a world what was universal and enduring in the Puritan view was kept; what was provisional and divisive rejected. It was a world in which the Greek and the man of the Renaissance temper could live as freely as the man of the Hebrew spirit. It follows, therefore, that the ethical order of Shakespeare's world must be found in the structure of that world, not in conventional or sectarian interpretations or expositions of its order. Shakespeare's morality is the morality of fundamental law, not of provisional rules; his righteousness is the righteousness of sane, wholesome, ordered living, not of conventional good behaviour.

To a mind of Shakespeare's breadth of view no conception of the ethical constitution of things less fundamental was possible; he saw too far to accept any local standards of right action or any provisional views of human duties. In the wide range of his vision of the fortunes of men the rigid and fixed bounds set to moral responsibility by sectarian moralists of every school lost their authority; the vast complexity of experience, the immense range of conditions, the influence of institutions on character, the pathetic and often tragic enfolding of a soul by circumstances which leave their stain and stamp upon it, the antagonistic elements which are at war in the noblest character — all these things touched Shakespeare's judgments with a great compassion, and, while unflinching in his disclosure of the penalty which lies in the heart of the evil deed, made him slow to measure out moral condemnation to the evil-doer. He could not fail to be aware, with all men of imagination and insight, of the vaster movement which enfolds the obvious ethical order of life. Like Goethe in "Faust," and Hawthorne in "The Marble Faun," he had glimpses of "a soul of goodness in things evil," divinations of a diviner reconciliation between conflicting elements than is accomplished on the narrow stage of the world. This deep mystery he could not probe; no man has sounded it; it enfolds us like an element of which we suspect the existence, but which our instruments of observation are not sensitive enough to discover. Its presence does not diminish the authority of the ethical order under which we live and from which no man escapes, but it ought to make us more tolerant, compassionate, and patient in judgment and in punishment.

"The web of our life is of a mingled yarn, good and ill together," says the dramatist in one of the group of plays which are most perplexing to the moralist who lacks this vision of a larger order; "our virtues would be proud if our faults whipped them not; and our crimes would despair if they were not cherished by our virtues."

This largeness of view gave Shakespeare the highest insight of the great tragic writer: the clear perception of the presence of a mediating element in life. Without this perception the highest form of tragedy is impossible of realization; for tragedy is not only an exhibition of tragic events, but an interpretation of their significance. Without this interpretation these events are blind happenings, — mere brutalities of fate, without order, meaning, or impressiveness. If Shakespeare's view of life was too broad to permit of a judgment of men from the standpoint of conventional morality, his insight was too deep and searching to rest in the violent collisions of contending principles, forces, and persons. He could not stop short of some kind of harmony; violence in its destructive aspect had only a minor interest for him; he cared for the storm because it cleared the air and prepared the way for a new and higher order of things. The deed reacts on the doer and brings doom with it, but the penalty is not inflicted as a matter of vengeance; it opens the door to a reorganization of character. For the evil-doer, the violator of the order of society, the real tragedy is to be found in the offence, not in the penalty; and the greatest disaster comes not when the punishment is borne, but when it is evaded. In this consistent representation of the inevitableness and necessity of the tragic disaster Shakespeare is in harmony with the soundest religious view of life and with the most intelligent psychology. As soon as personality is set free in society, directed by inward intelligence, will, or impulse, put under the necessity of subordinating impulse to intelligence, appetite to law, individual desire to the good of society, a series of tragic collisions is set in motion and a world of conflict rises into view. These conflicts are precipitated when individual passion, preference, or love is set in opposition to the family, as in "Romeo and Juliet" and "King Lear"; and when individual will, interest, or passion is set in opposition to the State, as in the historical plays, and in "Coriolanus," "Julius Cæsar," and "Macbeth." These are the two great classes of tragic conflict with which Shakespeare deals; and his point of view is consistent throughout. Society is striving, in a rude and halting fashion, toward the attainment of harmony; its institutions are often based on unrighteousness, they are perverted in their uses or they are outgrown; in each case some kind of conflict is inevitable and that conflict takes a tragic form.

Ethical Significance of the Tragedies

These institutions impose order upon society; to that order each individual must adjust himself, and in it he must find his place; if he sets his will against the general will as organized in these institutions he precipitates a conflict and becomes a tragic figure. These conflicts are not casual and accidental; they represent the working out of the moral and institutional order, and they must, therefore, find their ultimate issue in a deeper harmony.

This is the Shakespearean interpretation of the tragic collisions of society. It is the clearness with which Shakespeare sees and represents this principle of mediation, this process of reconciliation, which gives the Tragedies their authority as works of art and sets the dramatist among the masters of the knowledge of life.

CHAPTER XVI

THE ROMANCES

It was characteristic of Shakespeare that during the years in which the Tragedies were written, and while he was meditating upon the baffling problem of evil in the world, he was conducting his affairs with prudence and sagacity. The sanity of his nature, which held him to the great highways of human interest and rational human living, kept his genius in touch with reality at all points and contributed not a little to the richness and range of his creative activity. The assumption that the man of imagination cannot be a man of practical wisdom, and that there is an inherent antagonism between genius and sound judgment, has been disproved many times in the history of all the arts, and persists in the face of convincing historic refutation. There have been many men of rare and beautiful gifts who have lacked the capacity to deal strongly or intelligently with the practical side of life, and who have, therefore, been unable to make that adjustment to conditions and realities which is part of the problem of life and a chief part of its education. For this reason many men of noble imagination have missed the full unfolding of their genius and the complete harvesting of its fruits. Shakespeare

was not one of those pathetic figures who, through
some defect in spiritual organization, make splendid
tragic failures — figures with whom his imagination
was always busy, and who appear in nearly all the
plays. He was the sounder and therefore the greater
poet because in his life, as in his art, he held the balance between reality and ideality ; mounting into
high heaven with effortless wing, like the lark in the
meadows about Stratford, but returning with unerring
instinct to the familiar and solid earth.

During the decade between 1600 and 1610, Shakespeare was adding to his properties at Stratford, he
was making various investments, he was seeking to
recover by suits at law moneys loaned to others, and
he was steadily increasing his income from various
sources. His purchase of New Place has been
noted ; upon the death of his father the houses in
Henley Street came into his possession, and in one
of them his mother probably lived until her death in
1608. He enlarged by purchase the grounds of New
Place ; he acquired a property of nearly a hundred
and fifty acres in the neighbourhood of Stratford ; he
purchased an interest in the tithes of Stratford, Welcombe, and Bishopton ; and, both at Stratford and in
London, he brought suits for the recovery of small
debts. Like his father, he appears to have had no
aversion to litigation ; but, on the other hand, there
is nothing in the various records of the legal proceed
ings which he inaugurated, to show that he was oppres-
sive or unjust to those with whom he had business
dealings. In practical affairs he was sagacious, or-

derly, and businesslike. That a poet collected a debt which was due him hardly furnishes rational ground for the theory that he must therefore have been a hard and grasping person.

To the Tragedies succeeded a group of three plays commonly classed as Romances, which completed Shakespeare's work as a dramatist and which hold a place by themselves. It is true that "Henry VIII." came at the very end, but this spectacular play is Shakespeare's only in part, and is hardly to be counted among his representative and original works.

A new note was struck in the Romances, and that note is distinctly sounded in "Pericles," a play which is of Shakespearean authorship only in its idyllic passages. It seems to predict "The Tempest," "Cymbeline," "The Winter's Tale," as "The Two Gentlemen of Verona" predicts "Twelfth Night." Marina is of the same exquisite order of womanhood as Miranda and Perdita. The poet's work on this drama was done when the period of tragedy was drawing to a close but was not yet at an end. The play probably appeared about 1607, and was probably written in collaboration with some playwright of inferior taste and ability. The plot was derived from various sources; the story being one of great antiquity and having been very widely popular for several centuries before Shakespeare's time. It had been read on the Continent in the "Gesta Romanorum," and in England in Gower's "Confessio Amantis"; and it was retold in a prose romance by Lawrence Twine, which appeared in England in 1576. There is now substantial agreement that the repellent parts of "Pericles" were written by another hand than Shakespeare's, and that to his genius is due the exquisite episode and romance of Marina, conceived and worked out with a delicacy of feeling, a refinement of sentiment, and a pervading atmosphere of poetry which are unmistakably Shakespearean.

"Cymbeline" was included among the Tragedies by the editors of the First Folio; but its pervading spirit and its peaceful and happy ending place it among the Romances. Shakespeare had passed through the period of tragedy into a deep and abiding peace, but the gayety of the earlier mood of the Comedies was no longer possible. However serene and calm the spirit of the poet, he could never again look at life without seeing the element of tragedy at work in it. That element became subordinate and served chiefly to bring out certain gracious and beautiful qualities of nature, certain pure and almost spiritual personalities, but it was henceforth part of the mysterious experience of life to one who had sounded the depths of Hamlet's solitary melancholy and been abroad when all the fury of the elemental passions burst upon the head of Lear. In "Cymbeline," "The Winter's Tale," and "The Tempest," the tragic motive is introduced, and the tragic conflict would have worked out its inevitable wreckage if these later dramas had not been plays of reconciliation; plays, that is, in which the movement of the tragic forces is arrested by repentance, by the return, through penitence, to the true order of life. In these concluding dramas the

destructive forces, which run their course in the Tragedies, are set in motion in order that they may furnish a background for the presentation of the healing
and restoring power of remorse, penitence, reconciliation, forgiveness, and atonement. The dewy freshness
of the world in "The Winter's Tale" and "The Tempest" is more penetrating in its unstained purity because the lightning still plays from the clouds which
are fast dissolving along the horizon.

Shakespeare was a dramatist during the period
when his work touched its highest points of achievement, and it betrays the absence of even rudimentary
critical instinct to identify a dramatist with the wide
range of characters which his imagination creates in
a purely objective mood. There are individual plays
from which it would be an impertinence to attempt to
infer the ethical attitude or the personality of Shakespeare. On the other hand, it must also be remembered that Shakespeare was a poet before and after
the dramatic period; that the mask was not so consistently worn during the period of the Sonnets and of
the Romances as during that of the Tragedies; that he
left a large body of work behind him, and that through
this work there run certain consistent and fundamental conceptions of life and character; that this work,
conceding uncertainty with regard to the exact chronology of each play, can be divided into four distinct
periods. These facts have a bearing on the nature
of Shakespeare's personality and experience which it
is as uncritical to disregard as it is uncritical to hold
Shakespeare morally responsible for any sentiment put

The Romances

in the mouths of Iago and Richard III. However much or little the facts in Shakespeare's experience may have had to do with his work as a creative artist, it is beyond question that he passed through distinct stages of artistic and intellectual unfolding; and, accepting the psychology of genius, the history of the man of genius as it has been recorded in every art, and the revelation of the man of genius as it has been made by himself, Goethe serving as an example, it is rational to believe that the man and the artist in Shakespeare were in vital relationship from the beginning to the end.

In his life of sustained productivity Shakespeare passed through four periods : a period of apprenticeship, when he was learning both his trade and his art ; a period of joyous and many-sided contact with the world and with men, during which he made his approach to life ; the period of the Tragedies, when he entered into life, sounded its depths of experience, and faced its problems ; and a period of reconciliation or mediation, when the tragic elements found their place in a comprehensive and beneficent order. Out of this rich and vital contact with life the poet came at last into a mood at once serene, grave, and tender ; he looked upon men with a deep and beautiful pity ; fortitude under calamity, charity for human weakness, faith in the power of human sweetness and purity, pervade the Romances and give them an interior beauty of which the exquisite poetry in which they are steeped seems only an outward vesture. That beauty was the reflection of a nature of great richness, which, through deep and searching experience, had at last found peace in a wide vision, a catholic spirit, and a reverent faith in purity, goodness, and truth.

In these latest plays the poet shows also a great sense of freedom; a consciousness of inward power matched with outward skill which justifies him in becoming a law unto himself. The style is subordinated to the thought; rhyme almost disappears; weak endings increase in number; the iambic regularity of the blank verse is varied by new flexibility; the harmony of the line is subordinated to that of the paragraph, and the music of the verse gains a richer and fuller movement; and there is complete indifference to the traditional unities of time and place. These traditions had been modified or discarded at an early date, but in the Romances a new kind of unity is introduced, or at least illustrated, in an art so convincing that the mind accepts the new order of construction as if it were the order of nature. "The ideality of space which characterized the English stage of that time," writes Professor Ten Brink, "and of which the ideality of time was a necessary corollary, the ability of the prevailing drama to include a long chain of events throughout its entire course, permitted Shakespeare in tragedy to follow his inner bent, which impelled him to the psychological side of his subject. It permitted him to represent, as he loved to do, the evolution of a passion from its first beginnings to its climax; and not seldom reaching still further back, to show us the soil in which it was to take root. It permitted him to show us a character unfolding before our eyes under the reciprocal influence of deed and experience, of action and environment. It enabled him thus in his tragedies to lay the chief weight upon the connection between the character and the acts of the tragic hero, or, what is the same thing, to devote the best part of his powers and endeavours to the dramatic unfolding of his characters."

In the Tragedies this loosening of the bonds of time and place enabled Shakespeare to lay bare the very heart of the tragic conflict; in the Romances it made it possible to bring together, for the full disclosure of the drama of mediation, distant countries and times; to bring within the compass of a play the most exquisite poetry and the most rugged prose; to set on the same stage Perdita and Autolycus, Miranda and Caliban. "Cymbeline" marks the end of the period of tragedy, and the dominance of a new mood. It probably appeared about 1609. Dr. Forman, to whom reference has already been made, who combined the arts of a quack with the taste of a theatre-goer, and whose brief diary is an interesting comtemporary record, saw the play at the Globe Theatre, but made no record of the date. The plot was drawn from various sources, and these diverse materials were fused and combined by the dramatist with a free hand.

The story of Cymbeline and of his two sons was taken from Holinshed; the story of Imogen from Boccaccio's "Decameron"; while some details of the plot suggest that Shakespeare drew upon well-known and oft-used motives of current fairy tales. To this source he was probably indebted for some of the most delicate and poetic touches in the life of Imogen with her brothers in the cave of Belarius. This rude but hospitable home, full of kingly grace and nobleness in woodland disguise, is set in striking contrast to the court from which Imogen has fled. In this secluded cavern courage and integrity are preserved and trained against the day when they must bring in the new order, of which Imogen is the stainless and appealing protagonist. No lovelier image of chaste, self-sacrificing womanhood is to be found in the whole range of poetry. The poet has invested her with purity as with a garment which she wears without consciousness either of its value or its perishableness. It is so much a part of her nature that she could not separate it from herself. Her presence touches the rough lives of her brothers, and all their virtues shine through the disguise they wear. She mediates between her father and Belarius; and she reconciles Cymbeline and Posthumus. Her gentleness is emphasized by the savage temper, the hard spirit, which run through the play, and which at the end, with exquisite skill, are resolved into harmony by her spirit. Among all Shakespeare's lyrics there is none more noble than "Fear no more the heat of the sun," which is set like a gem in this drama of a woman's constancy.

Robert Greene had done what he could, when Shakespeare was serving his apprenticeship, to arrest the growing reputation of the young dramatist, and had failed. A "Groatsworth of Wit bought with a Million of Repentance" is of interest now chiefly because of the reference to the poet which was meant to do him harm, but which has served to settle some interesting questions of time, and to show that he had been successful enough to awaken envy. In 1588, five years before the attack on Shakespeare, Greene brought out a story which, under the unattractive title of "Pandasto: the Triumph of Time," became one of the most popular novels of the day, passing through at least fourteen editions. Its claims upon the interest of readers were set forth on the title-page: "Wherein is discovered by a pleasant history, that although by the means of sinister fortune, Truth may be concealed, yet by Time in spite of fortune it is most manifestly revealed: pleasant for age to avoid drowsy thoughts, profitable for youth to eschew other wanton pastimes, and bringing to both a desired content. *Temporis filia veritas.*" Time, if not in itself a mediating principle, is a necessary element in the work of mediation; and this old-fashioned romance furnished both the tragic introduction and the happy and peaceful issue upon which Shakespeare's mind fastened after the period of the Tragedies. His hand saved Greene's story from oblivion; it will always be remembered as the source from which "The Winter's Tale" was largely drawn, — the story having its roots in an incident in the history of Bohemia. The tale in the "Decameron," in which Shakespeare had found suggestions for parts of "Cymbeline," was also laid under contribution in "The Winter's Tale." Autolycus was the last of a long list of jesters who had no literary progenitors and have left no successors; they are the creatures of the play and overflow of Shakespeare's humour, his perception of the comic, his delight in contrasts and contradictions, with touches at times — as in the Fool in " King Lear " — of fathomless pathos. So far as the name is concerned, Autolycus was of historic ancestry. His character is sketched in the " Odyssey " in a few masterly strokes :

> Autolycus, who th' art
> Of theft and swearing (not out of the heart
> But by equivocation) first adorn'd,
> Your witty man withal, and was suborn'd
> By Jove's descend'nt, ingenious Mercury.

The witty thief could claim divine ancestry, and Shakespeare may have found this representative rascal in the pages of his Ovid. From these hints of classical characterization the poet expanded the rustic knavery, shrewdness, and inimitable self-assurance of this picturesque picker-up of other people's savings at country festivals and fairs.

Shakespeare accepted Greene's geography with delightful indifference to its accuracy, and so fell into the historic blunder of giving Bohemia a sea-coast. Ben Jonson was quick to fall upon this mistake, not so much from malice or ill-feeling, probably, as from the natural irritation of a careful and exact mind with a person of such marvellous spontaneity and such semi-humorous indifference to details as Shakespeare. " Shakespeare wanted art and sometimes sense," Drummond of Hawthornden reports him as saying ; " for in one of his plays he brought in a number of men saying they had suffered shipwreck in Bohemia, where is no sea nearly one hundred miles." Shake-

speare may have known this fact as definitely as
Jonson knew it; or he may have been as ignorant
of it as were many other well-informed men of his
time. His interest, it is clear, was fastened upon facts
of another order, and in a play in which the unity of
time was set at naught by an interval of sixteen years
between two acts, and the congruities of history are
quietly ignored in order to secure a free field for
a masterly drama of the imagination, geographical
accuracy was a small matter.

The play was produced about 1611. It was put
upon the stage of the Globe Theatre on the 15th of
May in that year, on which occasion Dr. Forman was
present and described it at some length in his "Book
of Plays and Notes thereof." In November of the
same year it was performed before the Court in the
palace at Whitehall; and two years later it was one
of the plays chosen for presentation in the elaborate
festivities with which the marriage of the Princess
Elizabeth was celebrated.

The early popularity of the play among theatre-
goers has not been revived in modern times. Its
essentially poetic quality has made "The Winter's
Tale," to modern taste, a reading rather than an acting play; a drama of the imagination rather than of
real life. The pastoral world in which Perdita moves
was the last of those lovely pastoral worlds which
Shakespeare created as refuges from the world of
reality and places of reconciliation between the ideals
and hopes of beautiful natures and the actualities
which surrounded them.

William Shakespeare

Perdita is half woman and half creature of fairyland; in her rare and exquisite spirit there is a subtle affiliation with nature which allies her with the flowers, whose succession she has set in an immortal calendar; in her sweet and patient devotion she personifies that spirit of goodness which in the end binds the shattered parts of her world into unity once more. In her speech, with its beguiling melody and its enchanting imagery, she is the personification of poetry. Among the Shakespearean women she represents the " eternal feminine " in its most poetic aspect; for she mediates, not only between conflicting persons, but between nature and man.

In power of pure invention, of creating plots, situations, and episodes, Shakespeare was inferior to many of his contemporaries; and if invention and originality were synonymous, as they are often taken to be, his rank would be below that of Jonson, Fletcher, Marston, or Middleton. The faculty of invention is, however, of small importance unless it be sustained by force of mind and inspired and directed by imagination. Many playwrights of the third or fourth rank have shown more fertility in inventing fresh situations and incidents than Shakespeare; none of them has approached him in originality. For originality does not consist in invention, but in insight, grasp, selection, arrangement, and, above all, in vitalization. The creative faculty does not disclose itself in dexterity or multiplicity of invention, but in the play of free, elemental power. " The great merit, it seems to me, of the old painters," wrote Mr. Lowell, " was that they did not try to be

James
read
on P-305
the marked
Paragraph

Al

original." "To say a thing that everybody has said before," said Goethe, "as quietly as if nobody had ever said it, *that* is originality."

Throughout his entire productive life, Shakespeare kept himself in closest touch with the experience of the race as that experience lies written in history and biography, and with the imaginative life of the race as that life has expressed itself in striking and significant figures, and in stories full of deep human feeling for humour or for poetry.

He knew the two chroniclers who were most popular in his time; he was familiar with Plutarch and with some of the notable contemporary translators; he had intimate acquaintance with such collections of stories as Paynter's "Palace of Pleasure"; and he read the novels or tales of his age with an artist's feeling for the truth of life or of poetry which they contained. He lived freely and deeply in his time; indifferent to conventionalities save as they conformed to his conception of sane living, and to literary traditions save as they harmonized with his artistic instinct and intelligence. His greatness as a poet lies in his extraordinary genius for seeing the concrete fact, and in his unrivalled power of irradiating that fact with the insight and vision of the imagination. No man of his time exhibited such fertility and audacity of imagination, and no man so firmly based his artistic work on clear, uncompromising perception of actualities. He was at the same time the closest observer and the most daring idealist of his age. Through each successive period of his productive career he touched phase after phase of experience and presented a long succession of characters. Beginning with the old chronicle plays, which he read with the truest historical perception and feeling, he passed on to the humorous aspects of life, and thence to a study of its most appalling aspects; and at each stage he laid hold upon some human document in history, legend, tradition, or romance. He never lost his touch with the realities of life; and he found so much that was of supreme significance that he rarely had occasion to use invention. The race in many lands and at many periods of time had been at work storing up the raw material of poetry for him; he entered into partnership with the race, and, by rationalizing its experience and giving it the beauty and order of art, repaid the race a thousand fold for the material of every sort which had been placed in his hands. In this masterful dealing, not with images of his own making, but with the actualities of human experience, is to be found his originality — an originality identical in its method and operation with the originality of Homer, Dante, and Goethe, who share with him the splendid loneliness of supreme literary achievement.

In "The Tempest" Shakespeare used existing material only in the remotest way; the play fashioned itself largely in his imagination. In the earlier dramas he had dealt entirely with past conditions and incidents; the "Merry Wives of Windsor" is the only one of his works which may be said to deal with contemporary society and manners. "The Tempest," however, so far as it was rooted in reality, was drawn by suggestion from stirring events in his own time. The poet, more than any of his contemporaries, personified the freedom, vitality, keen sense of reality, and wide discursive interests of the Elizabethan age; in "The Tempest" he touched the new world of wonder, adventure, and achievement fast coming to the knowledge of the old world. Strange tidings of new countries and peoples were coming up from time to time from the far seas, and marvellous stories of strange lands and perilous voyages were told by quiet English firesides. In the autumn of 1610 a great sensation was made in London by the arrival of a company of sailors who had been wrecked off the Bermudas, until that moment undiscovered. These sailors, like all men of their occupation, were lovers of marvels and spinners of strange tales; they had found the climate of the Bermudas charming, and they had heard many inexplicable sounds in the islands. These experiences were not dulled in colour by the homeward voyage; on the contrary, they gained in marvellous and mysterious accompaniments of sight and sound as the distance lengthened between the place where they befell the wrecked crew and the places in which they were heard with eager and uncritical ears.

The wreck of the *Sea-Venture*, Sir George Somers commanding, was described at length by several survivors, the most important of these accounts being that entitled "A Discovery of the Bermudas, otherwise called the Ile of Divels," which was reënforced by several pamphlets. According to these reports the island of Bermudas had never been "inhabited by any Christian or heathen people"; it was reported "a most prodigious and enchanted place," "still-vexed" with "monstrous thunder-storms and tempests." On the night the ship was wrecked the Admiral himself "had an apparition of a little, round light, like a faint star, trembling and streaming along with a sparkling blaze, half the height above the main-mast, and shooting sometimes from shroud to shroud, tempting to settle as it were upon any of the four shrouds."

The stories of this marvellous voyage were undoubtedly heard by Shakespeare, and he certainly read these narratives before writing of the "still-vexed Bermoothes," of the climate of the Island in "The Tempest," and of the spirits which frequented it. Traces of the reading of other books of travel are found in the play. It is possible also that Shakespeare may have heard from English actors, who had performed at Nuremberg a few years before this time, the plot of a comedy written by Jacob Ayrer, of that city, under the title "Die Schöne Sidea." It is also possible that there may have been an earlier play or novel of a somewhat similar plot, which has entirely disappeared. The famous description of an ideal commonwealth which is put in the mouth of Gonzalo was suggested to Shakespeare by an essay of Montaigne's which he read in Florio's translation; while the Invocation of Prospero may owe something to one of Ovid's "Metamorphoses," with which the poet had long been familiar.

After recognizing his indebtedness for certain details to various earlier and contemporary sources, "The

The Romances

Tempest" remains preëminently the creation of Shakespeare's imagination. In certain respects it is his masterpiece. As a drama it falls far below his earlier work; as a poem, cast in a dramatic form, it is one of the most beautiful creations in English poetry. The profound meditativeness and rich intellectual quality of "Hamlet" are fused in it with the lovely fancy of the "Midsummer Night's Dream," while in deep and sustained play of imagination, fashioning the play in its structure, shaping its parts to one high end, touching it everywhere with a kind of ultimate beauty, it stands alone not only in Shakespeare's work but in modern poetry. The nobleness of conception is matched throughout with a kindred nobleness of style; while the songs are full of the deep, spontaneous melody which issues out of the heart of the poet when sound and sense are perfectly mated in his imagination.

The profound seriousness of temper which pervades the play, the clearness with which its ethical bearings are disclosed, the deep philosophy which underlies it, convey an irresistible impression of something personal in the theme and the treatment. It is impossible to read "The Tempest" without a haunting sense of secondary meaning. Caliban, Miranda, and Prospero have been interpreted from many points of view; a final and convincing interpretation will never be made, but the instinct of Shakespeare's readers and lovers that in this last play from his hand the poet was bidding farewell to his art is probably sound. As a rule, critics err rather in diminishing than expanding the significance of great works of art.

William Shakespeare

"The Tempest" appeared about 1611. Shakespeare was then forty-seven years of age, and had nearly completed his work. When he set the noble figure of Prospero on the unknown island, and made him master of spirits and of men, with a knowledge of life which was so great that it easily passed on into magical art, he could not have been oblivious of the spiritual significance of the work, nor of its deep and vital symbolism in the development of his own mind and art.

The success of "The Tempest" appears to have been great; it was presented at Court, and was one of the plays performed during the marriage festivities of the Princess Elizabeth in 1613. One source of this popular interest was probably the charm of the songs which gave the movement pause and relief. There is good reason to believe that these songs were set to music by Robert Johnson, a popular composer of the day, and that two of them had been preserved in Wilson's "Cheerful Ayres and Ballads set for Three Voices."

Shakespeare completed no more plays after the appearance of "The Tempest," but he had a shaping hand in "Henry VIII.," which appeared about 1612 and is included among his works. This very uneven and very spectacular drama is based upon material found in Hall and Holinshed, in a life of Wolsey by George Cavendish, then in manuscript, and in Foxe's "Acts and Monuments of the Church." Its performance on June 29, 1613, led to the burning of the Globe Theatre — an event of which there are several contemporary accounts. The play was presented with unprecedented elaboration in scenery and dress — a first attempt, apparently, in the direction of the splendour of appointments which characterizes the modern stage. "Now King Henry making a Masque at the Cardinal Woolsey's House," writes Wotton, "and certain Canons being shot off at his entry, some of the paper or other stuff wherewith one of them was stopped, did light on the Thatch, where being thought at first but an idle smoak, and their eyes more attentive to the show, it kindled inwardly, and ran round like a train, consuming within less than an hour the whole House to the very grounds. This was the fatal period of that virtuous fabrique ; wherein yet nothing did perish, but wood and straw and a few forsaken cloaks." And the old chronicler of this first of many similar catastrophes adds with naive humour : "Only one man had his breeches set on fire, that would perhaps have broyled him, if he had not by the benefit of a provident wit put out with bottle ale."

Attention was directed in the last century to certain peculiarities of versification in " Henry VIII.," but it was not until the middle of the present century that Mr. Spedding set forth at length the theory that the play was Shakespeare's in part only, and that many passages were in the manner of Fletcher. It is interesting that these differences in style were recognized clearly, not by scholars, but by two men of sensitive literary feeling, Tennyson and Emerson. The English poet first made the suggestion to Mr. Spedding. Emerson's comments on the matter are full of insight :

William Shakespeare

"In Henry VIII. I think I see plainly the cropping out of the original work on which his own finer stratum was laid. The first play was written by a superior, thoughtful man, with a vicious ear. I can mark his lines, and know well their cadence. See Wolsey's soliloquy, and the following scene with Cromwell, where, instead of the metre of Shakespeare, whose secret is that the thought constructs the tune, so that reading for the sense will bring out the rhythm — here the lines are constructed on a given tune, and the verse has even a trace of pulpit eloquence. But the play contains through all its length unmistakable traits of Shakespeare's hand, and some passages, as the account of the coronation, are like autographs."

The view, presented with great skill by Mr. Spedding, that Shakespeare intended to make a "great historical drama on the subject of Henry VIII., which would have included the divorce of Katharine, the fall of Wolsey, the rise of Cranmer, the coronation of Anne Bullen, and the final separation of the English from the Roman Church;" that he worked out the first two acts, and that, for some unknown reason the manuscript was passed on to Fletcher, who expanded it into the play as we now have it, has been accepted by many students of the play. The three chief figures — the King, Queen Katharine, and the Cardinal — are unmistakably Shakespeare's in conception; and the trial scene is certainly his.

There are distinct traces of Shakespeare's hand in the "Two Noble Kinsmen," which the title-page

The Romances

declares was written by "Mr. John Fletcher and Mr. William Shakespeare, Gentlemen," and the play appears in some editions of the poet's works. It is impossible, however, to decide with any certainty the extent of Shakespeare's contribution to a drama which in many parts is clearly the production of another hand. It is not improbable, as has been suggested by some authorities, that when Shakespeare withdrew from active work in his profession he may have left some preliminary sketches for half-finished dramas behind him, and that it fell to the lot of Fletcher or some other contemporary dramatist to work over and complete what the poet had begun. With the writing of "Cymbeline" and "The Tempest" Shakespeare's work ended.

CHAPTER XVII

THE LAST YEARS AT STRATFORD

IT is impossible to overlook the recurrence of certain incidents and the reappearance of certain figures
in the Romances. "Pericles," "Cymbeline," "The
Winter's Tale," and "The Tempest" are all dramas
of reconciliation; tragic events occur in each of these
plays and tragic forces are set in motion, but the tragic
movement is arrested by confession and repentance and
the tragic forces are dissipated or turned to peaceful
ends by meditation and reconciliation. Coming close
upon the long-sustained absorption in tragic motives, the
singular unity of the Romances in organizing conception, in serenity of mood, and in faith in purity and
goodness and love as solvents of the problems of life,
make it impossible to escape the conclusion that the
later plays record and express the final attitude of the
poet towards the ultimate questions of life.

The chief figures in the Romances are men and
women who have borne heavy sorrows — Prospero,
Hermione, Imogen, Pericles, and the fair young creatures whose purity and sweetness typify the immortal
qualities of youth — Marina, Miranda, Perdita, Florizel,
Ferdinand, and the brothers of Imogen. Behind
these suffering or radiant figures there is, in each play,

314

a pastoral background of exquisite loveliness; a landscape so noble and serene that it throws the corruption of courts and of society into striking relief. In each play there is a trace of the old fairy story — the story of the lost prince or princess, condemned to exile, disguise, or servitude ; and in the end the lost are found, disguises are thrown off, evil plots are exposed and evil plotters brought to repentance; suffering is recognized and finds its sweet reward in the rebuilding of its shattered world on a sure foundation, and youth finds eager expectation merged in present happiness. Prospero does not break his magic staff or drown his book until he has reknit the order of life shattered in the Tragedies, and reunited the wisdom of long observation and mature knowledge with the fresh heart and the noble idealism of youth.

In such a mood Shakespeare returned to Stratford about 1611. He was forty-seven years of age, and therefore at the full maturity of his great powers. From the standpoint of to-day he was still a young man ; but men grew old much earlier three centuries ago. The poet had been in London twenty-five years, and had written thirty-six or thirty-seven plays, and a group of lyric poems. He was still in his prime, but he had lived through the whole range of experience, he was a man of considerable fortune, and he had a wholesome ambition to become a country gentleman, with the independence, ease, and respect with which landed proprietorship has always been regarded in England.

His sources of income had been his plays, which were paid for, in his earlier years, at rates varying from

William Shakespeare

twenty-five to sixty dollars — equivalent in present values to two hundred and fifty and six hundred dollars; his salary as an actor, which was probably not less than five hundred dollars a year, or about three thousand dollars in present values; the returns from the sale of his poems, which ran through many editions, and the profits of which his publisher undoubtedly divided with him on some acceptable basis; and, most important of all, his revenue from his shares in the Blackfriars and Globe theatres.

The Globe Theatre provided room for an audience of about two thousand people, and for a number of years before its destruction by fire in 1613 was almost continuously prosperous. The transference of public interest to the boy actors, though long enough to send Shakespeare's company into the provinces, was comparatively short-lived. It is estimated that the annual receipts of the Globe Theatre did not fall below the very considerable sum of two hundred thousand dollars in current values. After providing for the maintenance of the theatre, there must have remained a substantial profit. This profit was divided among the shareholders, among whom were Shakespeare, Burbage, Condell, Heminge, and Philips; all were actors and members of the company, and combined personal interest and practical knowledge in theatrical management. The profits of the Blackfriars Theatre were smaller. Shakespeare's great popularity after 1598 or 1600 probably enabled him to secure much larger returns from the sale of new plays than were paid to the majority of playwrights; while the fees

316

always distributed at Court performances must have amounted, in his case, to a very considerable sum. From these various sources Shakespeare probably received, during the later years of his life, not less than fifteen thousand dollars a year in current values. Mr. Lee, who has made a thorough investigation of the subject, thinks there is no inherent improbability in the tradition, reported by a vicar of Stratford in the following century, that Shakespeare " spent at the rate of a thousand a year."

The poet had become the owner of various properties at Stratford or in its neighbourhood. The houses in Henley Street had come into his possession. The house at New Place, in which he took up his residence, was a commodious and substantial building ; and the grounds, with the exception of a thin wedge of land on Chapel Lane, extended almost to the Avon. His circumstances were those of a country gentleman of ample income.

When Shakespeare left London, he probably withdrew from participation in the management of the two theatres in which he was a shareholder, but his plays continued to be presented. His popularity suffered no eclipse until the fortunes of the stage began to yield to the rising tide of Puritan sentiment. During the festivities attending the marriage of the Princess Elizabeth, seven of his plays were presented at Whitehall. That he made the three days' journey to London at short intervals and kept up his old associations is practically certain.

His son Hamnet had died in the summer of 1596 ;

his father died in the early autumn of 1601, and his
mother in September, 1608. When he took up his
residence in Stratford in 1611, his wife and two daughters constituted his family. The eldest daughter,
Susannah, had married, in June, 1607, Dr. John Hall,
a physician of unusual promise, who became at a later
day a man of very high standing and wide acquaintance
in Warwickshire. The house in which he lived is one
of the most picturesque buildings which have survived
from the Stratford of Shakespeare's time. Dr. Hall's
daughter, Elizabeth, the only granddaughter of the poet,
was born in 1608. Mrs. Hall made her home in her
later years at New Place ; there, in 1643, she entertained Queen Henrietta Maria ; and there, in 1649,
she died. In the inscription on her grave in the
churchyard of Holy Trinity both her father and
husband are described as " gentlemen." Of her it
was written :

> Witty above her sexe, but that's not all,
> Wise to Salvation was good Mistress Hall.
> Something of Shakespeare was in that, but this
> Wholly of him with whom she's now in blisse.

Her daughter Elizabeth married Thomas Nashe, a
Stratford man of education, and, after his death, John
Barnard, who was knighted by Charles II. soon after
the Restoration. Lady Barnard, who was the last
direct descendant of the poet, died in 1670. She had
come into possession, by various bequests, of New
Place, the Henley Street houses, the land in the
neighbourhood of Stratford, and a house in Blackfriars

purchased by Shakespeare in 1613. The houses in
Henley Street passed at her death into the possession
of the grandson of Shakespeare's sister Joan, and
remained in the family, as reported in a previous
chapter, until the present century. New Place was
sold after Lady Barnard's death, and subsequently came
again into the hands of the Clopton family.

Judith Shakespeare married, shortly before her
father's death in 1616, Thomas Quiney, a wine-dealer
of Stratford, and lived for thirty-six years in a house
still standing at the southeast corner of High and
Bridge streets in Stratford. It was known at that time
as The Cage, because it had been used at an earlier
period as a prison. The foundation walls of this
ancient house are four feet in thickness; books and
Shakespearean souvenirs of every kind are now sold in
the shop on the ground floor. Judith Shakespeare had
three sons, all of whom died in infancy or early youth.
She survived her family and her sister Susannah, and
died in 1661, at the age of seventy-six.

The records show that after his retirement to Stratford Shakespeare continued to give careful attention to
his affairs and to take part in local movements. In
1613 he bought the house in Blackfriars, not far from
the theatre, which subsequently passed into the possession of Lady Barnard. The deeds of conveyance,
bearing Shakespeare's signature, are still in existence.
Comment has sometimes been made on the fact that
the poet spelled his name in different ways, and that
other people spelled it with complete disregard of
consistency, and it has been inferred that he must

have been, therefore, an ignorant person. A little investigation would have shown that in the poet's time there was great variation in the spelling of proper names. Men of the eminence of Sidney, Spenser, Jonson, and Dekker were guilty of the same latitude of practice in this matter, and even Bacon, on one occasion at least, spelled his name Bakon.

Shakespeare's friend John Combe, at his death in 1614, left the poet a small bequest in money and a legal entanglement. The attempt of Combe's son to enclose certain fields at Welcombe which had long been common was vigorously opposed by the corporation of Stratford. Both as the owner of neighbouring property and as joint owner of the tithes of old Stratford, Welcombe, and Bishopton, Shakespeare had an interest in the matter which arrayed him at the start in active opposition to the plan to enclose the property. A record in the diary of Thomas Greene, the town clerk of Stratford, shows that Shakespeare was an influential person in the dispute, and that he was in London in the autumn of 1614.

There is reason to believe that Puritanism had gained many adherents in Stratford, and that the poet's son-in-law, Dr. Hall, was in sympathy with the movement. The town records indicate that in 1614 a clergyman was entertained at New Place; the entry is suggestive of hospitality: "Item, for one quart of sack and one quart of clarett wine geven to a preacher at New Place, xxd." It is probable that the preacher was a Puritan, but the fact furnishes no clew to Shakespeare's ecclesiastical leanings. Aside from the bent of his mind and his view of life, so clearly disclosed in the plays, he could hardly have been in sympathy with the Puritan attitude towards his own profession. The temper of Stratford had changed greatly since the days when, as a boy, he saw the companies of players receive open-handed hospitality at the hands of the town officials. Two years earlier, in 1612, the town council had passed a resolution declaring that plays were unlawful and " against the example of other well-governed cities and boroughs," and imposing a penalty on players.

Early in 1616 Shakespeare had a draft of his will prepared, and this document, after revision, was signed in March. On Tuesday, April 23, he died ; and two days later he was buried inside the chancel of Holy Trinity Church, near the northern wall. Over his grave were cut in the stone lines that have become familiar throughout the English-speaking world :

> Good friend, for Jesus' sake forebeare
> To dig the dust enclosed heare;
> Bleste be the man that spares these stones,
> And curst be he that moves my bones.

William Hall, who visited Stratford in 1694, declared that these words were written by the poet to protect his dust from clerks and sextons, " for the most part a very ignorant set of people," who might otherwise have consigned that dust to the charnel-house which was close at hand. The verse, by whomever written, has accomplished its purpose, and the sacred dust has never been disturbed. With a single exception, the line of graves which extends across the chancel pavement is given up to members of the poet's family. His wife, his daughter Susannah and her husband, and his granddaughter Elizabeth's first husband, Thomas Nashe, lie together behind the chancel rail in the venerable church which has become, to the English-speaking world, the mausoleum of its greatest poet. Shakespeare's father and mother were buried within the church, but their graves have not been located. His daughter Judith and his son Hamnet undoubtedly lie within the walls of the church or of the ancient burying-ground which surrounds it. His brother Edmund, who was a player, was buried in St. Saviour's Church, Southwark, in the heart of modern London. His brother Richard, who died in his early prime at Stratford in 1613, was probably buried in the churchyard of Holy Trinity. His brother Gilbert lived to a good age, and no record of his death or burial has been discovered.

Shakespeare's will, written on three sheets of paper, and signed at the bottom of each page, begins with the conventional phrases, bears a number of erasures and interlineations, and the three signatures indicate great weakness. Under its provisions the poet's wife received his second-best bed with its furnishings; his daughter Susannah inherited the greater part of the estate, including New Place, the properties in the neighbourhood of Stratford, and the house in Blackfriars, London; and she and her husband were made executors and residuary legatees. To his younger daughter Judith, who married Thomas Quiney earlier in the same year, he left a small property on Chapel Lane and money to an amount equal to about eight thousand dollars in current values, and certain pieces of plate. Bequests were made to his sister Joan and her three sons. To several of his Stratford friends, and to his old associates or " fellows " in London, John Heminge, Richard Burbage, and Henry Condell, small sums of money were bequeathed for the purchase of memorial rings. His godson, William Walker, was remembered, and a sum of money equivalent to about three hundred dollars in present values was left to the poor of Stratford. The omission of Shakespeare's wife from the distribution of his estate under the terms of his will has been accepted by some writers as evidence of the poet's waning regard ; the most reasonable inference from his action is that Dr. Hall, who was a man of unusual capacity, could be trusted to care for his wife's mother with more assurance than she could be left to manage her own affairs. She survived her husband seven years, dying on August 6, 1623. The Latin verses inscribed upon her tomb are affectionate in tone, and were probably written by Dr. Hall.

On the north wall of the chancel of Holy Trinity, at some time prior to 1623, the half-length bust of Shakespeare by Gerard Jonson, to which reference has been made, was erected. The poet is represented in the act of writing, and the inscription reads as follows :

Judicio Pylium, genio Socratem, arte Maronem
Terra tegit, populus mæret, Olympus habet.

William Shakespeare

Stay, passenger, why goest thou by so fast?
Read, if thou canst, whom envious death hath plast
Within this monument: Shakespeare: with whome
Quick Nature dide ; whose name doth deck ye tombe
Far more than cost ; sieth all y^t he hath writt
Leaves living art but page to serve his witt.

Obiit Ano. Doi. 1616. *Ætatis 53.* *Die 23. Ap.*

The bust was originally coloured, and was probably copied from a mask taken after death. The dress includes a scarlet doublet under a loose, sleeveless black gown. As a work of art the bust has no merit ; its interest lies in the fact that, despite its crude workmanship, it was accepted and placed in position by Shakespeare's children. It was whitewashed at the close of the last century, but the colours have been restored as far as possible.

The most important of the various portraits of the poet is that made by Martin Droeshout, and printed on the title-page of the First Folio in 1623. The engraver was a man of Flemish blood, born in London, and still in his boyhood when Shakespeare died. It is not probable that he ever saw the poet. This representation, crude as it is, was accepted by Shakespeare's friends and received the commendation of Ben Jonson. When Droeshout executed the engraving, he probably had before him a painting, and there is reason to believe that this painting was recently brought to light and now hangs in the Memorial Picture Gallery at Stratford. It is almost a facsimile of the Droeshout engraving, but shows some artistic skill and feeling.

The Last Years at Stratford

A much more attractive portrait is that known as the "Ely House" portrait, which now hangs in the Birthplace at Stratford, and was formerly the property of a Bishop of Ely. It was probably painted early in the seventeenth century. The well-known Chandos portrait, which hangs in the National Portrait Gallery in London, shows important variations from the bust and the Droeshout engraving, and was probably painted not many years after the poet's death from descriptions furnished by his friends and more or less imaginative in their details. Its origin is unknown, but its history has been traced. It was at one time the property of D'Avenant, whose father was landlord of the Crown Inn at Oxford in Shakespeare's time, and, later, of Betterton, Mrs. Barry, and the Duke of Chandos, becoming the property of the nation about the middle of the present century. The Janson portrait came to light about 1770, the Zoust portrait about 1725, and the Felton portrait about 1792; all show radical variations from the authenticated portraits. The portrait bust of terra-cotta now in the possession of the Garrick Club was found in 1845 in a wall which was put up on the site of the Duke's Theatre built by D'Avenant. Its general resemblance to other portraits furnishes the only basis for the claim that it reproduces the features of Shakespeare. The Kesselstadt death-mask, found in a junk-shop in Mayence in 1849, resembles a portrait in the possession of the Kesselstadt family, but neither the portrait nor the mask has been satisfactorily identified as a representation of the poet. The monument in the Poets'

William Shakespeare

Corner in Westminster Abbey was placed in position by popular subscription in 1741.

The most enduring memorial of Shakespeare was the complete edition of his works, known as the First Folio, published in 1623, seven years after his death. His early narrative poems, " Venus and Adonis " and " The Rape of Lucrece," were published under his direction and with his revision ; the Sonnets were printed without his sanction ; the " Passionate Pilgrim " was fraudulently issued as from his hand ; while of the sixteen plays which were published in quarto form before his death, it is believed that none was issued with his consent or revision. These publications were speculative ventures, and the text presented was made up either from reports of plays taken down in shorthand in the theatres, from separate parts, or complete plays surreptitiously secured, and hurried through the press without correction. Under these conditions the opportunities for errors of all kinds were practically without number ; and a further and prolific source of error was found in the custom which prevailed in the old printing-houses of reading the matter to be set up to the printers instead of placing it before them. The surprising fact about the text of the Shakespearean plays, when these circumstances are taken into consideration, is not that the difficulties, obscurities, and uncertainties are so many, but that they are so few relatively to the magnitude of his work.

In 1623 the poet's friends and fellow-actors, John Heminge and Henry Condell, at the suggestion of a small group of printers and publishers, brought

The Last Years at Stratford

together thirty-six plays under the three divisions of Comedies, Histories, and Tragedies. "Pericles" was omitted. The title-page declared that the plays were printed "according to the true originall copies"; the text was probably that of the acting versions in the possession of the company with which Shakespeare had been associated, in which there were great variations from the dramatist's original work. For this reason the text of the First Folio is in many places inferior to that of the sixteen quartos, which, although surreptitiously issued, gave the text of acting versions in use at an earlier date. The Droeshout portrait was engraved on the title-page of the First Folio, and the edition was dedicated to William Herbert, Earl of Pembroke, and to his brother Philip Herbert, Earl of Montgomery. The editors declared that their object in issuing the plays in this form was to "keepe the memory of so worthy a friend and fellow alive as was our Shakespeare." "I doubt," writes Mr. Lowell, "if posterity owes a greater debt to any two men living in 1623 than to the two obscure actors who in that year published the first folio edition of Shakespeare's plays. But for them it is more than likely that such of his works as had remained to that time unprinted would have been irrevocably lost, and among them were 'Julius Cæsar,' 'The Tempest,' and 'Macbeth.'"

The noble eulogy with which Ben Jonson enriched the First Folio was in the key of the entire body of contemporary comment on Shakespeare's nature and character. The adjective "sweet" was commonly applied to him; he was described as "friendly," as having "a civil demeanor" and "an open and free nature"; and tradition later affirmed that he was "very good company, and of a very ready and pleasant smooth wit." The two or three vague traditions of irregularity of life may be dismissed as unsubstantiated. The standards of his time, the habits of his profession, the circumstances of his early life, and the autobiographic note in the Sonnets make it probable that in his youth, at least, he was not impeccable. That he was essentially a sound man, living a normal, wholesome life, is rendered practically certain by his success in dealing with practical affairs, and by his long-sustained power of producing great works of art on the highest levels of thought and workmanship. Such industry, sagacity, and thrift as Shakespeare showed are never associated with disorderly living; while the consistent objectivity of his attitude toward life is impossible to any man whose moral or intellectual sanity is seriously impaired.

Shakespeare's resources, both material and spiritual, were harvested with a steady hand. While many men of his profession wasted their means and their strength in disorderly living, he invested the money earned in London in building up the fortunes of his family in Stratford. Generous by nature and richly endowed with imagination and passion, he was never prodigal either of his genius or his estate. Early in his career he laid the foundations of a solid prosperity, and when he had secured a competence he retired from active work to enjoy the harvest of a diligent and well-ordered life.

Among the many great qualities which combined to

make him a master of life and of art, sanity must be given a first place ; and sanity is as much a matter of character as of mind. When one takes into account the power of passion that was in him, and the license and extravagance of his time, his poise and balance become as marvellous as his genius. He avoided as if by instinct those eccentricities of taste, interest, subject, and manner to which many of his contemporaries fell victims, and which men of sensitive imagination often mistake for evidences and manifestations of genius.

Shakespeare kept resolutely to the main highways of life, where the interest of the great human movement is always deepest and richest if one has adequate range of vision. He dealt with the elemental and universal experiences in broad, simple, vital forms, and in a language which was familiar and yet of the largest compass. There was nothing esoteric in his thought or his method ; he was too great to depend upon secret processes, or to content himself with any degree of knowledge short of that which had the highest power of diffusion. Although the keenest of practical psychologists, he did not concern himself with curious questions of mental condition, nor with spiritual problems which are elusive and subtle rather than vital and profound. He was too great an artist to mistake psychological analysis, however skilful and interesting, for literature.

As he studied life and passed through its experiences he saw with increasing clearness the moral order of the world, the ethical relation of the individual to society and to his environment, the significance of character as the product of will, and the gradation of qualities in a scale of spiritual values. His work as an artist deepened and widened as he grew in the wisdom of life. Such wisdom, and its expression in work of sustained power, come to those only whose natures are harmonious with the fundamental laws of life, and who keep themselves in wholesome relations with their kind.

Too great in himself to become a cynic, and of a vision too broad and penetrating to rest in any kind of pessimism, Shakespeare grew in charity as he increased in knowledge. He loved much because he knew men so well. A deep and tender pity was distilled out of his vast experience, and his last work was the ripe fruit of the beautiful humanization of his genius accomplished in him by the discipline and the revelation of life in his personal history. "The Tempest" and "The Winter's Tale," coming at the end of a long and arduous career, are the convincing witnesses of the harmony of life and art in which resides the secret of Shakespeare's noble fertility and sustained power. The path which led from "Titus Andronicus" to "The Tempest" must have been one of gradual but unbroken ascent. To keep in one's soul the freshness of perception and imagination which touches "The Tempest" with the light that never fades, one must be great in heart and in life as well as in creative power. When Prometheus brought the arts of life to men, he did not leave them skill without inspiration; he brought them hope also. Shakespeare's genius, shining on the darkest ways, seems to touch the sky beyond the horizon with light.

INDEX

Actor, Shakespeare as an, 80, 91.

Actors, professional, created by the Moralities, 13; their position by the middle of the sixteenth century; Elizabeth a patron of, 82; Leicester's company of, 82–83, 89; a performance described, 84–86; Shakespeare's name on lists of, 90; the address to, in "Hamlet," 91; opposition of the City to, 99–101; in the "War of the Theatres," 221–223, 248; boys as, 83, 248–251, 316; reference in "Hamlet" to the strife between boy and adult, 248.

Adam, in "As You Like It" played by Shakespeare, 90.

Adaptation of his own plays, 160, 208.

Adaption of plays by Shakespeare, 105–106, 107–112, 115.

Alleyne, Edward, the star of the Admiral's Men, 89, 90.

"All's Well that Ends Well," source of its plot, 250–252; alluded to, 253.

"A Lover's Complaint" alluded to among the poetical writings of Shakespeare, 106, 138; published with the Sonnets, but little else is known of it, 177.

"A Midsummer Night's Dream," Warwickshire in, 49; alluded to, 48, 72, 138, 143, 309; sources of, 159; metre, 160; the great popularity of, 161.

Analysis of special characters in Shakespeare's plays: Talbot, 119; Biron, 131; Falstaff, 187–189, 210; Shylock, 200–202; Jaques, 214; Hamlet, 245–249; Helena, 251, 252; Othello, 322; Macbeth, 262–265; Lear, 267, 268; Timon, 269; Coriolanus, 274.

Angelo, Michael, alluded to, 153.

"Antony and Cleopatra," alluded to, 234; the source of, 234, 270–273.

Arden, Mary. See Shakespeare, Mary.

Arden, Robert, of Wilmcote, grandfather of the poet, 28, 204.

"Arden of Feversham," credited to Shakespeare by some critics, 21.

Armada, the, alluded to, 20, 107.

Armado in "Love's Labour's Lost," 130.

"Arte of English Poesie," by Puttenham, 78, 106.

"As You Like It," Warwickshire in, 49, 212; Shakespeare as Adam in, 90; its plot, etc., 212–214; alluded to, 133.

Aubrey, authority for the report that Shakespeare assisted his

331

Index

father after leaving school, 41; quoted, 72.

Autographs of the poet, 319.

Ayrer, Jacob, 308; his "Die Schöne Sidea" very similar in plot to "The Tempest," 308.

Bacon, Francis, Lord Verulam, alluded to, 320.

Baker, Mrs., late custodian of the Birthplace, 66.

Bale, —, author of "King Johan" and other Chronicle plays, 20.

Ballad-dance, the, 3.

Bandello, the story of Romeo and Juliet in a "*nouvelle*" by, 157; some of the plot of "Much Ado About Nothing" due to, 211; the ultimate source of "Twelfth Night," 215.

Barnard, Sir John, of Abingdon, second husband of Elizabeth Hall, the poet's granddaughter, 205, 318.

Barnfield, Richard, lines by, on Shakespeare's "Venus" and "Lucrece," 154.

Beaumont, Francis, alluded to, 189; lines by, on the Mermaid Tavern, 218.

Belleforest, the story of Hamlet in the *Histoires Tragiques* of, 242.

Bermudas, the, and "The Tempest," 307, 308.

Bible, Shakespeare's study of the, 38.

Birthplace, the, of Shakespeare, detailed description of, 29-31; inherited by Shakespeare, 293, 317; by his daughter, 318; by his sister's grandson, 29, 319.

Blackfriars, Vautrollier a publisher

in, 77; Shakespeare's house in, 318, 319, 322.

Blackfriars Theatre, built by the elder Burbage, 90; secured for the use of the Children of the Chapel, 248; Shakespeare's income from, 316.

Boccaccio, the source of "All's Well that Ends Well," 250; and of "Cymbeline," 299.

Bond, the marriage, of Shakespeare and Anne Hathaway, 66, 67.

Boy actors, 83; the strife between adults and, 248, 249, 316; the reference to, in "Hamlet," 248.

Brandes, Mr. Georg, on Shakespeare's visiting Italy, 92-94.

Brooke, Arthur, author of a poetical version of the story of "Romeo and Juliet," 157.

Burbage, James, actor and a liveryman in the neighbourhood of Smithfield, 71, 79; a Stratford man by birth, 78; owner of The Theatre, 79; builder of Blackfriars Theatre, 90, 248.

Burbage, Richard, son of James, 71, 79; a member of the King's Players, 83; of Shakespeare's company, 89; builder of the Globe Theatre, 89, 323; alluded to, 222.

Bushnell, Dr., quoted, 199.

Camden, William, 223.

Cavendish, George, 310.

Cecil, Sir Robert, Raleigh's letter to, 127.

Chamberlain, the Lord, his company of players, 90, 215.

Chapman, George, his Homer,

332

Index

Index

Index

Index

Index

26; alluded to, 55, 57, 68, 207; bust of Shakespeare in, 217, 323, 324.

Holy Trinity Churchyard, 204, 318, 322.

"Hotspur," 20.

Inferences from a dramatist's work dangerous, 68–70.

Interlude, the, 15, 16.

Italian, Shakespeare's knowledge of, 37, 38.

Italy, the teacher of western Europe, 17–18; its influence on England in the sixteenth century, 92, 93; possible visit of Shakespeare to, 92, 95; its influence on Chaucer and others, 93; and on the English imagination, 102–103; its general influence on Europe, 125, 126, 164.

Jaggard, William, 178.

James I. on the growth of London, 76; a patron of the stage, 257, 265; alluded to, 232.

Jew, the, in 1596, 201, 202.

Johnson, Robert, 310.

Jonson, Ben, ridiculed for including plays among his "Works," 109; prices paid for his plays, 109; his "Irene," 147; a contributor to Chester's "Love's Martyr," 178; a combatant in the "War of the Theatres," 221–222; a sketch of the life of, 223–226; his personal appearance, 224; his character, 224–225; his criticism of Shakespeare's lack of scholarship, 225; his tribute to Shakespeare, 226; the "Poetaster," 227; his "Sejanus" and "Cati-

line," 239; the spelling of his name, 320 ; his Eulogy of Shakespeare in the First Folio, 327; alluded to, 38, 181, 189, 304.

Jonson, Gerard, 217, 323.

"Julius Cæsar," criticised by Jonson, 225; political situation when it was written, 232; source of, in Plutarch, 234; modification of the original in, 235; publication of, 236; analysis of the play, 237, 239, 272; preserved in the First Folio, 327.

Kempe, 222.

Kenilworth Castle, 42; the entertainment of Queen Elizabeth at, 42–43, 45; alluded to, 46, 51; Mervyn's Tower, 46; the loveliness of its ruins, 48.

"King Johan," 20.

"King John," the prelude of the historical plays, 182; completed about 1595, 184; a recast, 184; has no hero, 185.

"King Lear," description of Dover cliff in, 37; its landscape exceptional, 49; the sublimest height of the poet's tragic art, 265; performed before the King, 265; sources of, 265, 266; analysis of, 266, 267; alluded to, 20, 261, 302.

King's servants, the, 257, 258.

Kyd, Thomas, one of Shakespeare's immediate predecessors as a playwright, 21, 181; his "Spanish Tragedy," 242.

Landor, Walter Savage, his "Citation and Examination of William Shakespeare," 65.

Index

Landscape, influence of, on the verse of Scott, Burns, Wordsworth, 49; the Italian, 50.

Latin, Shakespeare's knowledge of, 36, 37.

Law, Shakespeare's knowledge of, 38.

Lee, Sidney, on Shakespeare's Sonnets, 172 ; on his acting before King James, 258; on his expenditures, 317.

Leicester, the Earl of, his entertainment of Queen Elizabeth, 42–43, 45, 48; his company of players, 81–83, 88.

Leicester Hospital, 51.

Lodge, his death in 1625, 21; his plays, 20; one of the group in possession of the stage on the arrival of Shakespeare, 21, 120, 181 ; his " Rosalynde " the source of the plot of " As You Like It," 212; his allusion to an early Hamlet, 242; alluded to, 121, 213.

London, Shakespeare's journey to, 71 ; in the sixteenth century, 73; streets, 74; the city, 75; its growth, 76; alluded to, 69, 125.

London Bridge, 74.

" Lord Chamberlain's Men," the, 90, 215.

" Love's Labour's Lost," the first touches of the poet's hand shown in, among others, 113; betrays the influence of Lyly, 125, 130 ; played before the Queen, 128 ; satirizes the times, 128, 143 ; betrays the youth of the writer, 130; analysis of, 130–133; three poems from, in " The Passionate Pilgrim," 179; alluded to, 160, 198.

" Love's Labour's Won," mentioned by Meres, probably the same as " All's Well that Ends Well," 250.

Lucy, Sir Peter, 64.

Lucy, Sir Thomas, of Charlecote, 42, 64, 65.

Lydgate, his Troy Book, 255.

Lyly, John, a sketch of, 125–127; his influence on Shakespeare's " Love's Labour's Lost," 125, 130, 139; one of the group in possession of the stage on Shakespeare's arrival in London, 181; his " Euphues," 21, 106, 127.

Lyrical poetry, Shakespeare's contribution to, 164.

" Macbeth," contrast of landscape in this and other plays, 49; contains traces of the older drama, 114; sources of, 261; analysis of, 262; parts of, said to be by Middleton, 263; De Quincey on the introduction of the comic element, 263; Dr. Forman's account of the performance of, in 1611, 264; unprinted until in the First Folio, 327.

Magdalen College, Oxford, 125.

Malone, on the authorship of " Henry VI.," 118.

Manningham, John, quoted, 214, 215.

Marlowe, Christopher, leader of the group of men who controlled the stage at the time of Shakespeare's arrival in London, 21, 107, 120, 181; a sketch of, 23; his writings, 23; his influence on English poetry, 104, 114; his death, 106; credited with part authorship of

Index

Index

Index

Raleigh, Sir Walter, 107, 127.

"Ralph Roister Doister," 16.

Ravenscroft, Edward, 113.

Register of the Stationers Company, 61, 112, 200.

Religion in the fifteenth century, 11, 12.

Renaissance influence, the, at its height in Shakespeare's time, 36; Italy the birthplace of, 92; surprisingly wholesome considering the moral life of Italy at the time, 102–103; made Europe a community in intellectual interests, 125; the suggestiveness of, 141; freedom secured by, 143, 144, 276, 287; love of beauty a characteristic of, 149, 276.

"Richard II.," published in 1597, 115; reflects the genius of Marlowe, 124, 182, 183; revived at the Globe, 229; its outline taken from Holinshed, 235.

"Richard III.," published in 1597, 115; reflects the genius of Marlowe, 124, 183; Holinshed followed in, 183, 235.

Richardson, Locke, 39.

Robsart, Amy, imprisoned in Mervyn's Tower, 46.

Romances, the, 294, 296, 298, 314; "Pericles," 294, 295; "Cymbeline," 295; "The Winter's Tale," 301–304; "The Tempest," 306–310.

Rome, the theatre of, 4, 5.

"Romeo and Juliet," mistakes in, 94; shows among the first touches of the poet's hand, 113; published in 1597, 115; in the front rank of English poetry, 143; shows the poet's development, 143; sources, 156, 157; analysis of, 157–159; affiliated to "A Midsummer Night's Dream" in lyric quality, 160; alluded to, 260.

Rose, the, 89, 110, 156; production of "Henry VI." at, 119, 193.

Rowe, his story of Shakespeare's poaching, 63; quoted again, 79, 90, 208.

Sackville, one of the authors of "Gorbordoc," 18.

Sandells, Fulk, 66.

Schlegel, quoted, on the historical plays, 194.

Sea-Venture, the, 307.

Shakespeare, Edmund, 322.

Shakespeare, Gilbert, 322.

Shakespeare, Hamnet, 71; his death, 182, 204, 231, 317; his grave, 322.

Shakespeare, Joan, sister of William, 29, 319, 323; the grandson of, 319; three sons of, 323. See Hart.

Shakespeare, John, 27; his marriage to Mary Arden, 28; his public offices, 29; his children, 29; his means, 32; financial embarrassments, 40, 203; alluded to, 77, 204; his coat-of-arms, 27, 204; his death, 231, 318.

Shakespeare, Judith, the poet's youngest daughter, 31, 319; baptized, 71; married Thomas Quiney, 31, 207, 319, 322; her sons, 319; bequest to, in the poet's will, 322; her death, 319; her grave, 322.

Shakespeare, Mary, the poet's mother, wife of John, 28; heiress of Robert Arden of Wilmcote, 204; death of, 318.

341

Index

Index

spelling of his name, 319; his religion unknown, 320; his will, 321–323; his death, 321; lines over his grave, 321; the Stratford bust and other portraits of, 323–325; the First Folio, 326, 327; his personal character, 327–330.

Shallow, Justice, 42, 53, 64, 65, 66.

Shaw, Julius, 206.

Shottery, 26, 48, 56, 66, 67.

Sidney, Sir Philip, his "Arcadia," and "Apologie for Poesie," 106, 181, 257; alluded to, 18, 212, 230, 320.

Sill, Mr., quoted, 190.

Snider, Denton, quoted, 276.

Somers, Sir George, and the *Sea-Venture*, 307.

Sonnets, a favourite poetic form in the closing decade of the sixteenth century, 162, 163; introduced from Italy by Surrey and Wyatt, 164; their translations of Petrarch's, 164; other collections of, 165; modern sequences of, 166.

Sonnets of Shakespeare, the, 162; published, 163; a sequence, 166; analysis of, 168; interpretations of, 172–174; alluded to, 217, 278, 296, 328.

Sonneteers of Shakespeare's time, 165.

Southampton, Earl of. See Wriothesley.

Spedding, Mr., 311, 312.

Spenser, Edmund, a well-known name in Shakespeare's time, 107, 181; Shakespeare's love of pastoral life shared by, 212, 213; his laxity in spelling of names, even his own, 320; his "Colin Clout," 181; his "Epi-thalamium," 181; alluded to, 230.

Still, John, 17.

St. Pancras, 75.

St. Paul's Cathedral, 73, 75.

St. Paul's Churchyard, 150.

Stratford-on-Avon, its charm, 25; Shakespearean associations, 25; in 1564, 26; its population, 27; Henley Street, 28–31; its love of the drama, 33; the Grammar School and Guild Chapel, 35, 57; the landscape between Kenilworth and, 43, 46, 51; the byways about, 47, 48; Warwick from, 51; between Hampton Lucy and, 55; events which led to the poet's departure from, 63–66, 70; men from, among Shakespeare's friends, 77, 78, 146; touches of, in the poems or plays of Shakespeare, 145, 203; Shakespeare's return to, 204, 232, 315; his restoration of New Place in, 205, 293; later history of New Place, 205–207, 317, 318, 322; the bust of Shakespeare in the church at, 217; the poet's property at, 293, 317–319.

Stuart, Mary, 44.

Surrey, 93, 126, 164, 165.

Symonds, quoted, 122.

Tableaux of New Testament scenes in the fifth century, 7.

Talbot Inn, Chaucer's "Tabard," alluded to, 89.

Ten Brink, quoted, 298.

Thames, the principal thoroughfare, 75.

"The Atheist's Tragedy," 102.

Theatre, the, 77, 79, 83, 89, 193; the library of, 110, 115.

Index

Index

Cæsar," 233–240; "Hamlet,"
240–249; "All's Well that Ends
Well," 250–252; "Measure for
Measure," 253, 254; "Troilus
and Cressida," 254–257;
"Othello," 259–261; "Mac-
beth," 261–265; "King Lear,"
265–268; "Timon of Athens,"
268, 269; "Antony and Cleopatra," 270–272; "Coriolanus,"
273–275; ethical significance
of, 276–291; the highest point
of Shakespeare's art, 284; the
great insight of, due to Shakespeare's largeness of view,
289.

" Troilus and Cressida," supposed to have had a part in
the "War of the Theatres,"
222; painful and repellent, 254;
belongs to the year 1603, 254;
sources, 255; analysis of, 254–
256; alluded to, 278.

" Twelfth Night," produced, 1601,
214; source of, 214, 215;
analysis of, 215; alluded to,
294.

Twine, Lawrence, 294.

Udall, Nicholas, 16.

Vautrollier, Thomas, 77.
" Venus and Adonis," 77, 106,
143, 145–155.

Walker, William, godson of
Shakespeare, 323.
" War of the Theatres," the, 221,
223, 248, 256.
Warner, William, 134.
Warwick, the town of, 51.
Warwick Castle, 52.
Warwickshire landscape, the, 43,
46–58; Shakespeare's familiar-
ity with, 46, 48, 62, 207; in mid-
summer, 47; the footpaths in,
47, 48; touches of, in all Shake-
speare's work, 49; its special
charm, 50; along the Avon
below the bridge, 52; references
to, in "Henry VI.," 190; in
"The Merry Wives of Wind-
sor " and " The Taming of the
Shrew," 203.
Webster, alluded to, 93, 102.
Weever, John, 154, 155.
Whitehall, the old Palace at, 215;
acting before the King at, 258,
265, 303.
Wilmcote, 28, 40.
Wilson, his " Cheerful Ayres and
Ballads," 310.
Wilton House, 257.
Wotton, on the Masque at Car-
dinal Wolsey's, 311.
Wriothesley, Henry, Earl of
Southampton, 146, 150, 176,
228–230, 232.
Wyatt, 93, 164, 165.

345